CULTURAL HUMILITY

CULTURAL HUMILITY

ENGAGING DIVERSE IDENTITIES IN THERAPY

JOSHUA N. HOOK,
DON DAVIS, JESSE OWEN,
AND CIRLEEN DeBLAERE

AMERICAN PSYCHOLOGICAL ASSOCIATION • *Washington, DC*

Published by
American Psychological Association
750 First Street, NE
Washington, DC 20002
www.apa.org

To order
APA Order Department
P.O. Box 92984
Washington, DC 20090-2984
Tel: (800) 374-2721; Direct: (202) 336-5510
Fax: (202) 336-5502; TDD/TTY: (202) 336-6123
Online: www.apa.org/pubs/books
E-mail: order@apa.org

In the U.K., Europe, Africa, and the Middle East, copies may be ordered from
American Psychological Association
3 Henrietta Street
Covent Garden, London
WC2E 8LU England

Typeset in Meridien by Circle Graphics, Inc., Columbia, MD

Printer: Bookmasters, Ashland, OH
Cover Designer: Naylor Design, Washington, DC

The opinions and statements published are the responsibility of the authors, and such opinions and statements do not necessarily represent the policies of the American Psychological Association.

Library of Congress Cataloging-in-Publication Data

Names: Hook, Joshua N., author. | Davis, Donald D., 1950- author. | Owen, Jesse, author. | DeBlaere, Cirleen, author.
Title: Cultural humility : engaging diverse identities in therapy / Joshua N. Hook, Don Davis, Jesse Owen, and Cirleen DeBlaere.
Description: First edition. | Washington, DC : American Psychological Association, [2017] | Includes bibliographical references and index.
Identifiers: LCCN 2016054958 | ISBN 9781433827778 | ISBN 1433827778
Subjects: LCSH: Psychotherapy—Cross-cultural studies. | Cross-cultural counseling. | Psychology—Case studies.
Classification: LCC RC455.4.E8 H66 2017 | DDC 616.89/14—dc23 LC record available at https://lccn.loc.gov/2016054958

British Library Cataloguing-in-Publication Data
A CIP record is available from the British Library.

Printed in the United States of America
First Edition

10 9 8 7 6 5 4 3 2

http://dx.doi.org/10.1037/0000037-000

To Dr. Micah McCreary, who encouraged me to engage with people
who were different from me, move toward
my discomfort, and trust myself.
—Joshua N. Hook

To my training director, Harold Stevens (who recently passed of cancer),
and two fellow interns, Parker Mott and Chris Ruth.
My contribution to this book is just an extension
of the friendship, trust, and conversations
we had with Hal.
—Don Davis

To my family, friends, colleagues, students, and clients who
have taught me many lessons of humility over the years.
Also, to Drs. S. A. Fras and Hank T. T. for inspiring
me to be a better version of myself every day.
—Jesse Owen

To my dad, Dennis D. DeBlaere, who nurtured my curiosity and,
from my earliest memories, taught me to value and respect others,
their experiences, their cultures, and their worldviews.
—Cirleen DeBlaere

Contents

Preface

Culture plays a complex role in our society and world. Our cultural identities enrich our lives and make our cities, workplaces, churches, and neighborhoods more exciting and engaging, but our cultural identities can also be a source of disagreement, division, and conflict. In our current cultural context, disagreements about cultural identities and worldviews dominate news coverage (e.g., the Black Lives Matter movement and its opposition; attitudes toward Syrian refugees and immigrants; disagreement and conflict about lesbian, gay, bisexual, and transgender rights).

As counseling psychologists, our hope is that the therapy context can be a place where therapists and clients can engage in deep discussion and analysis of clients' cultural identities, beliefs, values, and attitudes, as well as the intersection between clients' and therapists' cultural identities. Unfortunately, many therapists struggle to understand how to meaningfully address and engage the cultural identities of clients when they come up in therapy. They may ask themselves, How do I ask about a client's cultural background? How do I communicate that I value my client's culture? What do I do when I make a cultural misstep or mistake? How should I proceed when I have a strong negative reaction toward a part of my client's cultural values or worldview?

It is with these questions in mind that we set out to write this book. We wanted to write a book that would be practical—that would help therapists who were struggling to address or engage culture in the therapy room. We wanted a book that would be integrative—that would connect theory and research from multicultural counseling with the primary tasks of psychotherapy, such as developing a working alliance with a client and dealing with ruptures when they occur in therapy. Finally, we wanted a book that was respectful of various cultural identities, rather than relying on generalizations or stereotypes.

We decided to use cultural humility as the guiding theoretical framework for our writing. Humility is an interesting theoretical perspective from which to write a book because it focuses on acknowledging what we don't know rather than the more typical approach in psychology of discussing what we (believe we) know. But when it comes to engaging culture and exploring an individual's cultural identity, humility is a great tool and represents a worthwhile place to begin. Engaging with an attitude of humility avoids some of the common pitfalls that can disrupt relationships, such as stereotyping or making assumptions. In contrast, humility involves an openness to explore and an inherent valuing of cultural diversity.

Humility isn't easy. In fact, we intentionally put together a writing team representing a variety of cultural identities. We knew we would have different perspectives, and we hoped this would lead to stronger ideas. The process was challenging, and the book ended up being more nuanced than the book we set out to write. But in the end, we think our experience mirrored the costs and benefits of engaging cultural identities in therapy. Engaging cultural identities can be difficult, challenging, and messy. Cultural missteps or mistakes can feel awkward and painful. But if you stick with it, commit to consistent dialogue even when uncomfortable, and engage with humility, the benefits are profound and include a deeper, richer experience of connection, learning, and growth. Thanks for taking this journey with us.

In writing this book, we want to acknowledge and thank several people. Professionally, we are thankful to our mentors who showed us the way—Ev Worthington, Karen Kitchener, and Bonnie Moradi. We are indebted to the courageous researchers and clinicians who started and maintained the multicultural counseling movement over the past several decades. In our education, we were taught to think about and value culture as an important aspect of therapy, and we are thankful to those who came before us and paved the way. Finally, we are thankful to our families, who provided us with our own cultural story to share.

CULTURAL
HUMILITY

Introduction
Beginning the Journey of Cultural Humility

> The beginning is the most important part of the work.
> —Plato, *The Republic*

Culture is full of rich histories and shared stories that exist within the larger sociopolitical context that influences the power, privilege, and opportunities we have in everyday life. People who share a cultural identity at some level share a similar story, although they have important differences and unique characteristics as well. Engaging with clients and their cultural identities involves understanding and honoring our cultural stories and those of our clients.

As you begin reading this book, we encourage you to think about your cultural story and how it intersects with the cultural stories of your clients. Maybe you are a therapist who would like to improve your ability to connect and work with clients from different cultural backgrounds. Perhaps you want to learn how to honor and respect the cultural identities of your clients. Or maybe you are a therapist-in-training, entering your work with clients and culture with a mix of excitement and fear. Wherever you are in your journey as a therapist, we are hopeful that you will find this

http://dx.doi.org/10.1037/0000037-001
Cultural Humility: Engaging Diverse Identities in Therapy, by J. N. Hook, D. Davis, J. Owen, and C. DeBlaere

book helpful. This book presents a theoretical foundation and framework for how to think about your work with diverse clients and honor their cultural identities in the therapy room. Throughout the book, we encourage you to take a close, hard look at yourself. If you are like most people, you probably have certain areas of strength for working with clients and their cultural identities, but you probably also have certain areas for growth, including struggles and biases. We encourage you to step into these areas of growth with courage, rather than retreating into your areas of comfort and avoiding the discussion. Finally, we discuss practical strategies for engaging with clients and their cultural identities, including repairing mistakes that threaten the therapeutic relationship.

Culture and Therapy

There has been a growing recognition by mental health professionals over the years that clients' and therapists' cultural identities are an important aspect of therapy (American Psychological Association [APA], 2003; Comas-Díaz, 2012). Historically, an assumption of most theoretical approaches was that people were more similar than different. Psychological disorders were thought to occur on the basis of a series of universal principles. According to this conceptualization, treatment followed a one-size-fits-all approach, which was typically tailored according to the type of psychological disorder (e.g., depression, anxiety, personality disorder). For example, Freud focused on internal drives toward aggression and sex, as well as defense mechanisms such as repression and projection, and he believed these principles were universal regardless of a person's cultural identities (Freud & Strachey, 1964). Skinner described human behavior in terms of behavioral reinforcement (Skinner, 1953). Principles such as shaping and extinction were thought to work similarly for all people (and animals) regardless of clients' cultural identities (e.g., race, ethnicity, religion, gender, sexual orientation).

Looking back, it is hard to believe that culture was not a bigger part of the conversation. Culture is now widely accepted as a potent force that underlies and shapes all human thought, emotion, and behavior (Pedersen, 1990). Throughout this book, we discuss culture in more detail. Culture involves the ways in which we think, feel, behave, and interact with others. Culture provides us with a lens or point of view with which we see the world. Culture affects almost all our decisions: where we choose to live, what we do for a living, who (or whether) we decide to marry, and whether we believe in God or a higher power.

When mental health professionals first started to think about culture, they focused on race and ethnicity. This was a good place to start because racial and ethnic differences form some of the strongest group memberships in our society. Race and ethnicity have a complex history, both in our country and around the world, and these group memberships continue to exert powerful effects on individuals today. As mental health professionals continued to work and study culture, theory and research necessarily became more complex. Mental health professionals expanded the scope of culture to include other cultural identities, including nationality, language, gender, religion, sexual orientation, socioeconomic status, disability or ability status, and size (Cornish, Schreier, Nadkarni, Metzger, & Rodolfa, 2010). They also began to explore the fact that a person's various cultural identities were presented in conjunction with each other and exerted reciprocal effects on one another. This led to theory and research examining the intersectionality of various types of cultural identities (Cole, 2009). As such, culture, as a broader term, reflects the fact that people belong to and identify with different cultural groups. This sense of belonging to different cultural groups influences every aspect of one's life, including beliefs, values, attitudes, and worldviews.

In examining culture in therapy, some important research on health disparities was conducted in the 1970s and 1980s (e.g., S. Sue, 1976; S. Sue, McKinney, & Allen, 1976). This work documented that racial and ethnic minority clients had worse therapy outcomes compared with White clients (S. Sue, 1977). Moreover, racial and ethnic minority clients were not seeking therapeutic services as much as White clients. When they did seek services, they had higher rates of premature termination and dropout and also reported smaller levels of symptom improvement relative to White clients. These findings disturbed many mental health professionals, who devoted their careers to thinking and writing about why therapy did not seem to be working as well for racial and ethnic minority clients and what could be done to improve the situation.

This enterprise led mental health professionals to realize that many therapists were doing a poor job of addressing cultural identities in therapy (S. Sue & Zane, 1987). This finding was not surprising; mental health professionals were just beginning to write about the idea that cultural identities might be important to explore in therapy. Thus, therapists entering the field did not have the necessary training for how to think about or address cultural identities in the therapy room.

These mental health professionals critiqued many therapeutic models and techniques. They pointed out important limitations of therapeutic models that were aimed at all people, regardless of cultural background. They worked to articulate the role of culture in shaping individuals' beliefs, values, thoughts, feelings, behaviors, and interpersonal relationships. Likewise, they highlighted the role of culture in how clients and therapists understand some of the key variables in the therapy process, including the presenting problem, goals, interventions, and even the idea of what therapy should look like. This line of theory and research coalesced into a body of work on how to train therapists to be effective or competent in their work with culturally diverse clients (D. W. Sue, 2001; D. W. Sue, Arredondo, & McDavis, 1992; D. W. Sue et al., 1982).

Multicultural Competence

The first major model of multicultural competencies was developed by Derald Wing Sue and colleagues in the early 1980s (D. W. Sue et al., 1982). The model involved three components. First, therapists were encouraged to develop *self-awareness* of their own cultural background and experiences and gain a better understanding of how these identities affected others. For example, some White individuals in the United States might not necessarily think of themselves as having a "culture" because culture can be invisible for people who are members of privileged groups (i.e., groups that have greater collective bargaining power to negotiate formal structuring of institutions and subtle expression of social norms to prioritize their values and interests; McIntosh, 1988). This aspect of multicultural competencies encouraged therapists to acknowledge and explore their cultural background and to note points of connection or disconnection regarding their own and the client's cultural background.

Second, therapists were encouraged to develop *knowledge* for working with various cultural groups. As we noted previously, culture has a large influence on one's way of thinking, feeling, behaving, and interacting. Therapists were encouraged to learn all they could about various cultural groups so they could better understand and help their clients.

Third, therapists were encouraged to develop specific *skills* for working with culturally diverse clients. Psychologists noted that certain kinds of interventions were likely to work better or worse with clients from different cultural backgrounds. For example, encouraging a client to be more independent and to disregard the wishes of their family may be a misguided suggestion in some cultures that are more collectivistic. Also, therapists should realize that certain skills may be required to address and discuss culture and cultural identities in the therapy room.

This model of multicultural competencies has had important effects on the field of psychology and other helping professions, including medicine, psychiatry, social work, and counseling (APA, 2003). To become a therapist in almost any discipline requires completing coursework in multicultural counseling. Much of this coursework is based on D. W. Sue and colleagues' (1982) three-part model of multicultural competence.

Although this model of multicultural competence is popular and widely disseminated in several mental health fields, it is not without its critics (Owen, 2013; Weinrach & Thomas, 2002). Most of the critiques of this model have focused on the research base supporting its use, implementation, and effectiveness. First, measures of multicultural competence have been difficult to develop and validate. For example, researchers and clinicians have questioned the validity of self-report measures of multicultural competence. Self-report measures of multicultural competencies have been linked to social desirability (Constantine & Ladany, 2000). Therapists who rate themselves as "very high" in multicultural competence may be accurate or may perhaps lack self-awareness, demonstrating a lack of humility in their overconfidence.

Given these concerns, the majority of research in this area has used client-report measures, in which the client rates the therapist on perceived multicultural competence (Tao, Owen, Pace, & Imel, 2015). Although these other-report measures seem to fare better than self-reports, they have their issues as well. Namely, some aspects of multicultural competence (e.g., the therapist's knowledge of racial identity models) involve jargon that is likely unfamiliar to clients and may be difficult or impossible for clients to rate (see Drinane, Owen, Adelson, & Rodolfa, 2016). Furthermore, ratings of perceived multicultural competence may be confounded with measures of general competence or closeness with the therapist. Taken together, because measurement is crucial to a solid scientific foundation, the major concerns regarding measurement of multicultural competencies have undermined the confidence in this body of work.

Perhaps just as concerning, mental health professionals have noted the absence of scientific support for the hypothesis that multicultural competence, as a quality of the therapist, predicts better outcomes in therapy (Owen, Leach, Wampold, & Rodolfa, 2011). When clients rate their therapist as low in multicultural competence, this corresponds with negative outcomes in therapy. However, most studies in this area have looked at single pairings of therapists and clients, so ratings of multicultural competencies are likely mixed up with factors that are specific to the particular relationship between the therapist and client. In studies that have looked at multicultural competence as a quality of the therapist (measured by aggregating ratings across clients), this construct does not reliably predict client outcomes (Owen et al., 2011). These findings ought to make therapists question the scientific basis for models promoting multicultural competence given that there is currently no established link between this construct (as a quality of the therapist) and better therapy outcomes.

In our work with therapists-in-training, we have noted another difficulty with the dominant model of multicultural competence: The focus on competence denotes a particular end state at which the therapist-in-training reaches a certain level of knowledge or skill for their work with culturally diverse clients. This language gives the impression that therapists can "arrive" in a sense in their work with diverse clients. We have started to question the usefulness of this language for thinking about and training therapists to work with diverse clients. The language sets therapists up for having unrealistic standards that may exaggerate perfectionistic striving and evaluative concerns that undermine desired qualities and behaviors. Some therapists-in-training may become preoccupied with working toward an ill-defined state of "competence." Given that this end state of competence remains vague, therapists who are honest with themselves about their limitations may feel anxious and fear negative evaluation from supervisors. Therapists may try to avoid appearing "incompetent," rather than leaning into their discomfort and anxiety about cultural identities, which is an important prerequisite for growth.

These practical issues, combined with the well-established theoretical and empirical gaps in work on multicultural competence, have led us to develop a framework that focuses on therapists' development and values regarding working with diversity. As such, for both practical and scientific reasons, we prefer the language of *humility* to *competence*. Humility encourages therapists to approach their work with culturally diverse clients with an attitude of openness, being engaged in a dynamic process of growth (Hook, Davis, Owen, Worthington, & Utsey, 2013). This process is characterized by acknowledging and owning limitations and striving to express openness and interest in the client's salient cultural identities. There is no end state of competence. There is only humility and continued growth and development over time.

On the basis of this humility framework, we have developed an approach to integrating cultural considerations into therapy that addresses some of the limitations of the existing models of multicultural approaches to therapy. Our framework is developmental in nature and acknowledges that therapists will have struggles and growth edges. We invite therapists to be honest about their growth edges and work on them, rather than aiming to achieve an unrealistic end goal of competence. Also, our framework is flexible. Rather than focusing on specific approaches for particular cultural identities, which may be unrealistic given recent theory and research on the importance of considering the intersectionality of identities, our framework provides a general structure for how to think about respecting and integrating cultural considerations into therapy. Finally, past approaches have not done a good job of integrating theory and research on diversity issues and psychotherapy. Our framework explicitly integrates cultural considerations with theory and research on the process of psychotherapy, focusing on important topics such as developing a strong working alliance and dealing with ruptures in the alliance.

Multicultural Orientation

This shift in focus from competence to humility aligns with recent theory and research on the importance of developing a strong multicultural orientation for work with diverse clients (Owen, 2013; Owen, Tao, Leach, & Rodolfa, 2011). A *multicultural orientation* refers to how a therapist thinks about and values diversity, which necessarily affects the therapist's work with diverse clients. *Multicultural competence* focuses on "ways of doing" therapy with diverse clients, including the effective implementation of cultural knowledge and skills. Multicultural orientation, however, focuses on "ways of being" with diverse clients and includes cultural humility, cultural comfort, and taking advantage of cultural opportunities (Owen, 2013).

Cultural humility is the bedrock of developing a strong multicultural orientation and reflects the focus and title of this book (Hook et al., 2013). Cultural humility involves an awareness of one's limitations to understanding a client's cultural background and experience. Cultural humility also involves an interpersonal stance that is other oriented rather than self-focused in regard to the cultural background and experience of the client. The culturally humble therapist is interested in and open to exploring the client's cultural background and experience. The culturally humble therapist does not assume their cultural perspective is "the correct one"; rather, the culturally humble therapist recognizes that there are several valid ways of viewing the world and developing a sense of one's beliefs and values.

The second aspect of multicultural orientation involves attending to and eliciting cultural opportunities in one's work with clients (Owen, 2013; Owen, Tao, et al., 2016). This is also a specific expression of cultural humility. Therapists have several decision points during therapy, and many of these decisions involve deciding whether to engage a discussion about the client's cultural background and identities. These choice points, which are guided by the therapist's multicultural orientation, can directly or indirectly communicate to the client that the therapist views the client's culture as an important aspect of the client's life that should be addressed in therapy. However, avoiding or moving away from a cultural opportunity can communicate that the client's cultural identity is unimportant or invalid.

Finally, the third aspect of multicultural orientation involves cultural comfort. This is an expression of cultural humility that involves the therapist's sense of ease when addressing cultural topics and engaging the client in cultural discussion (Owen, 2013; Owen et al., 2017). Cultural comfort is expected to directly influence a therapist's likelihood of initiating cultural dialogue with a client, and it is also expected to relate positively to the quality of a discussion with a client about culture. Cultural comfort can be developed through experiences both inside and outside the therapy room.

Who We Are

As authors, we bring four different sets of cultural stories and perspectives to bear on this book. Thus, here in the Introduction, we decided to share a bit about our own stories and how we became interested in multicultural counseling and cultural humility.

Josh: Looking back, I did not think too much about culture and diversity before I attended graduate school. A lot of this had to do with privilege. I belong to certain groups and communities that have historically had greater power, so their values and interests are disproportionally reflected in both the structure of formal societal institutions and more subtle social norms. As a cisgender (i.e., my gender identity matches my biological sex) White man, I did not have to think a lot about my cultural background and identity when I was younger. I grew up in a suburb of Chicago, in a town that consisted of people who mostly looked like me and believed the same things I did. I went to college at a large state university that was more diverse, but it was so big that I was able to surround myself with people who looked like me and viewed the world similarly to me. The most in touch I got with my ethnic heritage growing up was eating traditional Norwegian and Swedish foods during the holidays. I had the privilege to engage with and think about my cultural identity as much (or as little) as I wanted.

Culture became more salient for me when I entered graduate school. First, there was the professional side. I dove headfirst into multicultural counseling training, and I also began to develop relationships with supervisors, colleagues, and clients who identified with a variety of cultural identities. There was also the personal side. A lot of this had to do with my identity as a Christian and my growing awareness that relatively few psychologists also identified as religious. During my training, I struggled to align beliefs I had been taught growing up with new values I was developing as a counseling psychologist. This was not an easy process, and for a time I thought I would have to either give up my identity as a Christian or my identity as a psychologist.

My professional interests in multicultural counseling and cultural humility emerged from a mix of personal interest and some unexpected events along the way. I love hearing people's stories, including those about their families and cultures. I am naturally curious, and I was interested in exploring how people's cultural backgrounds influenced the problems in their lives, as well as how culture could be used as a source of support. I was interested in how or why people believed certain aspects of life were valuable and important, especially those aspects that were different from my own.

When I first got to graduate school, my advisor was on sabbatical, so I worked with a different advisor at first, which focused some of my early research on the experience of racism in African Americans, as well as cultural protective factors that buffered African Americans from the deleterious effects of race-related stress. I also spent a lot of time studying the intersection of religion and psychology—partly due to my professional interest and partly in the hope I could work out my struggles between my two seemingly conflicting identities as a person of faith and a counseling psychologist.

When I took my first faculty position, my department chair asked whether I would teach multicultural counseling. I was not sure what I was getting myself into, but I knew I was interested and passionate about the topic, so I said yes. It has been a wonderful and challenging journey over the past several years, working with students to help them navigate their struggles with cultural issues to help serve their clients. I am grateful to my students for trusting me with their process and stories; my experience teaching this class has strongly influenced my thoughts about cultural humility and working with cultural identities in therapy.

Donnie: I was home schooled through the sixth grade, in part because my parents did not trust the public school system to reflect their religious values. My mom was a devout Christian—in fact, her father and all three of her brothers were pastors. I wonder whether she would have been a pastor if that was allowed within her tradition, but as it turns out, raising her children to love Jesus was at the center of her sense of calling. When I was about 12 years old, she became depressed. As a result of several years of therapy, she explored her identities as a woman and a daughter. Over the course of her work in therapy, my mom realized she had become an expert at intuiting and responding to the needs and wants of others, for which she earned approval. But to have a greater sense of wholeness, she had to discover and honor her own interests, hopes, and dreams.

One of the ways she did this was through art. We took lessons from an artist in Atlanta who was very good. (I stopped after a few years, but my mom continued to develop into an outstanding artist.) As her four kids grew up, she also explored possibilities for a second career. She aced her GREs and got a scholarship to a counseling program near our home. Before she actualized some of these dreams, however, she was diagnosed with ovarian cancer. I was a senior in college at the time, and as soon as I graduated, I came home and worked for my dad's small home-building company and went to school with my mom. Just before finishing her internship, she died— her life cut short at age 48.

My mom is often the first person I think about when trying to understand intersecting cultural identities. I wonder what she would have done with her life if she had grown up in a cultural environment with less strict rules related to gender roles. She got to explore and expand her identity, gifts, and talents later in her life, but I wish she had gotten to do that sooner.

My interest in multiculturalism is deeply grounded in my relationship with my mom. I feel ambivalent, which I think is OK. On the one hand, I sometimes feel sad (and even angry) that certain perspectives may have limited her options and her sense of freedom to explore her calling in life. On the other hand, I do not think she viewed her sacrifice as I have come to, which gives me pause. I received many benefits from my mother's commitment to and integrity in how she understood what it meant to be a loving wife and mother. I wonder how to honor her commitments and the way she invested her life in line with her values. I think this intuition is somehow important for the work we do as therapists. We are not dealing just in the theoretical. Our clients come to us and trust us with their deepest dreams and disappointments.

Holding this tension is what I want to spend my life learning about. I want to learn to honor the strengths of cultural identities and systems to provide people with meaning and purpose, but I also want to be honest about how certain cultural values can sometimes exploit and stifle human flourishing. I want to understand how to listen to people's pain related to identity and begin to explore what it might mean to flourish as a person in the face of cultural hurts and wounds. I want to learn how to build trust even when it is hard. I want to understand how to actively participate with others to develop systems in which people have a chance to develop and grow.

Jesse: Over my life, I have come to learn that I have a complex relationship with the institutions of power, privilege, inequities, and justice. My mother is an immigrant to the United States from Malaysia, and my father is from the United States (preceded by multiple generations). They met in England, and their relationship began because of the Vietnam War (my father was in the Navy). Although I am fortunate they were able to meet, the context in which that occurred has never been lost on me. Indeed, the larger sociopolitical contexts and systems continue to define the way I understand myself, others, and the world.

In my youth, there were times when I ignored the racial and ethnic teasing from my friends, and there were times where I even joined in. At times, I did not stand up for justice or the inequitable treatment of others. Those memories sit with me to this day. As I grew up, I faced situations in which individuals called me racist terms, such as *sandnigger* and *terrorist*. Although these memories are painful, it made me wonder how many other individuals are thinking the same thing but not vocalizing their views (at least in public).

As I entered graduate school, I remember learning about cultural dynamics and how they might influence the therapy process. The lessons were rife with stereotypes, surface-level exposure, and a focus on deficit-based models of learning. Moreover, the focus tended to be largely on race and ethnicity and tended to ignore the true complexity of culture—in particular, the concept of intersectionality. What was even more disconcerting to me was the lack of empirical data guiding the treatment suggestions. In addition, the treatment suggestions appeared to lack a connection to how actual therapy is conducted (not to mention missing how to conceptualize cultural exchanges based on modern empirically supported treatments). In my private practice, I tend to find a more natural way of being with clients to truly honor the complexities of cultural dynamics.

From these experiences, I have dedicated my professional and personal life to better understanding how I relate to the institutions and systems that influence the lived experiences of minority and majority identified individuals. I know I do not have the answers to these complex issues, but I am dedicated to being part of the discussion.

Cirleen: I feel like culture was a salient construct to me before I even had the words to articulate the ways in which my identities and worldview reflected my cultural experiences. I identify as a biracial Asian American cisgender woman. I would add my identities as an ally, first-generation college student, and daughter of an immigrant as salient as well. My mother emigrated from Taiwan to the United States in her mid-20s and met and married my father, a Belgian American from Ohio. I lived in four countries (Japan, Taiwan, Saudi Arabia, the United States) before I was 8 years old. The transition from Saudi Arabia to the United States was the most challenging. I went from attending an international school at which cultural and ethnic diversity were inherently present and celebrated to attending an elementary school in a small town in Florida where there were few Asian or multiracial families. I recall my younger sisters being the only other Asian children at my school. So I went from not seeing my ethnicity or biracial identity as the defining characteristic of my person to being a "chink" in a transition that was extremely painful. The one question I constantly asked myself was: "Why?" "Why did people see me so differently here?" "Why did they see something wrong with me?" and, eventually, "What was wrong with me?" I think my educational journey has been one of trying to understand these questions.

I did not plan on getting a PhD. I did not see the point in spending 5 years of my life pursuing a degree if I did not find something I was passionate about and would want to study with that level of intensity. However, I did pursue a master's degree, and in my second year, I took my first multicultural psychology course. My diversity course with Dr. Adelbert Jenkins was an absolute awakening for me. For the first time in my life, I had language for my experience—my identity development, the complexity of my multiple ethnicities, racism, systemic oppression, and privilege. It was all there. I felt like I took my first real breath as a psychologist. I had found my passion. I wanted to do that—to explore identity, to combat oppression, to do work that would elucidate the pervasive and insidious impact of discrimination. I think on a basic level, my work as a researcher, teacher, mentor, and therapist is an answer to the question I asked as a kid—"What is wrong with me?" The answer was "Nothing!" We are all cultural beings who deserve the opportunity to develop authentically and be genuinely seen and known.

Structure and Outline of This Book

The focus on multicultural orientation has important ramifications for training and work with diverse clients, as well as the organization of this volume. The focus of this book is different from that of many texts on multicultural competence, which tend to have a chapter devoted to various types of clients (e.g., one chapter on counseling African American clients, one chapter on counseling lesbian, gay, bisexual, and transgender clients). It is not that we view developing knowledge and skills for work with specific types of clients to be unimportant. Other texts have done a good job providing baseline knowledge and skill. Also, attempting to apply knowledge and skills about general groups without a baseline value of cultural humility can easily devolve into stereotyping or other cultural problems. The existing body of work reflects valuable resources of a diverse profession, but what is needed is an approach for engaging these resources and contextualizing them to the specific needs of the client who is sitting in the therapy room. Each client has a unique identity that is based on their personality, experience, and intersecting cultural identities. Something new is needed to clarify and explore what this task requires.

Instead of focusing one chapter on various types of cultural backgrounds, we organize this book into two main sections. First, in Part I (Chapters 1–3), we present the theoretical foundation of our book, focusing on self-awareness and the importance of developing a strong multicultural orientation that values diversity in all forms. Specifically, in Chapter 1, we explore in detail the concepts of cultural humility, cultural comfort, and cultural opportunities and what they mean for us as therapists. In Chapters 2 and 3, we shift our focus to the person of the therapist and delve into the therapist's cultural identity, background, and experiences. In Chapter 2, we invite you to explore your cultural identities, as well as the relationship or intersection between your cultural identities and systems of power and privilege. In Chapter 3, we work with you to develop a plan for working on becoming more comfortable with cultural differences, reducing your cultural biases, and exploring what to do with your experiences of power and privilege. In this section, we set the groundwork for you to develop cultural humility in your life, to better prepare you for engaging in your work with culturally diverse clients.

Then, in Part II (Chapters 4–9), we shift our focus to the therapy room and explore how cultural humility shows up in the interpersonal interactions between therapist and client. In this second section, we first present an overview of the connections between having a multicultural orientation and the various tasks of therapy, such as intake procedures, diagnosis, case conceptualization, treatment planning, and the use of interventions (Chapter 4). Then we present a detailed discussion about four core ways in which you can integrate cultural humility and the multicultural orientation model with the key processes of therapy: developing a strong working alliance with clients of various cultural identities (Chapter 5), avoiding cultural ruptures and microaggressions and repairing the therapeutic relationship if and when they do occur (Chapter 6), navigating value conflicts when they occur in therapy (Chapter 7), and understanding and addressing your limits when you face them in therapy (Chapter 8). We conclude the book by discussing cultural humility as a lifelong learning process, and we share some of our stories of continued growth (Chapter 9).

The chapters follow a similar structure. We begin with a personal story from one of the authors. Each of us is involved in teaching and training graduate students, and we focus on issues related to diversity in our teaching and training work. (When these personal stories involve work with clients, the identifying information and some details about the clients have been changed to protect client confidentiality.) Second, we describe the main content of the chapter, integrating recent research supporting the link between each topic and effective work with culturally diverse clients. Third, integrated throughout each chapter, we present practical exercises to aid in application and training. The practical exercises are designed to help you meaningfully incorporate the concepts described in each chapter into your work with clients. Our hope is that this text will actively engage you as the reader, and we encourage you to actively engage with your thoughts and feelings as you read the material and complete the exercises. At times, this engagement may bring up strong feelings or reactions, which is normal and to be expected. It may be helpful to be mindful of your environment and the psychological space you are in as you read the text and do the exercises. Finally, throughout the text, we provide several case examples[1] from a variety of settings. The case examples illustrate therapists working with the concepts presented in their work with clients, in supervision, and in consultation with other colleagues. The case examples present therapists working with varying levels of cultural humility. We hope these case examples will both normalize struggles with the material in this book and provide snapshots of therapists working to develop a strong multicultural orientation and connecting with clients and their cultural identities.

Conclusion

Improving one's therapeutic work with clients is a worthy goal. There are not many constants in the world of therapy, but one constant is that issues related to your clients' cultural identities will come up in therapy. These issues will intersect with your cultural identities in complex ways. Cultural differences may cause struggles or misunderstandings with your clients, or they may lead to an enriched therapeutic relationship that results in increased growth. Likewise, cultural similarities may lead to overidentification with your clients, or they may result in a close bond. Our goal is to explore how to engage your clients' cultural identities in a way that promotes connection rather than alienation. The main theme is this: Learn to get comfortable with acknowledging your limitations, owning them, and viewing them as opportunities to grow and connect with your clients at a deeper level. Becoming a better therapist is not an end state to be achieved through striving, but rather a continued process of growth in humility, openness, interest, and flexibility.

---

[1]Case examples have been disguised to protect client confidentiality.

THEORETICAL FOUNDATION AND SELF-AWARENESS

Multicultural Orientation

1

Humility is the solid foundation of all the virtues.
—Confucius

Josh: I remember beginning to prepare to teach my
first graduate course in multicultural counseling as
a new faculty member. I had done some research
in graduate school about the intersection of religion
and therapy, as well as the experience of race-related
stress in African American college students. My chair
asked me whether I would consider teaching the
course. I thought about for a bit, and then I said yes.
Even though I tried to appear confident as I agreed to
teach the course, on the inside I felt afraid and anxious.

I doubted my abilities. Sure, I had written some
articles on a couple of different aspects of cultural
diversity, and I was interested in culture and diversity
issues, but did that make me an expert? Probably not.
I wondered whether I was way out of my league. I
was not sure how my students would react to having
a White man as the instructor. I also felt a lot of
pressure to do a good job teaching the course. I knew
that effectively engaging with clients' cultural identities
was an essential aspect of being a strong clinician. I felt

http://dx.doi.org/10.1037/0000037-002
Cultural Humility: Engaging Diverse Identities in Therapy, by J. N. Hook, D. Davis,
J. Owen, and C. DeBlaere

that, at least in some areas, I possessed a certain degree of competence, but I was not at all certain I was ready to consistently help students with a variety of identities deal with the many areas and issues that fall under the topic of multicultural counseling.

As I prepared to teach the course, I did what most beginning faculty members do—I read works by leaders in the field and gathered materials from other professors I respected. Most of the models of graduate multicultural education focused on multicultural competence. This made sense to me at first. I wanted my students to get to a place where they could competently counsel their clients. Navigating cultural identities was an important part of effective therapy, so it made sense that multicultural competence would likewise play a large role in effective therapy.

But what did multicultural competence mean? The main models of multicultural competence focused on multicultural awareness, knowledge, and skills, but which aspects were most important? My students all seemed to be in different places in their process of developing their multicultural awareness, knowledge, and skills—how much was enough to be deemed "competent"? I also started to struggle with the idea of multicultural competence. Competence seemed to focus on an end goal and achieving a certain status. But this language did not align well with my experience of growth in dealing with various aspects of culture and diversity. Often the more I learned, the more I realized I did not know. In fact, many people talk about how multicultural learning is a lifelong developmental process. I was looking for a language that captured this pursuit of ongoing learning and growth about cultural identities. In fact, when my students were worried about how they were doing (e.g., they were focused on competence and grades), they seemed less willing to share their limitations and struggles, which inhibited the learning process. I wanted my students to recognize and own their limitations instead of just trying to appear as competent as possible. These experiences led me (and others) to explore the language of humility as an alternative to competence in our research, clinical work, and training.

Multicultural Orientation Framework

This chapter outlines the multicultural orientation framework that serves as the theoretical foundation for the rest of the book. Theory guides practice. A good theory provides a framework or explanation for why we do what we do as therapists. It provides a common language for talking about clients and guides our interventions and decisions. Thus, before we get into some of the personal work of developing cultural humility, as well as practical ways to engage clients with cultural humility, it is important to discuss the theoretical foundation that guides this work. First, we critique the multicultural competency framework, which sets the stage for the development of the multicultural orientation framework that we use in this book. Second, we describe the foundational assumptions of the multicultural orientation framework. Finally, we explain the core tenets of the multicultural orientation framework. In doing so, we hope to provide you with a sense of how the multicultural orientation model can assist in the process of therapy. In addition, we highlight how cultural humility is one of the foundational aspects of this framework.

CRITIQUE OF MULTICULTURAL COUNSELING COMPETENCIES

For decades, theorists and researchers have investigated the multicultural counseling competencies of therapists (D. W. Sue et al., 1998; Whaley & Davis, 2007). A primary impetus for the multicultural competencies movement was that psychologists had mostly disregarded the needs of racial and ethnic minority clients in psychotherapy research, theoretical models, training, and practice. As mentioned in the Introduction to this volume, the multicultural competencies model defined three core aspects that professional counselors and psychologists had to demonstrate (i.e., awareness, knowledge, and skills).

Most existing models of multicultural counseling and training are based on this definition of multicultural competencies. Summarizing various multicultural competencies definitions, Whaley and Davis (2007) shared the following:

> We view cultural competence as a set of problem-solving
> skills that includes (a) the ability to recognize and understand
> the dynamic interplay between the heritage and adaptation
> dimensions of culture in shaping human behavior; (b) the ability
> to use the knowledge acquired about an individual's heritage
> and adaptational challenges to maximize the effectiveness of
> assessment, diagnosis, and treatment; and (c) internalization (i.e.,
> incorporation into one's clinical problem-solving repertoire) of this
> process of recognition, acquisition, and use of cultural dynamics so
> that it can be routinely applied to diverse groups. (p. 565)

The multicultural competencies have greatly shaped the field of psychology in many positive ways.

Although the multicultural competencies catalyzed a cross-disciplinary explosion of interest and scholarly research on how to work with culturally diverse clients (see Huey, Tilley, Jones, & Smith, 2014; D. W. Sue, 2010), the language itself has led to several well-known limitations. Some limitations are practical, such as some of the personal struggles

Josh shared about integrating the idea of competencies in his work and training. Other limitations are based on scientific research and involve major limitations in the scientific basis of multicultural competencies. For example, profound concerns regarding the accuracy of certain measurement strategies persist (Drinane, Owen, Adelson, & Rodolfa, 2016). Likewise, there is little evidence that multicultural competencies can be reliably measured as a quality of a therapist (i.e., they seem to vary by relationship and show low convergence across clients). Also, multicultural competencies as a quality of the therapist has not been associated with better therapy outcomes (e.g., higher levels of symptom improvement; see Owen, Leach, Wampold, & Rodolfa, 2011), which suggests that adopting models that purport to increase multicultural competencies may not work to improve outcomes for culturally diverse clients.

As psychologists who have committed our careers to some of the underlying values and the mission reflected in the multicultural competencies movement, we were deeply concerned with these practical and scientific limitations, and we set out to do something about it. Accordingly, Jesse Owen and colleagues (Owen, 2013; Owen, Tao, Leach, & Rodolfa, 2011) began to reexamine what constitutes effective psychotherapy practice with clients from various cultural backgrounds.

Recent work on the intersectionality of identities led us to become increasingly convinced that we might need a theoretical change rather than just a minor tweaking of the multicultural competencies model. If cultural identities intersect with each other (e.g., Black gay cisgender man, South Korean Christian cisgender woman from a lower socioeconomic status [SES] background), and these intersections are meaningful and important, then the task of identifying multicultural competencies for specific intersections of cultural identities became difficult, if not impossible, to clarify. For example, what would it mean to assess a therapist's multicultural competencies for a configuration of a client's intersecting identities involving varying levels of privilege and marginalization? The main objective of our efforts was to develop a theoretical framework that appreciates the complexities of individual differences within any social identity (e.g., race, ethnicity, gender, SES) while also providing a way forward that was easily understood, therapeutically sound, and empirically testable.

Before we start this reexamination of foundational assumptions, we should first consider the meaning of *multicultural competencies*. We are clearly in a training era in which competencies are a prevalent and guiding force. We also place a high priority on the importance of providing effective therapy services to clients from underprivileged and marginalized groups. So the question of multicultural competence is an important one. As a thought exercise, consider the following questions related to the term *competent*. What does it mean to be multiculturally competent? Specifically, what actions or behaviors would a therapist have to demonstrate to be competent? How much knowledge does a therapist need to have to be deemed multiculturally competent? Does a therapist need to have a wide breadth of knowledge (e.g., information about a wide variety of cultural groups)? Or is depth of cultural knowledge equally or even more important? How much cultural self-awareness is necessary for competence? If a therapist has some cultural biases or areas of growth, are they not competent?

Also, defining how to be multiculturally competent is a complex endeavor. When Jesse was trained in multicultural counseling, he took a course in which the instructor focused each week on one of several cultural identities. For example, they spent 1 week on counseling African American clients, 1 week on counseling lesbian, gay, bisexual, and transgender clients, 1 week on counseling clients with disabilities, and so on. This information was augmented by lectures, readings, and discussions regarding privilege, power, and oppression. On the one hand, Jesse found this information helpful, and he gained a better appreciation for his assumptions and biases. On the other hand, Jesse often found the information presented to be superficial and potentially reinforcing of stereotypes.

Where the training really fell flat was in the therapy room. Jesse had learned generalized information about various groups, but he was left largely on his own to figure out how to contextualize this collection of knowledge (about himself and various groups) to each client—and no two clients were alike. Jesse suspected the course was taught this way because this is how many authors organize their textbooks on multicultural counseling (e.g., Cornish, Schreier, Nadkarni, Metzger, & Rodolfa, 2010; D. W. Sue & Sue, 2013). But he started to wonder whether our existing training models might have overlooked a fundamental aspect of what good therapists learn to do when they engage cultural issues in therapy.

There are also other related multicultural competency terms, such as *culturally sensitive* or *culturally responsive* treatments in the literature (Whaley & Davis, 2007). Although these terms are well-intentioned, there are some shortcomings in their definitions. For instance, culturally responsive treatment seems to suggest that therapists have to be reactive (or responsive) to cultural factors in session, compared with being proactive and engaging with clients regarding their cultural identity. In addition, culturally sensitive treatments propose that therapy with culturally diverse clients has to be approached cautiously or delicately. In contrast, we suggest that therapists should have a multicultural orientation that is encompassing of the entire therapy process.

The empirical approaches to understanding cultural processes in psychotherapy do not provide many answers to the question of how to be multiculturally competent. Following the manualized treatment approach, several researchers have tailored standard treatments, such as cognitive behavioral therapy, to the cultural background of clients with specific cultural identities (see Benish, Quintana, & Wampold, 2011; Huey et al., 2014, for reviews). For example, a culturally adapted treatment could take the form of using interpersonal therapy for men who never married (e.g., Waehler, 1996) or adjusting psychodynamic therapy with lesbian, gay, and bisexual individuals (e.g., Cornett, 1993). Many of these treatments focus on panethnic groups and ignore important differences or complexities within those groups (e.g., focusing on Hispanic clients without acknowledging the differences among Hispanic clients' countries of origin). These treatments assume that therapists can learn the appropriate techniques and approaches with clients according to their social identity.

Dozens of studies comparing culturally adapted treatments (i.e., interventions that are modified to be more consistent with the cultural worldview of a particular cultural group) with standard nonadapted treatments produced results that seem equivocal. Some studies favor the culturally adapted treatments, some favor the nonadapted treatments, and some studies show no differences between treatments (for a review, see Huey et al., 2014). These results are less surprising when compared with the broader literature on psychotherapy. For example, therapists who adhere more closely to a treatment manual or who are rated as more competent (presumably because they possess more knowledge and skills; Webb, DeRubeis, & Barber, 2010) do not have better outcomes with clients. Cultural adaptation of interventions joins a variety of other seemingly good ideas that have weak empirical support.

Even if these findings on culturally adapted treatments were more promising, they focus on approaches that are more effective across therapists, rather than informing our understanding of what makes some therapists better than others when engaging with clients from various cultural backgrounds. Indeed, recent work has shown that therapists do vary in their effectiveness with clients according to their own or the client's race or ethnicity (Hayes, McAleavey, Castonguay, & Locke, 2016; Imel et al., 2011; Owen, Imel, Adelson, & Rodolfa, 2012). For example, Black clients are more likely to drop out of therapy with some White therapists compared with other White therapists. Although multicultural competencies do not explain this variability, these findings suggest that something is happening and it has to do with the therapist (see Hayes, Owen, & Nissen-Lie, 2017). We need to understand these processes better, and what we propose in this chapter is aimed to help us do that.

Taken together, these studies highlight the importance of focusing on psychotherapy outcomes when assessing our ability to work with clients with diverse cultural identities. We assume that a framework regarding working with diversity should be evaluated on the degree to which it can explain variability in therapist outcomes with clients from particular cultural identities. Therapists can assess their strengths and weaknesses for working with clients from various cultural groups (aggregated across a large number of clients) through examining client outcomes—a potentially humbling and scary process.

At an even more vital level, what inspired the multicultural orientation framework was the lack of practical guidance for therapists when facing various questions about multicultural competencies. For example, are there specific skills that a therapist should use with an Asian American client that are different from those necessary to work with a Hispanic client? Are there different skills that should be used when working with Asian American women versus Asian American men? Or Asian American gay men who are first generation to the United States compared with upper middle class Asian American transgender women?

The challenge can feel untenable when one truly takes the influence of intersecting cultural identities on the psychotherapy process seriously. The identities under consideration grow exponentially as one integrates race and ethnicity, gender, religion and spirituality, social class, sexual orientation, ability, and other identities into one's conceptualization, treatment plan, and interventions. The challenge is even more daunting when one considers the interaction of cultural identities with mental health symptoms. For example, what about generalized anxiety disorder treatment for Asian American cisgender men versus generalized anxiety disorder treatment for African American women who identify as genderqueer? Considering intersectionality in conjunction with different symptoms adds layers of complexity that may limit the effective applicability of the traditional model of multicultural competencies.

The challenge of this task led Jesse to explore an entirely different approach. Instead of using the language of competencies, the multicultural orientation framework uses the language of *orientation*. A therapist's orientation provides a lens through which one sees the world. In a way, an orientation is its own type of identity. It involves a way of being with clients and informs one's understanding of how change is possible. A parallel example to consider is that through training, therapists develop theoretical orientations (e.g., cognitive behavioral, psychodynamic, humanistic). The primary purpose of possessing and using a theoretical orientation is to organize how one understands a client's personality, presenting problem, and life context, as well as to guide the therapy process. Like other theoretical orientations in psychology and therapy, the multicultural orientation framework is intended to be an orientation that can be used alongside other therapeutic models (e.g., cognitive therapy, emotion-focused therapy, psychodynamic therapy). The multicultural orientation we hope you will embrace is grounded in a belief that by attending to, infusing, and integrating the cultural dynamics that naturally occur between therapist and client into the psychotherapy process, client therapy outcomes can be enhanced.

ASSUMPTIONS OF THE MULTICULTURAL ORIENTATION FRAMEWORK

The multicultural orientation framework has three main pillars: cultural humility, cultural opportunities, and cultural comfort (Owen, 2013). These three pillars involve one's attitudes and motivations, as well as behaviors and reactions, both within and outside the therapy space. Before we elaborate on these three pillars, we first acknowledge four foundational assumptions of the multicultural orientation framework.

First, we assume that clients and therapists cocreate cultural expressions. Wachtel (1993) noted that some therapists approach therapy with a one-person model, which focuses mainly on the client, and the person of therapist is largely ignored (except to facilitate change through techniques and relational bond). Other therapists approach therapy with a two-person model, which assumes who the therapist is can be a powerful and meaningful factor in the therapy process. In our view, the therapist is not simply a person who reflects feelings, challenges cognitive errors, and facilitates the development of insights in the client. Rather, the cultural identities of therapists can influence a variety of factors such as what clients say and do not say, how safe clients feel in the room, and so on. For example, a cisgender African American female client might relate differently to a therapist who is a cisgender African American man than to a therapist who is a cisgender African American woman. The interaction between the cultural heritages of clients and therapists can vary according to a host of factors, such as the presenting problem of the client or the personalities and socialization histories of both the therapist and client.

Take a few minutes and consider how you generally think about the therapy process, especially as it pertains to the client, the therapist, and the relationship between the therapist and client. Is there a particular metaphor you like to use to describe the client, therapist, or therapeutic relationship? For example, you might think of the therapist as a blank slate or a pillar of support. Maybe you think of the therapist as a guide who is leading the client in a process of exploration. Perhaps you think of the therapy relationship as similar to a doctor–patient relationship or an equal partnership. Take a step back and consider the metaphor you like to use. If you like to express yourself through art, draw a picture or create a work of art that reflects your metaphor. Does your metaphor reflect more of a one-person model of therapy or more of a two-person model of therapy? How might your metaphor for therapy influence how you work with clients to cocreate cultural expressions in the therapy room?

As clients and therapists cocreate cultural expressions in therapy, we assume that therapists can influence the cultural identities that are more or less salient for clients, how culturally safe the therapeutic environment feels, and the degree to which clients' cultural heritage is integrated into the therapy process. Also, therapists vary in the degree to which they discuss the therapeutic relationship with clients. Some theoretical orientations are designed to have these interactions occur more explicitly because they are thought to be part of the mechanisms for change (e.g., psychodynamic, interpersonal; Ackerman, Hilsenroth, Baity, & Blagys, 2000; Hilsenroth, Ackerman, Clemence, Strassle, & Handler, 2002). Accordingly, we assume that effective therapy requires therapists to attend to and use these cultural interpersonal dynamics in their work with clients. How therapists go about doing so (e.g., discussions of the therapeutic relationship, self-disclosures, informing the conceptualization) varies according to the needs of the client, the comfort level of the therapist, and the theoretical beliefs of the therapist. Our approach in this book is flexible regarding theoretical approach—we do not prescribe one theoretical orientation or perspective. Further, we assume that therapists will use clinical judgment for how to integrate the material that is presented in this book with their own theoretical approach. At the same time, it is likely that, regardless of theoretical orientation, discussions of cultural beliefs and values will be front and center during some therapy sessions. How those discussions are managed (i.e., with humility and comfort) will likely be of utmost importance.

Second, we assume that multicultural orientation involves a way of being with clients rather than a way of doing therapy (Owen, 2013; Owen, Tao, et al., 2011). In other words, the multicultural orientation framework is less about the actual interventions that are implemented with clients with specific cultural identities and more about the therapist's values regarding culture and the integration of those values throughout the therapeutic process. Values consistent with the multicultural orientation framework include engaging conversations about culture in a genuine, natural, curious, and real way. Integration of this value involves finding one's voice in the therapy room and having cultural conversations in a manner that is congruent with one's values and identity. Throughout this book, we provide examples of how to engage clients in cultural conversations, but these examples are intended to be guides and suggestions because you will have to find the words that work best for you.

Third, we assume that cultural processes (e.g., cultural humility) are especially important for connecting with the client's most salient cultural identities; feeling deeply known and accepted sets the stage for effective therapy. For example, Owen, Jordan, et al. (2014) found that clients' rating of their therapists' cultural humility was a significant predictor of therapy outcomes only for clients for whom their cultural identity was most salient. A key feature of this assumption is that clients have the right to define for themselves what cultural identities are most salient to them personally. This is an important distinction from other approaches in which the theorists, researchers, and therapists have assumed the importance of certain cultural identities. For example, should we presume that being a racial or ethnic minority equates to a client's racial or ethnic identity's being a primary identity for them? It could be, but we should not assume that to be the case. Moreover, it could be that for a particular racial or ethnic minority client, sexual orientation, generational status, nationality, or gender identity is a more salient identity. In addition, like the first assumption (i.e., that clients and therapists cocreate cultural expressions), for some clients, it may be that gender identity is more salient when they are discussing issues with an individual of a particular gender (e.g., men) rather than the other (e.g., women).

Fourth, we assume that having a strong multicultural orientation motivates therapists to learn new things about their own and their clients' cultural perspectives and worldviews. The values that underlie a multicultural orientation framework affect one's motivational system as a therapist. Multicultural orientation values motivate one to (a) understand one's cultural limits (e.g., gaps in knowledge, feeling uncomfortable during cultural discussions) and (b) learn and experience more about culture and diversity more broadly. Of course, some therapeutic encounters require cultural knowledge. For example, Budge (2015) described best practices in writing letters for transgender clients to obtain medical treatments. Therapists are asked to be gatekeepers in helping transgender clients to obtain gender-affirming treatments, such as gender transitioning. This level of knowledge is critical to providing adequate care for transgender clients who are seeking medical treatment. However, to state the obvious, it is impossible to know everything about every cultural group and every possible intersection of cultural identities.

Thus, the multicultural orientation framework emphasizes one's metacognition about what one does and does not know. In addition, multicultural orientation values intrinsically motivate therapists to learn more about the dynamics of their own cultural perspective and those of other cultural groups, both in their personal and professional lives. Consider for a moment: What was the last cultural experience you had that expanded your perspective? What type of documentaries are you drawn to? How diverse is your social network? How motivated are you to learn about different cultures? What proactive things are you doing to learn more about culturally diverse others? The answers to these questions are sometimes not easy to arrive at or even evaluate. For instance, we sometimes have a tendency to surround ourselves with people who look like and think similarly to us because it can feel more comfortable. These questions are intended to highlight that we all have room to grow.

CORE PILLARS OF THE MULTICULTURAL ORIENTATION FRAMEWORK

There are three core pillars of the multicultural orientation framework: cultural humility, cultural opportunities, and cultural comfort. In this section, we describe each of these pillars in detail, offer examples of therapist and client interactions that highlight each pillar, and provide an opportunity for you to assess how you are doing with each aspect of the multicultural orientation framework.

Cultural Humility

Cultural humility encompasses the intrapersonal and interpersonal spirit inherent in the multicultural orientation framework. This aspect of the multicultural orientation framework is the foundational concept that drives the other two important parts of the model: cultural opportunities and cultural comfort. Culturally humble therapists are able to have an accurate perception of their own cultural values as well as maintain an other-oriented perspective that involves respect, lack of superiority, and attunement regarding their own cultural beliefs and values (Davis, Worthington, & Hook, 2010; Hook, Davis, Owen, Worthington, & Utsey, 2013). To date, there are data on over 2,000 clients who evaluated their therapist's degree of cultural humility toward the cultural identities that were most salient to the client. The findings from these studies demonstrate that clients who view their therapist as more culturally humble have better therapy outcomes, including key therapeutic processes such as the working alliance (e.g., Davis et al., 2016; Hook et al., 2013; Hook, Farrell, et al., 2016; Owen, Jordan, et al., 2014).

The *intrapersonal* aspect of cultural humility captures how therapists are able to view themselves culturally, including their biases, strengths, limitations, areas for growth, beliefs, values, attitudes, and assumptions. In doing so, culturally humble therapists should be open to feedback from others. The use of feedback in training from supervisors, peers, and clients is commonplace. The ability to incorporate this information in a nondefensive, open stance is the hallmark of intrapersonal humility. This process of self-evaluation can be challenging, but it is critical work. Indeed, humility can be most difficult to embody during times that are most stressful. Engaging with a client in a discussion about cultural beliefs and values can be difficult. It is important to accurately gauge your reactions to various cultural issues. While doing so, attune to your true feelings, be present with the thoughts that automatically enter your mind, and resist the urge to explain or defend your reactions. For example, what is your initial reaction to a client who would like your assistance in deciding on whether she should have an abortion? Is it possible to stay neutral in such a case? What is your honest, accurate view of this issue? What are the barriers, if any, to accepting your viewpoint? What are the barriers, if any, to accepting your client's viewpoint?

The *interpersonal* aspect of cultural humility describes a way of being with others that is open to and curious about others' cultural beliefs and values rather than presumptuous or arrogant (Davis et al., 2010; Hook et al., 2013). Of course, being open to others' values and identities does not entail unconditional acceptance. As a professional community, psychologists view some beliefs and ideologies as morally inferior (e.g., viewing certain races or ethnicities as inherently superior to others). Also, you are likely to have a personal set of values that views some beliefs and ideologies as better or worse than others. The interpersonal aspect of cultural humility involves the process by which we engage beliefs and values that are different from our own. To continue our example, did you have any initial assumptions about a person who was seeking an abortion? What do these assumptions say about your beliefs and values? Again, it is important to understand and have an accurate sense of self and then contemplate how those initial reactions might impede an open, humble stance with others.

Case Example: Laura and Cesar

Consider the following therapy example of Cesar, a 31-year-old Mexican American, heterosexual, cisgender male client, and Laura, his 33-year-old White, heterosexual, cisgender female therapist. Cesar is struggling with some symptoms of depression, as well as feeling isolated at his workplace. The following is a portion of the dialogue between Cesar and Laura. As you read, think about whether Laura is engaging with Cesar in a culturally humble manner. After you read the dialogue, you will be asked to rate the therapist on her level of cultural humility.

> *Laura:* You know, you mentioned earlier that you are feeling hopeless at work, but also that things might be looking up. I wonder how you are feeling about your work situation now.
>
> *Cesar:* Well, I guess I am not feeling totally hopeless—getting a good review definitely helped a lot there—but I still feel this kind of sick feeling in my stomach when I

think about going to work each week. I just don't
know if it's the right place for me, and that worries
me because I had to fight really hard to get here.

Laura: That does sound particularly hard—I know your
parents are proud . . . but what was challenging this
week?

Cesar: Especially over this past week, I've been trying to
stay upbeat and keep myself motivated. These past
few months have just sucked—I can't kick these
negative feelings. Even when I'm really putting
in the effort, I go to work, push through the day,
and [*sighs*] when I get home, I just have to unwind
and reboot, and it doesn't feel like enough. It takes
everything I've got just to tolerate my day, and then
I just settle in in front of the TV, which makes my
girlfriend upset, but I just don't want to deal with it. I
can't explain it to her, but all I want to do is veg out.

Laura: Hmm, yeah, it sounds like you are spending so much
energy at work that you aren't able to take care of
yourself when you get home. Does that sound right
to you?

Cesar: Exactly, work takes it out of me, and I don't have the
motivation to work on my relationship or to spend
time with my family, and that's what I really want
to do. I miss them, and I miss feeling like myself.

Laura: So you are in survival mode, just trying to make it
through? Sounds hard to keep this up. What do you
think is contributing to that?

Cesar: I think it has to do in part with my being the only
Mexican man in my office. Like I feel so on edge
without a feeling of community and connection
with my colleagues, and it wears on me all the time.
I'm on my own, and people aren't really reaching out. It's exhausting trying to make it all come
together and being by myself.

Laura: Well, after listening to you these past few sessions,
I'm not really sure if your being Mexican has anything to do with it. . . . A lot of people experiencing
depression like you are feel lonely and isolated. Don't
be so hard on yourself.

What do you think? Was the therapist culturally humble or not?
What parts of the dialogue indicated that the therapist was culturally
humble (or not)? Try using the scale in Exhibit 1.1 to rate your impression of the therapists' cultural humility. It is important to know that these

EXHIBIT 1.1

Cultural Humility Scale

Regarding the client's cultural background, the therapist . . .	Strongly disagree (1)	Mildly disagree (2)	Neutral (3)	Mildly agree (4)	Strongly agree (5)
1. Was respectful.	1	2	3	4	5
2. Was open to explore.	1	2	3	4	5
3. Assumed she already knows a lot.	1	2	3	4	5
4. Was considerate.	1	2	3	4	5
5. Was genuinely interested in learning more.	1	2	3	4	5
6. Acted superior.	1	2	3	4	5
7. Was open to seeing things from the client's perspective.	1	2	3	4	5
8. Made assumptions about the client.	1	2	3	4	5
9. Was open-minded.	1	2	3	4	5
10. Was a know-it-all.	1	2	3	4	5
11. Thought she understood more than she actually did.	1	2	3	4	5
12. Asked questions when she was uncertain.	1	2	3	4	5

Note. To score the scale, first reverse code Items 3, 6, 8, 10, and 11. Then add up the scores. Higher scores indicate higher levels of cultural humility. Adapted from "Cultural Humility: Measuring Openness to Culturally Diverse Clients," by J. N. Hook, D. E. Davis, J. Owen, E. L. Worthington, Jr., and S. O. Utsey, 2013, *Journal of Counseling Psychology, 60*, p. 366. Copyright 2013 by American Psychological Association.

are just your initial reactions. We understand that it can be challenging to rate a dialogue without seeing it on video (or live), but try your best. If you are working through this book with a group or class, take some time to discuss your perspective with others. How did you come up with your scores? What statements in the dialogue led you to rate the therapist as more or less culturally humble? Was there any disagreement in the group about whether Laura was more or less culturally humble?

Cultural Opportunities

Cultural opportunities are the second pillar of the multicultural orientation framework. Cultural opportunities are markers that occur in therapy in which the client's cultural beliefs, values, or other aspects of the client's cultural identity could be explored (Owen, 2013; Owen, Tao, et al., 2016). Each therapy session provides multiple opportunities to explore and integrate a client's cultural heritage, but for a variety of reasons many of these opportunities go unrealized.

Consider the example of Cesar and Laura. When Cesar mentioned that he thought his struggles might have to do with being the only Mexican man at his office, Laura had the opportunity to explore more about his cultural experience as a Mexican American man in an office in which most of his colleagues are White. Instead, Laura assumed that Cesar's distress was rooted in his depressive symptomology and wanted to focus on the depressive symptoms instead.

There could be many reasons why Laura decided to go this route. Perhaps Cesar had displayed a pattern in the past of avoiding discussion of his depressive symptoms, and Laura wanted to encourage him to maintain focus on the depression. Maybe she felt anxious about the cultural comment and was not sure how to address it. Perhaps Laura was experiencing some racial or ethnic prejudice (unconscious or conscious) and did not want to admit that her client's problems could have been partially caused by a difficult, stressful, and potentially racist work environment. Whatever the reason, by taking the route she did, Laura could have missed a cultural opportunity to connect with Cesar. Furthermore, by not addressing the cultural comment, Laura likely minimized Cesar's feelings about his cultural identity. In doing so, she committed a *micro-aggression*, a subtle discriminatory insult to or invalidation of Cesar's cultural identity (D. W. Sue et al., 2007).

Cultural opportunities and cultural humility work in tandem during therapy sessions. For example, Owen, Tao, et al. (2016) found that clients who reported that their therapists missed cultural opportunities reported poorer therapy outcomes. However, those negative effects were mitigated if clients viewed the therapist as high in cultural humility. These findings suggest that maintaining a culturally humble stance can offset some cultural mistakes or missteps.

Cultural opportunities arise when clients mention a cultural belief, value, or some other aspect of their cultural heritage. These moments provide natural chances for the therapist to transition to a deeper exploration of a client's cultural identity. Other times, the therapist may initiate cultural opportunities. For example, in a session in which a client describes the loss of a family member to suicide, the therapist might say, "Sometimes when people face tragedy, they turn to religion or spirituality to cope. I am wondering if that is true for you?" In this example, the therapist relies on previous knowledge about grief and loss to create an opportunity for cultural exploration. What is nice about this intervention is the therapist does not make assumptions about the client's cultural worldview. If the question does not fit for the client, the therapist and client can move on to more relevant clinical material. But if it does fit, it may facilitate an important discussion about a cultural identity that is important for the client.

We invite you to engage in an exercise that will help you notice cultural opportunities in your everyday life. Today, during your conversations with family, friends, and colleagues, pay particular attention to cultural opportunities that may come up. For example, make a note if someone you are talking with mentions an aspect of their cultural identity. Also, try to think about how you could link the various experiences or topics that people talk about to aspects of their cultural identity. If a cultural opportunity comes up, try to pursue the cultural opportunity and ask a question about the person's cultural identity. Do not force the conversation in that direction; just ask a question and see where the conversation goes. At the end of the day, spend some time thinking, reflecting, and journaling about what happened. How many cultural opportunities did you notice throughout your day? Was it helpful to be more attentive to the cultural opportunities that came up?

We view cultural opportunities to be a naturally unfolding process over the course of therapy, rather than a specific rule or set of rules to which all therapists must rigidly adhere. For example, some therapists advocate for having explicit conversations about certain cultural identities in the first session. This recommendation is difficult to reconcile with research showing that some clients do not want or need therapists to address cultural concerns in therapy (Chang & Berk, 2009; Maxie, Arnold, & Stephenson, 2006). Similarly, initial evidence has suggested that discussing race or ethnicity within the first session is unrelated to therapy outcomes with racial or ethnic minority clients (Thompson & Alexander, 2006).

These findings suggest that greater nuance may be needed regarding when and how therapists decide to explore cultural opportunities. We revisit this issue in greater depth in Chapter 5, but for now, suffice it to say that perhaps it is better to look for organic ways to address cultural issues in therapy rather than force abrupt transitions that may unsettle clients and distract from the natural flow of therapy. Any given moment can provide a variety of inroads to explore the client's cultural heritage. Within the multicultural orientation framework, the critical issue is the degree to which clients perceive their therapist is willing and motivated to explore their cultural identity (Owen, Tao, et al., 2016). As a therapist, it is important to explore your decisions about whether to engage in cultural opportunities (or not) in your sessions with clients, as well as the motivations behind them. Especially for beginning therapists, there can sometimes be a tendency to avoid discussion of cultural topics because of inexperience, anxiety, or discomfort. Thus, although we encourage therapists to engage in organic discussions of cultural opportunities, it is important to consider and challenge one's thoughts, feelings, and motivations for not addressing cultural topics in session.

Case Examples

In the following examples, we provide client statements to which there could be multiple therapeutic responses. Specifically, these client statements afford an opportunity for the therapist to address the client's culture or move the conversation in an alternate direction without engaging the client's culture. We would like you first to read the client statement and then consider how you might respond. We start with an excerpt from the earlier example and provide an example response statement. After that, we provide another client example for you to try out for yourself.

Cesar:	I think it has to do in part with my being the only Mexican man in my office. Like I feel so on edge without a feeling of community and connection with my colleagues, and it wears on me all the time. I'm on my own, and people aren't really reaching out. It's exhausting trying to make it all come together and being by myself.
Laura—Symptom focus:	I can see it on your face; you seem exhausted just talking about this. I am wondering how this experience is affecting your ability to make changes, both in your home life and in your office.
Laura—Cultural focus:	I can see it on your face; you seem exhausted just talking about this. I am curious what it means for you to be the only Mexican man in the office.

As you can see, there is a decision to be made about the direction of the therapeutic discussion. The focus of Laura's first comment was to check in about how the client's level of distress was inhibiting his ability to apply what he was learning in therapy to make changes in his home and work life. It was not necessarily an error, but it did not take advantage of the cultural opportunity the client presented. Her second comment highlighted the impact of the client's cultural identity. This approach could lead to new insights about the client's level of distress, as well as other ways of being in the therapy room and the workplace.

Now we invite you to try this second example. The client is Kristi, a 35-year-old Chinese American, heterosexual, cisgender woman who has been married for 7 years. She has two children with her husband. Her family lives with her parents, who are immigrants from China. The client and her family identify as Christian.

Kristi:	I have been feeling very down lately. I don't know why, but I have now been feeling more anxious since we chatted last week. I know this is only our third session, but I am just feeling nervous every day. I can't stay focused at work, and it is really affecting my

relationship with my husband. I guess I have been questioning my relationship with him . . . but I could never think about being divorced.

Therapist Statement—
Symptom focus: _____

Therapist Statement—
Cultural focus: _____

How was it to come up with a symptom-focused response, as well as a culture-focused response? Which response was easier to write? Which response felt more natural to you? Try to brainstorm some benefits and drawbacks for each response. If you were the therapist in this scenario, which one do you think you would be more likely to use? Which response would be more likely to promote a deeper connection and discussion about the client's cultural identities?

Next, we would like you to evaluate each response using the scale in Exhibit 1.2, the cultural opportunity scale from our research. It might be hard to evaluate your own work, so you may want to complete this exercise with a peer. Try to evaluate each response using the cultural opportunity items. You can see that some responses are more or less culturally focused. You can use this rubric to help evaluate other therapist comments throughout the book.

EXHIBIT 1.2

Cultural Opportunities Scale

	Strongly disagree	Mildly disagree	Neutral	Mildly agree	Strongly agree
1. The therapist encouraged the client to discuss the client's cultural background more.	1	2	3	4	5
2. The therapist discussed the client's cultural background in a way that seemed to work.	1	2	3	4	5
3. The therapist avoided topics related to the client's cultural background.	5	4	3	2	1
4. There were many chances to have deeper discussions about the client's cultural background that never happened.	5	4	3	2	1
5. The therapist missed opportunities to discuss the client's cultural background.	5	4	3	2	1

Note. To score the scale, first reverse code Items 3, 4, and 5. Then add up the scores. Higher scores indicate that more cultural opportunities were explored. Adapted from "Client Perceptions of Therapists' Multicultural Orientation: Cultural (Missed) Opportunities and Cultural Humility," by J. Owen, K. W. Tao, J. M. Drinane, J. Hook, D. E. Davis, and N. Foo Kune, 2016, *Professional Psychology: Research and Practice, 47*, p. 33. Copyright 2016 by the American Psychological Association.

Cultural Comfort

Cultural comfort is the third pillar of the multicultural orientation framework. Cultural comfort relates to the feelings that arise before, during, and after culturally relevant conversations in session between the therapist and client. The emotional states of feeling at ease, open, calm, and relaxed are hallmarks of cultural comfort. Discussing issues related to culture can sometimes feel difficult and uncomfortable, and some therapists may feel awkward or tense when having these discussions. Therapists with high levels of cultural comfort can moderate their anxiety when having cultural conversations and instead engage the client in a composed, relaxed, and connected manner. Owen et al. (2017) found that therapists' cultural comfort helped explain the racial and ethnic disparities in treatment dropout within therapists' caseloads. In other words, some therapists were better at retaining their White clients than their racial or ethnic minority (REM) clients, whereas other therapists showed the opposite pattern (see Figure 1.1). Therapists who were less culturally comfortable with REM clients had a higher rate of dropout for

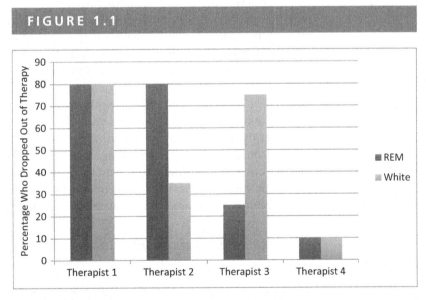

FIGURE 1.1

Percentage of racial and ethnic minority and White clients who dropped out of therapy. REM = racial and ethnic minority. Adapted from "'No-Show': Therapist Racial/Ethnic Disparities in Client Unilateral Termination," by J. Owen, Z. Imel, J. Adelson, and E. Rodolfa, 2012, *Journal of Counseling Psychology*, *59*, p. 318. Copyright 2012 by the American Psychological Association.

their REM clients than their White clients. Also, cultural comfort can interact with cultural humility—it is difficult to be culturally humble if one does not feel comfortable being open or curious about a client's cultural heritage.

Emotional states provide important signals for therapists. Therapists who are higher in cultural comfort are more likely to have cultural conversations with their clients. They are also more likely to respond to cultural markers during sessions (i.e., cultural opportunities). In addition, their clients are more likely to discuss cultural topics because the therapists have established a safe, positive, cultural therapeutic environment (Owen, Drinane, et al., 2016; Tao, Whiteley, Noel, & Ozawa-Kirk, 2016; Tao, Whiteley, Noel, Ozawa-Kirk, & Owen, 2016). Emotional states are also signals for clients. For example, clients' sense of emotional safety in session is paramount because many REM clients do not trust the medical and/or psychological community (Whaley & Davis, 2007). Accordingly, therapists' cultural comfort sends a signal to clients that it is OK to discuss cultural issues in session.

Cultural discomfort can provide vital feedback to therapists about areas that are in need of further exploration and development. For example, if a therapist feels uneasy about discussing sex with a gay couple, the therapist may want to seek out consultation or supervision to figure out why the discomfort is occurring. Cultural discussions may elicit strong emotional reactions, some of which may be uncomfortable because of a lack of familiarity, conflicting values, and so on. Although it may be difficult to explore these emotions, we urge you throughout this book to lean into the discomfort rather than avoid or run away from the uneasiness. These feelings are excellent windows into new insights about the cultural dynamics between you and your client, and they also may help you identify areas for future growth. However, to benefit most thoroughly from these emotions, therapists need cultural humility to be willing and open to listening to and exploring the uncomfortable feelings. Moreover, therapists have to be aware of the cultural topics they tend to avoid because avoidance is a typical defense against discomfort.

Case Example: Graham and Adam

Consider the following supervision example between Graham, a 49-year-old White, heterosexual, cisgender male supervisor and Adam, a 25-year-old White, heterosexual, cisgender male therapist. They discuss Adam's most recent session with Arthur, a 56-year-old White, heterosexual, cisgender male client. Arthur is a nontraditional student who returned to school after having to quit his job as a carpenter because of the physical symptoms of Parkinson's disease.

> *Graham:* We haven't talked much about your work with Arthur lately. How did your session go this past week?

Adam:	I guess it went OK.
Graham:	Just OK? How are you feeling about it?
Adam:	Well, we're still in the beginning stages, still trying to get to know one another. But I guess it's just been challenging because he's really struggling with trying to get back into school, and I don't blame him. I mean, he's been out of school for 35 years! I couldn't imagine doing that.
Graham:	Yeah, it does sound like a tough situation. How does his physical disability impact the goals he is working toward in therapy?
Adam:	I'm sure it has to make his schoolwork more difficult. I mean, he needed a lot of help with filling out the intake paperwork. I bet it's difficult to take exams and take notes in class.
Graham:	How has it been to discuss those things in therapy with him?
Adam:	Well, to be honest, it hasn't come up a whole lot thus far. We talked about it a little bit at the beginning when he was talking about his reasons for the career change and going back to school because he couldn't maintain his manual labor job because of his disability. But lately we've been talking more about his goals, what types of careers he might be interested in, adjustment to college, things like that.
Graham:	Interesting. . . . I'm curious if you have any thoughts about why you haven't talked more about his disability. It seems like it might be pretty important to what he's presenting with in therapy.
Adam:	I don't know. I guess, to be honest, I didn't want to make him feel self-conscious about the disability, and I thought maybe talking about it more would draw attention to it. But maybe I'm a little uncomfortable talking about it myself.

Did you have any reactions to the dialogue between Graham and Adam? What do you make of the fact that Arthur's disability has not come up often in therapy? How comfortable did Adam appear to be when discussing Arthur's disability? If you were Adam's supervisor, how could you help him to work on becoming more comfortable in his work with Arthur specifically and with disability or ability status issues more generally?

Exploring Your Cultural Comfort

Changes in cultural comfort are also important markers. Shifts in cultural comfort or discomfort within a session may indicate topics that require further exploration. Certainly, reactions within the session can guide one's therapy, especially within certain theoretical approaches. For example, a therapist might notice a growing discomfort and tension as a client discusses his family's attitudes toward discussing money. Beginning therapists might be tempted to ignore such shifts or seek to reduce the uncomfortable feelings, but sometimes these emotions can provide important clues to what is happening within the therapeutic relationship, and they may indicate subtle experiences of the client that deserve further exploration. The therapist might disclose noticing a shift, which could provide an opportunity to understand the client at a deeper level. In this way, therapists' cultural comfort might inform cultural opportunities within a session, which should be met with a level of cultural humility. Accordingly, these three pillars should work in combination for the greater good of the client.

In this next exercise, we would like you to think about your level of cultural comfort with various cultural identities. Specifically, we would like you to watch a series of videos (e.g., documentary, social media clip). We encourage you to watch videos that represent new or novel cultural topics for you. If you are stuck on what type of video to watch, pick one video from several categories of various cultural identities (e.g., race, ethnicity, gender, sexual orientation, religion, disability or ability status, progressive chronic illness, SES). It would be good to watch some videos that are within your cultural comfort zone as well as some that are outside of it. After watching each video, complete the items in Exhibit 1.3.

EXHIBIT 1.3

Cultural Comfort Scale

Overall, how comfortable did you feel watching the video?	Strongly disagree (1)	Mildly disagree (2)	Neutral (3)	Mildly agree (4)	Strongly agree (5)
1. Comfortable	1	2	3	4	5
2. Awkward	5	4	3	2	1
3. Tense	5	4	3	2	1
4. Nervous	5	4	3	2	1
5. Confident	1	2	3	4	5
6. Uneasy	5	4	3	2	1
7. Relaxed	1	2	3	4	5
8. Calm	1	2	3	4	5
9. Edgy	5	4	3	2	1
10. Genuine	1	2	3	4	5

Note. To score this measure, first reverse code Items 2, 3, 4, 6, and 9. Then add up the total values. Higher scores indicate higher levels of cultural comfort. From "Racial/Ethnic Disparities in Client Unilateral Termination: The Role of Therapists' Cultural Comfort," by J. Owen, J. Drinane, K. W. Tao, J. L. Adelson, J. N. Hook, D. Davis, and N. Foo Kune, 2017, *Psychotherapy Research, 27*, p. 106. Copyright 2017 by Taylor & Francis. Reprinted with permission.

After you finish watching the videos and rate your degree of cultural comfort with each one, spend some time discussing your experience with a friend or colleague. Which videos were more comfortable for you to watch? Which videos were less comfortable for you to watch? What did you learn about your degree of cultural comfort with various types of cultural identities? After you have spent some time sharing your experiences, ask your discussion partner if they have any feedback for you. In particular, do they have any feedback about how comfortable or uncomfortable you appeared during the discussion of the various videos and types of cultural identities?

Conclusion

We hope this chapter has provided you with a new framework to understand cultural dynamics in psychotherapy. We continue to expand on these principles throughout the book, with a particular focus on cultural humility. We focus more on this aspect of the multicultural orientation framework because this pillar is truly the foundation for the framework. At this point, we have provided information regarding (a) why the multicultural orientation framework is different from the multicultural competencies approach, (b) the core assumptions of the multicultural orientation framework, and (c) the three main pillars of the multicultural orientation framework. In the next chapter, we shift our focus to self-awareness and invite you to explore your own cultural identity, as well as the relationships between your cultural identity and systems of power and privilege.

Exploring Your Cultural Identity 2

Who in the world am I? Ah, that's the great puzzle.
—Lewis Carroll, *Alice's Adventures in Wonderland*

Jesse: My paternal grandfather had many great qualities—he served in World War II, he was a successful businessman, he was handy with construction (he even built a two-story garage), and he raised my father, just to name a few of his notable accomplishments. However, he was quite biased—racist—against racial and ethnic minorities. He is responsible for a notable memory highlighting my awareness of being a racial and ethnic minority (biracial, Malaysian—my mother is an immigrant to the United States—and European—my father's side of the family) when I was young.

It was around the time of the first Gulf War, and we (my father, mother, older brother, and I) were sitting with my grandfather watching the news about the war. He made a remark about the Iraqi army in a negative racist term and then quickly looked over at my mother and asked, "Where are you from again?" He continued with a few more disparaging remarks, and then my mother encouraged my brother and me to go and play in the yard. What I remember

http://dx.doi.org/10.1037/0000037-003
Cultural Humility: Engaging Diverse Identities in Therapy, by J. N. Hook, D. Davis, J. Owen, and C. DeBlaere

the most about this experience is the steadfastness, strength, patience, and thoughtfulness of my mother. She seemed unfazed by his comments and quickly turned to protecting us. These types of events would continue throughout my life in more and less overt and intentional ways. In most situations, I try to channel my mother's spirit of strength. Moreover, these situations have fueled my passion to not only know and understand my cultural identity but also to help eliminate the hatred that can divide us.

Cultural Humility and Self-Awareness

Mental health professionals place a high value on personal insight and self-awareness (Richardson & Molinaro, 1996; D. W. Sue, Arredondo, & McDavis, 1992). In this chapter, our goal is to help you explore and better understand your cultural identity, worldview, beliefs, values, and attitudes. Some of you might wonder what the point of self-awareness and cultural exploration is. In our view, the purpose is not just to increase your knowledge about yourself for the sake of gaining knowledge, but the hope is that as you increase your self-awareness and understanding, you will have a better sense of how your cultural identities and values affect your sense of self and your interactions with others, especially your clients. A core aspect of cultural humility involves knowing yourself well, including awareness and ownership of your strengths and limitations.

We hope you will push yourself to be as real and honest as you can when you complete the activities in this chapter. At times, you might experience discomfort, shame, anger, or sadness in exploring these topics—that is normal. At other times you might feel proud and appreciative of exploring your cultural identity—that is normal too. Regardless of the feelings that come up, we hope you sit with your feelings, avoid the temptation to run from any negative emotions you may experience, and be mindful of how your positive emotions can fuel your motivation to do more work in this area. This motivation should also lead you to have conversations with others about their experiences as well. We hope you have the courage to take risks in being vulnerable with others (assuming it is safe to do so).

Cultural self-awareness is an important component of cultural humility and developing a strong multicultural orientation (Hook, Davis, Owen, Worthington, & Utsey, 2013; Owen, 2013). An important part of cultural humility involves an awareness of your cultural identities, beliefs, and values. This is where the work of self-awareness starts. Taking time to honor where your cultural identity originates and reflecting on the roots of your cultural heritage is crucial. These foundational lived experiences of your family members provided valuable lessons and also reflect the sociopolitical environment of the times in which you grew up. Of course, these experiences and lessons teach and guide our way of being. At the same time, there are other lessons and experiences your family and you did not experience. This is a reminder that we cannot fully know the lived experiences of others. Accordingly, knowing the scope of your cultural awareness, as well the limits of your ability to truly understand the cultural experiences of others, is a key aspect of cultural humility. Understanding yourself as a cultural being, as well as how your cultural identities intersect with experiences of power, privilege, and oppression, is an important step in this process.

What does cultural self-awareness look like in practice? How much self-awareness is necessary to be effective in therapy? Should there ever be an end to self-exploration? It can be overwhelming to consider all of the origins, histories, intersecting values, and expressions within your own set of cultural identities. This becomes even more complex when you consider the interactions of your cultural identities and those of your clients. Accordingly, we want to be clear about what, why, and how cultural self-awareness can be harnessed to promote cultural humility.

We consider cultural self-awareness to contain four main components: (a) knowledge structures (e.g., knowledge of your cultural identity), (b) motivational processes (e.g., the process of learning), (c) relational experiences (e.g., how your cultural identity intersects with others and the sociopolitical systems of power, privilege, and equity), and (d) meta- and epistemic cognitions (e.g., reflective capacity). Our hope is that by better understanding your cultural identities in these four areas, you will be able to feel more secure in yourself culturally and be able to engage in cultural discussions, knowing your perspective and vantage point.

KNOWLEDGE STRUCTURES

First, the starting point to cultural self-awareness begins with increasing cultural knowledge and understanding about your particular cultural identities. However, we encourage you to go deeper than simply identifying the cultural identities that are important to you. Indeed, your cultural identities include your personal, family, and sociopolitical histories that help inform the broader contexts of your cultural heritage. Importantly, we encourage you to consider the relationships and connections between your cultural identities and your experiences of privilege, power, and oppression, as well as how your cultural identities intersect and work together to create your cultural self. In most cases, there are social norms that also inform how you understand your cultural identities, as well as how others understand your cultural identities (e.g., Mahalik, Good, & Englar-Carlson, 2003). Sometimes those social norms may feel congruent to how you view yourself; other times they will not feel congruent, and they can be a source of distress and misunderstanding. Also, we would like you to consider your most important and fundamental cultural beliefs, values, and attitudes and how these are connected or related to your cultural identities and experiences. In doing so, we encourage you to think about the development of your cultural identities. Most cultural identities change over time, some in predictable ways. Accordingly, it can be useful to read more about developmental models that describe how cultural identities can shift or develop over time (e.g., Cross, 1995; Helms, 1990; Peek, 2005; Rosario, Schrimshaw, & Hunter, 2011).

Sociocultural Identity Wheel

In this first exercise, we begin the process of cultural self-exploration by identifying the cultural identities that make up who you are. Take a look at the sociocultural identity wheel (adapted from Metzger, Nadkarni, & Cornish, 2010) in Figure 2.1. Think of this wheel as a cultural picture of your life. The center represents the essence of who you are. The six blank circles surrounding the center represent various aspects of your cultural identity. Take some time and think about the aspects of your cultural identity that are important to you. These are the cultural identities that describe who you are. Write one part of your cultural identity in each circle. If you cannot come up with six things right now, that's OK. Just write down as many as you can. After you write down your cultural identities, think about which cultural identities are more or less salient to you. Which do you feel are core to who you are as a person, and which cultural identities are more peripheral?

When you are finished, take a few minutes and look at your cultural identity wheel. Feel free to write down any reactions or reflections you had while doing this exercise. Consider the following questions: What identities were most salient and least salient to you (and how are they expressed on a daily basis)? What meaning do you make about the saliency of your cultural identities? How have these cultural identities changed or shifted over time? What privileges, advantages, inequities, or discrimination have you experienced on the basis of your cultural identities? What messages do you receive about your cultural identities from the media? How do you think other people view your cultural identities? Did any feelings (e.g., sad, angry, scared, happy, excited) come up for you as you completed the exercise?

There are several aspects of culture that you could have used to fill out your cultural identity wheel, including race, ethnicity, gender, sexual orientation, religion, social class, age, disability or ability status, progressive chronic illness, size, and political affiliation, among others.

FIGURE 2.1

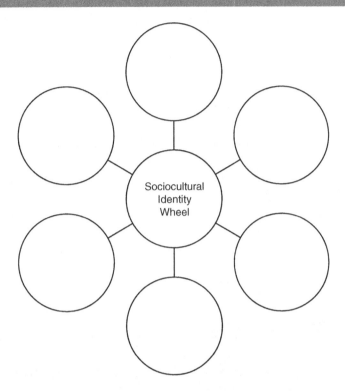

Sociocultural identity wheel. From *Handbook of Multicultural Counseling Competencies* (p. 14), by J. A. E. Cornish, B. A. Schreier, L. I. Nadkarni, L. H. Metzger, and E. R. Rodolfa (Eds.), 2010, Hoboken, NJ: John Wiley & Sons. Copyright 2010 by John Wiley & Sons. Adapted with permission.

Perhaps you included other aspects of your identity, such as your role as a mental health professional or graduate student.

As you reflect on your wheel, were there any aspects of your cultural identity that did not come to mind when you were completing the sociocultural identity wheel? Such an omission might be an indication that this aspect of your culture is not important or salient to you. However, sometimes an aspect of our cultural background is not salient to us because it represents a privileged aspect of our cultural background (McIntosh, 1988). Sometimes we are not aware of the privileged parts of our cultural identity because they just seem "normal" to us. These parts of our identity might have a big impact on us, but the impact might be invisible. For example, if you are White, did you put down "White" on your sociocultural identity wheel? Sometimes White people leave it off. If you are heterosexual, did you put down "heterosexual" on your wheel? Sometimes heterosexual people leave it off. If you are able bodied, did you put down "able bodied" on your wheel? Sometimes people who do not have a disability or progressive chronic illness do not think about it.

Next, take a look at your sociocultural identity wheel and think about how the cultural identities you listed intersect with experiences of privilege. We want you to think about your relationship with privilege. There are clear sociopolitical privileges that come with some cultural identities (e.g., White men typically have more privilege than racial minority women). However, our relationship with these institutes of privilege might cause us to see our relationship differently. For example, a White man might view his relationship with power as accepting of the power but channeling it into a mission to be an ally and to fight for social justice. This stance does not mitigate the power afforded him, but it also honors his position in society. In addition, there may be other identities that are less or more advantaged that could also influence his perspective. How would you describe your relationship with systems of power, privilege, and equity based on your salient cultural identities?

For each of your cultural identities, write a *P* if it represents a privileged identity in the United States, and write a *D* if it represents a disadvantaged identity in the United States. How did it feel to mark certain aspects of your cultural identity as privileged or disadvantaged? Did your classification of your cultural identities into privileged or disadvantaged ring true for you? Which of these labels are consistent or inconsistent with your experience? For the labels that are inconsistent, what do you make of this difference? Do you think it is possible that there is a part of you that is not in touch with your experiences of privilege or disadvantage related to a particular aspect of your cultural identity? Perhaps there are more powerful or salient aspects of your cultural identity that buffer your experience of a different cultural identity? For example, if you identify as Black but grew up in a wealthy home, your socioeconomic privilege may have buffered your racial disadvantage. Conversely, if you identify as White but grew up in a poor home, your socioeconomic disadvantage may have overshadowed your racial advantage. Spend some time thinking, reflecting, and journaling about these questions.

Case Example: Becky and Grant

Having a clear sense of your cultural identities, as well as how these identities are connected with experiences of power, privilege, and oppression, can be important in the therapy room. It can be especially helpful to consider the intersection between our identities as therapists and our clients' identities, as seen in the following supervision case example between Becky, a 28-year-old White, heterosexual, cisgender female therapist, who is in her third year of a PhD program in clinical psychology, and Grant, a 51-year-old White, heterosexual, cisgender male supervisor, who works in the counseling center at Becky's university. They discuss Becky's third session with Luis, a 45-year-old Latino, heterosexual cisgender male client. The following is the dialogue between them. As you read, think about the intersection of cultural identities between the supervisor, therapist, and client.

Grant: You mentioned before that you felt like you were struggling to connect with Luis—could you say more about how you experience that?

Becky: Yeah, well, sometimes I feel like we're just not on the same page. Like I try really hard during session to understand his perspective and get a sense of what he's going through, but it's tough. I think we both realize we're pretty different from each other. We do our best to connect and help each other, but it doesn't always happen.

Grant: When you say you're different, what do you mean by that?

Becky: Well, there are the obvious differences between us. We have different racial/ethnic backgrounds; he's a man and I'm a woman. But I think the biggest difference is where we are at in our life situations. He's older, he has a wife and child, and he's trying to balance all of that, along with work and school part time. It's just a lot. Sometimes I feel overwhelmed just listening to him, and I'm honestly not sure what I would do in his situation. Sometimes I just don't know how to help.

Grant: It does sound like he has a lot going on. Is that the part you're having trouble connecting with— that he has all these different responsibilities and is pulled in all these different directions? It sounds like maybe your experience has been different, so it's hard to connect.

Becky: Yeah, I mean, I've had my share of problems, but for the most part, things have been pretty easy. My family always had enough money, and my parents really stressed that getting an education and doing well was important, so I was able to pretty much focus on that. Even now, you know, some of my classmates have to wait tables to make ends meet. I still have support from my parents, so I'm able to focus on my schoolwork and not get too stressed out.

Grant: So it sounds like there might be a difference between you and Luis in regard to privilege and opportunities, especially around money. It seems to be getting in the way of you connecting with Luis. I wonder what feelings come up for you when you consider your privilege in this case?

Becky: Yeah, I feel a little awkward in session, because I don't know how he is connecting with me . . . and I guess I feel kind of angry in general. I don't know what to do about my privilege. It's just something that I am not aware of on a day-to-day basis.

What did you think of this exchange between Becky and her supervisor? What cultural identities and issues were salient to you as you considered this case? What cultural processes might be helpful for Becky to consider in her relationship with her client? If you were Becky's supervisor, what additional questions might you have asked to help her in her work with Luis?

Cultural Identity Salience

As you completed the sociocultural identity wheel exercise, you probably noticed that some of your cultural identities were more salient to you, and other cultural identities were less salient to you. The salience of various cultural identities is an important thing to consider as we work on engaging clients and their cultural identities. As noted in Chapter 1, it is important to be humble and listen to how clients describe the cultural identities that are most salient to them, rather than enforcing our own views on which cultural identities should be salient for our clients. In the following exercise, we provide one example to help you (and your clients) think about the salience of your cultural identities.

In this next exercise, we invite you to complete the Multigroup Ethnic Identity Measure (Phinney & Ong, 2007) in Exhibit 2.1 to help you understand the salience of various cultural identities in your life, as well as in the lives of your clients. Note that this measure focuses on ethnic identity, but you could ask similar questions about other aspects of your cultural identity.

EXHIBIT 2.1

Multigroup Ethnic Identity Measure

In terms of ethnic group, I consider myself to be: _____

Use the numbers below to indicate how much you agree or disagree with each statement.

	Strongly disagree	Mildly disagree	Neutral	Mildly agree	Strongly agree
	(1)	(2)	(3)	(4)	(5)
1. I have spent time trying to find out more about my ethnic group, such as its history, traditions, and customs.	1	2	3	4	5
2. I have a strong sense of belonging to my ethnic group.	1	2	3	4	5
3. I understand pretty well what my ethnic group membership means to me.	1	2	3	4	5
4. I have often done things that will help me understand my ethnic background better.	1	2	3	4	5
5. I have often talked to other people to learn more about my ethnic group.	1	2	3	4	5
6. I feel a strong attachment to my ethnic group.	1	2	3	4	5

My ethnicity is

☐ Asian or Asian American, including Chinese, Japanese, and others
☐ Black or African American
☐ Hispanic or Latino, including Mexican American, Central American, and others
☐ White, Caucasian, Anglo, European American; not Hispanic
☐ American Indian or Native American
☐ Mixed; parents are from two different groups
☐ Other (specify): _____

My father's ethnicity is (use ethnicity list): _____

My mother's ethnicity is (use ethnicity list): _____

Note. To score this measure, add the scores from Items 1, 4, and 5. These items reflect exploration. Next add the scores from Items 2, 3, and 6. These items reflect commitment. Adapted from "Conceptualization and Measurement of Ethnic Identity: Current Status and Future Directions," by J. S. Phinney and A. D. Ong, 2007, *Journal of Counseling Psychology, 54,* p. 276. Copyright 2007 by the American Psychological Association.

After you complete the Multigroup Ethnic Identity Measure, take some time to think and reflect on your experience. Did your scores line up with how salient you view your ethnicity to be? Did you notice any differences in your scores on exploration versus commitment? Could you think of ways in which you could use questions such as these in your work with clients? Could you think of ways in which you could adapt these questions to explore other aspects of your cultural identity?

Cultural Beliefs, Values, and Attitudes

In addition to recognizing our salient cultural identities and those of our clients, it is important to explore our most important cultural beliefs, values, and attitudes. These aspects make up our cultural worldview and have a strong effect on our everyday lives and decisions. It is important to be able to understand our cultural worldview and also recognize how our cultural worldview is similar or different from that of our clients.

In this next exercise, we ask you to describe your current cultural worldview and reflect on how it is consistent (or not) with the cultural worldview of your family. Take out a blank sheet of paper. Begin journaling about the most important beliefs, values, and attitudes you learned in your family growing up. *Beliefs* are broad and refer to things you believe to be true about yourself, other people, and the world. *Values* are the things you think are most important in your life; they serve as guiding principles and affect your judgments of right and wrong (Schwartz, 1992). *Attitudes* are more specific and refer to thoughts or opinions on various subjects (Myers & Twenge, 2012). If you need help getting started, think about what you were taught by your parents or caregivers about the following topics: politics, money and possessions, family, romantic relationships, crisis, fun and friendship, gender roles, sexual orientation, education, work, religion, and diversity.

After you have spent some time journaling about what you were taught by your parents or caregivers when you were growing up, take out another sheet of paper, and describe what you believe currently about these topics. For example, perhaps your family valued education strongly, and you do as well. Alternatively, perhaps your family was very religious, but religion is not an important aspect of your life currently.

Take a few minutes and reflect on this exercise. Do you think your description of your beliefs, values, and attitudes do a good job of describing your cultural worldview? Does it reflect the things that are most important to you? Does it capture how you tend to view the world? What was it like to compare your current cultural worldview with the cultural worldview of your family? Was your current cultural worldview mostly consistent with the cultural worldview of your family of origin, or were there quite a few differences?

MOTIVATIONAL PROCESSES

In addition to growing in self-awareness about our cultural identities and worldview, it can be helpful to get in tune with our motivations about how we engage with culture in our professional and personal lives. We believe that cultural self-awareness at its core is a motivational process, not an outcome. Conceptually, understanding cultural self-awareness as a process raises considerations of what is activated while contemplating the self or self–other interactions. We hope that by encouraging you to begin the process of exploring your cultural identities and worldview, you will develop a natural tendency to be interested and curious about your cultural experiences, as well as the cultural experiences of others. Accordingly, we hope that the process of developing cultural self-awareness will be a lifelong endeavor. This motivational process should continue to develop with each new person we are fortunate enough to meet and develop a relationship with. At the same time, there may be some experiences in which you get protective, defensive, guarded, or prideful in your reactions. These reactions are a normal part of the process, and we encourage you to sit with them and fully explore and make meaning of them. Ultimately, we hope that by engaging in this process you will develop new motivations to be multiculturally oriented.

In this next exercise, we invite you to consider some of your motivations for engaging in cultural work and exploration. *Motivation* refers to the factors that activate, direct, and sustain behavior toward particular goals (Nevid, 2013). Motivation gets at why you do something. Motivation asks questions about the needs or wants that drive what you do.

To begin, think about your current degree of motivation regarding cultural exploration and engaging with others who are different from you. You cannot really "see" your motivation per se, but you can infer your level of motivation by observing your behavior in certain areas. For example, how much personal work have you done to understand your cultural identities and worldview? Do you generally hang out with people who are similar to you, or do you push yourself to engage with and understand people who are different? Take a look at your family and friends. Who are your friends on social media? Do they reflect a range of cultural identities? What about the kinds of books, documentaries, and movies you watch? Are you curious to learn about people who are different from you, or do you stay away because of your discomfort? What about the news channels you watch and listen to? If you are liberal, have you watched and listened to more conservative news outlets? If you are conservative, have you watched and listened to more liberal news outlets?

Next, think about your motivations for the current cultural work and exploration you are doing now. Why are you reading this book? Is it required reading for a course you have to take? Are you intrinsically interested in the subject matter? Do you want to improve your ability to work with culturally diverse clients? Maybe your motivation comes from a different source. Think about the needs and wants that underlie the cultural work and exploration you are doing now. What professional and personal needs and wants fuel your motivation?

As you engage in this work, be aware of your motivations. Sometimes our motivations are not truly respectful of others' cultural identities. For instance, it can be useful to engage with others who have different cultural identities. However, it is important to understand why you are doing this and how others feel about your motivations. For instance, going to a Black Republican's meeting can provide new insights for some individuals who hold different political and/or racial identities. At the same time, if not welcomed, trying to enter a new group for your own enlightenment can be tokenizing and selfish.

RELATIONAL EXPERIENCES

In addition to understanding our cultural identities, worldview, and motivations, the third important part of cultural self-awareness is to understand how you experience your cultural identities in relationship to others and within society. Our cultural identities do not exist in a vacuum; rather, they are partially defined by shared rituals and histories. To honor the past and have an active relationship with the traditions that define us can be a vital source of enrichment. There is also value in connecting with others through cultural dialogues. At times these dialogues can affirm our cultural self, and at other times they can push us to think differently. They can also highlight the limits of our knowledge and push us to be more mindful about the lived experiences of other individuals.

Case Example: Mark and Jamie

Consider the following consultation case example between Mark, a 31-year-old White, heterosexual, cisgender male therapist, and Jamie, a 37-year-old biracial (Cuban and White), gay, cisgender male therapist. They discuss Mark's work with Brian, a 20-year-old, White, gay, cisgender man. The following dialogue is from a consultation meeting following Mark's eighth session with Brian.

> Mark: I'd like to get your thoughts on something that has been bothering me a little bit with one of my clients, if that's OK.
>
> Jamie: Sure, what's on your mind?
>
> Mark: Well, overall, I've been pretty happy with our work together. I think we have a strong connection, and he has been doing some good work. But he keeps saying he wants to work on his struggles with romantic relationships, but when I try to ask him about that topic, we kind of get off track.
>
> Jamie: Hmm, so what tends to happen exactly?

Mark: My sense is that Brian feels like dating will never work for him. He has some very rigid views, in my opinion, about what he has to look like or be like in order to date. It's almost like he thinks that to date in the gay community here, you have to look like a model or professional athlete. He doesn't see himself that way, so he kind of gives up on the whole thing.

Jamie: Do you think there's any truth to what he is saying?

Mark: Well, to be honest, I guess I don't know that much about what it's like to date in the gay community. But I guess my thought was that it's probably on a continuum, like most things. I'm sure there are people who are looking for people who look like models, but I'm sure there are people who are OK with normal-looking people.

Jamie: My guess is that you are probably right that there's some variability there. But it sounds like Brian's experience has been one of struggle trying to date. Your hypothesis is that it has something to do with rigid ways of thinking, which is possible. But I wonder if it might be helpful to remain open to Brian's experience and honor that as you continue to explore this issue with him.

What is your reaction to the dialogue between Jamie and Mark? What did you think of Mark's perspective on his client? In what ways was Mark culturally humble? In what ways was Mark not culturally humble? How do you think Mark's cultural identities influenced his perspective? If you were consulting with Mark on this client, how could you encourage him to more fully explore the relationship between his cultural identity and his client's cultural identity to best serve his client?

Relationship With Power and Privilege

There is another type of relationship we would like you to consider: your relationship with systems of power, privilege, and equity. It may be harder to think about a relationship with systems of power, for example. Yet, being aware of these systems and working to promote justice in the face of bias are at the heart of the multicultural orientation framework. For example, how do you feel about the power (or lack thereof) afforded you based on the gender with which you identify? What other cultural identities do you hold that influence the power you may (or may not) have through your gender identity? How do you use (intentionally or not) your power (or lack thereof) in social interactions? What would do you do to support others who are in a position of less power?

A good example that has received a lot of recent attention in the news relates to bathroom accessibility for transgender individuals (Seelman, 2014). Nontransgender individuals likely do not think about which bathroom to use or how safe they feel in the bathroom. For transgender individuals, this is a much different experience (with state laws prohibiting use). What role do we have in this discussion on a national level? If we do nothing, what does that say about our relationship with power and privilege?

In this next exercise, you will continue your reflection about the relationship or intersection between your cultural identities and power and privilege. For some, the various parts of cultural identity afford a certain amount of power and privilege. For others, this may not be the case. Some aspects of your cultural identity may grant you quite a lot of power and privilege, whereas other aspects of your cultural identity may not grant you much power and privilege at all. For other aspects of our cultural identity, you may even experience prejudice, discrimination, and oppression.

In Figure 2.2, there is one large oval at the top of the page that is labeled "Power." Near the bottom of the page, there are six rectangles. Pick six aspects of your cultural identity—perhaps use the six identities you wrote down in your sociocultural identity wheel—and write down these identities in the rectangles—one identity in each box. Then spend some time thinking and reflecting about each cultural identity. Does this particular identity afford you a high, medium, or low amount of power and privilege? Then make a mark on the "power line" that connects the box to the large power oval at the top of the page. If the identity affords you a large amount of power and privilege, make a

FIGURE 2.2

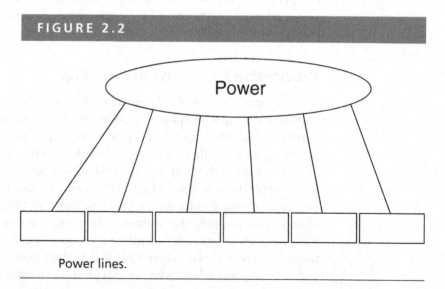

Power lines.

mark near the top of the line, close to the power oval. If the identity affords you a low amount of power and privilege, make a mark near the bottom of the line, far away from the power oval. If the identity affords you a medium amount of power and privilege, make a mark near the middle of the line.

In Figure 2.3, Jesse has given an example of the power lines exercise for his set of cultural identities. In regard to gender, Jesse identifies as a cisgender male. This identity affords him a high amount of power and privilege, so he made a mark near the top. In regard to race, Jesse identifies as biracial—Malaysian and White. This identity affords him a low amount of power and privilege, so he made a mark near the bottom. In regard to socioeconomic status, Jesse identifies as middle class—a medium amount of power and privilege. In regard to ability, Jesse identifies as able bodied—a high amount of power and privilege. In regard to sexual orientation, Jesse identifies as heterosexual—a high amount of power and privilege. In regard to religion, Jesse identifies as agnostic—a medium amount of power and privilege.

After you have finished marking your power lines for each aspect of your cultural identity, take some time and think and reflect on the

FIGURE 2.3

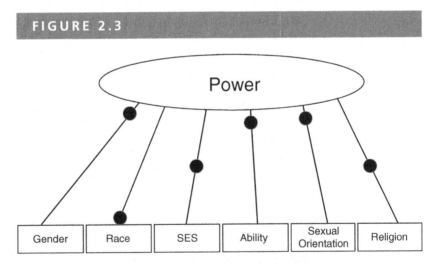

Power lines (Jesse's example). The boxes at the bottom of the figure represent six aspects of Jesse's cultural identity. The dots represent Jesse's relationship with power and privilege for each of the cultural identities. A dot near the top of the line indicates that the cultural identity provides Jesse with a large amount of power and privilege; a dot near the bottom of the line indicates that the cultural identity provides Jesse with a low amount of power and privilege. SES = socioeconomic status.

connections between your cultural identity and your experiences of power, privilege, and oppression in our society. Did anything new come up for you while completing this exercise? Did any feelings (e.g., sad, angry, scared, happy, excited) come up for you as you reflected on these connections and your experiences with power, privilege, and oppression? Can you identify an experience in which you were more aware of your power and privilege (or lack thereof)? Have there been times when you have been an ally to someone who has less power and privilege? Overall, how do you feel about your relationship with the power systems in society?

Part of the reason we are encouraging you to think about and consider the deeper meanings and connections associated with your cultural identities is that research has shown that more simplistic considerations of culture and cultural identities may not be helpful in promoting positive outcomes with culturally diverse clients (Cabral & Smith, 2011). For example, early research in this field focused on whether it was helpful to match therapists and clients on their racial or ethnic identity (S. Sue, Fujino, Hu, Takeuchi, & Zane, 1991). The idea was that culture was important, so perhaps having a therapist who shared one's cultural identity would lead to a stronger working alliance and more effective therapy outcomes. In general, the research findings did not provide strong support for the matching hypothesis to promote therapy outcomes (see Cabral & Smith, 2011).

In contrast, there is a growing set of studies that have found engaging clients with cultural humility can be beneficial to the process and outcome of psychotherapy (e.g., Davis et al., 2016; Hook et al., 2013; Hook, Farrell, et al., 2016; Owen, Jordan, et al., 2014; Owen, Tao, et al., 2016). Specifically, in engaging with clients from different cultural backgrounds, cultural humility (including having an awareness of the limitations of one's cultural worldview and ability to understand another person's cultural background and experience) has been linked to being able to develop a stronger working alliance with diverse clients (Davis et al., 2016; Hook et al., 2013), achieving higher rates of improvement (Hook et al., 2013; Owen, Jordan, et al., 2014), and being able to repair relationships with clients following microaggressions in counseling (Davis et al., 2016; Hook, Farrell, et al., 2016). Importantly, these studies approached the study of clients' cultural identities by allowing clients to self-identify their intersecting and salient cultural identities.

These differences in research findings have shifted the way we tend to think about self-awareness of cultural identities in therapy. Instead of focusing on superficially noticing differences (e.g., I'm Black, you're Asian—what do you think about that?) or trying to maximize similarities (e.g., We're both gay, so we should be able to understand each other), we encourage you to develop a deep understanding of how your cultural identities relate to or intersect with your experiences in the world, such as power, privilege, and oppression. We take these relationships into the therapy room, where we then interact with our clients who bring a similar set of relationships or intersections between their cultural identities and experiences of power, privilege, and oppression. Developing an awareness of these cultural considerations is key to cultural humility and effective therapy.

Case Example: Jasmine and Lucy

Consider the following supervision example between Jasmine, a 35-year-old African American, heterosexual, cisgender female therapist, and Lucy, a 44-year-old Asian American, heterosexual, cisgender female supervisor. They discuss Jasmine's most recent session with Darla, a 28-year-old African American, heterosexual cisgender female client. The following is the dialogue between them as they watched the tape from the most recent session. As you read, think about the intersection of cultural identities between the supervisor, therapist, and client, particularly as it relates to experiences of privilege and oppression.

Lucy:	What jumps out at you the most as you watch this session?
Jasmine:	Well, she definitely seems engaged, which is good. And she's sharing something that I know is really important to her—her struggles with her dating relationships. But, I don't know—I mean, sometimes when we talk, I'm just not sure where we're going—you know what I mean?
Lucy:	Like you don't necessarily have a clear direction?
Jasmine:	Yeah, maybe. I do feel like we have a good connection, but sometimes it feels like we're just chatting about things. It seems more informal than with my other clients.
Lucy:	Yeah, I got that sense too. When I was watching, what popped into my mind was that it seemed like you were hanging out with one of your girlfriends. I think it's definitely more than that, but that thought did pop into my mind. Any thoughts on why you might have this dynamic with this client and not your other clients?
Jasmine:	Well, I think I definitely feel like I understand what she's going through. We both know what it's like to be discriminated against and not treated well. When she's sharing some of her stories, I just want so badly for things to be different for her.

> *Lucy:* It sounds like when you hear some of her struggles with discrimination and racism, you're connecting with some of your own experiences around that. And what I'm hearing is that you feel a lot of empathy for her, and you want things to be different for her. Maybe like you want things to be different for yourself?
>
> *Jasmine:* Ha ha, now we're really getting into it! Yeah, I think that's accurate. It's not easy being a Black woman, trying to be a professional, trying to navigate a workplace that can be less than ideal. So I think I'm wanting certain things for myself, and to a certain extent, I have made a place for myself. She's a few years behind me, maybe, so I'm wanting her to have those same things too. And maybe I'm trying to protect her in a way, from experiencing some of the same things I did.
>
> *Lucy:* And how do you connect those wants and needs that you have with what we're watching on the tape?
>
> *Jasmine:* Well, I think because we connect on some of the same experiences around being Black, the stuff we have to go through—there's a really close connection. So I think that's evident. But I also think that sometimes I hold back from maybe challenging her as much? Like this session, I probably could have called her out more for how she just let Dave [her boyfriend] pretty much take advantage of her, but instead it turned into more like a gab session.

What did you think of this exchange between Jasmine and her supervisor? What cultural identities were most salient for Jasmine in her relationship with her client? What cultural identities might Jasmine and her supervisor have missed? How did Jasmine's experiences with power, privilege, and oppression come up in the supervision session? How did Jasmine's experiences with power, privilege, and oppression affect her work with Darla? If you were Jasmine's supervisor, what additional questions might you have asked to help her in her work with Darla?

Experiences of Privilege and Oppression

As you continue to explore the relationships between your cultural identities and experiences of power, privilege, and oppression, it can be helpful to reflect on some of your personal experiences in a deeper way. In the power lines exercise, you spent some time connecting each of your cultural identities with the degree of power and privilege it affords you in society. In what follows, we invite you to consider some of your personal experiences of power, privilege, and oppression in more depth.

On the basis of the intersection of your various cultural identities, it is likely that you experience some privilege and power in certain areas of your life. In this next exercise, consider and reflect on an experience of privilege. (Again, we define *privilege* as an identity in which belonging to a group or community affords you certain unearned benefits based on the power of that group to influence social institutions and social norms.) Think about an area of your life in which you believe you have received an advantage or benefit based on one part of your cultural identity or a cultural group you belong to. If you belong to one or more historically marginalized groups, you may find it difficult to identify a part of your cultural identity that is associated with privilege. If this is your experience, we encourage you to push yourself a bit and consider other aspects of your identities that might reflect an aspect of privilege, even if they are not salient to you. For example, perhaps you identify as cisgender or able bodied. Perhaps you have educational or socioeconomic privilege.

What comes to mind? Spend some time reflecting and journaling about the experience. Describe what happened. If you like to express yourself through art, draw a picture or create a work of art that reflects your experience. When you became aware of the benefit or advantage you received, how did you feel about it? What did your family or other communities teach you to do with your awareness of privilege? Did your experience of privilege motivate you to do anything? Does it motivate you to do anything now? How do you feel toward others who do not experience the privilege in the same way you do?

In addition to experiencing privilege, you may have had experiences of prejudice, discrimination, or oppression based on one or more of the cultural identities with which you identify. For the next part of this exercise, consider and reflect on an experience of oppression. Think about an area of your life in which you believe you have experienced prejudice or discrimination based on one part of your cultural identity or a cultural group to which you belong. If you cannot think of a time when you personally experienced prejudice, discrimination, or oppression, think about a situation in which you saw someone else experiencing prejudice, discrimination, or oppression.

What comes to mind? Spend some time journaling about the experience. Describe what happened. If you like to express yourself through art, draw a picture or create a work of art that reflects your experience. When you became aware of the prejudice or discrimination, how did you feel about it? Did your experience of oppression motivate you to do anything? Does it motivate you to do anything now? Do you wish someone would have stepped in or intervened on your behalf? If so, how would you have liked them to intervene? How do you feel toward others who do not experience oppression in the same way you do?

META- AND EPISTEMIC COGNITIONS

The fourth and final aspect of cultural self-awareness is to engage meta- and epistemic cognitions. *Metaprocessing* involves the ability to reflect on what is happening in the moment (see King & Kitchener, 1994; Owen & Lindley, 2010). Specifically, Owen and Lindley (2010) noted that

> Metacognition reflects four abilities: (a) Self: Self-monitoring personal thoughts in therapy generally reflect a heavy focus on the self. . . . (b) Self-other: Self-other monitoring describes the ability to observe the impact of the self in relation to clients (e.g., "When I made that comment my client started to cry"); (c) Self-other-time: Self-other-time monitoring reflects the ability to have perspective of one's thoughts in relations to clients over time (e.g., "My relationship with the client has gone through some ups and downs over the course of therapy" or "I felt very close to this client at the beginning of the session but now I feel a barrier between us"); and (d) Self-other-time-settings: Self-other time-settings monitoring simply adds the perspective of monitoring one's abilities and thoughts from setting to setting (e.g., practicum settings, clients, supervisors). (pp. 131–132)

This framework applies well for building cultural self-awareness because therapists need to be able to see their actions in a variety of interactions, across individuals, time, and settings. Accordingly, therapists can engage in critical inquiry about their ability to culturally connect with others across sessions with the same client, across clients, across settings, as well as within the various structures provided (e.g., supervisors, consult teams). This meta-process also involves several contexts that can be rich sources of learning.

Epistemic cognitions reflect how you think about cultural learning. For example, do you turn to authorities for a better understanding of your cultural identities? Do you turn to psychological theory? Do you believe there are clear-cut answers to questions that may have multiple competing answers (e.g., abortion, health care, immigration)? What is the best source of information to answer value-based questions? How quickly do you feel we should be able to gain cultural self-awareness? All of these questions reflect how we come to think about the nature of cultural knowledge. By reflecting on this level of thinking, we can gain a larger appreciation for the various ways of approaching and understanding cultural differences.

In the next exercise, we hope to help you start to think about your cultural identity across different settings and relationships by gaining insight into how someone else views you and your cultural identities. Sometimes there can be a difference in how we view ourselves culturally and how other people experience us. For example, during his growing up years, Josh did not think too much about his racial identity (White), but once he got to graduate school, he realized that other people viewed his racial identity as having a deeper meaning. Likewise, sometimes it can be helpful to get a sense of how others view us. In this exercise, you will have the opportunity to get a sense of how another person experiences you and your cultural identities.

Pick someone who is willing to work with you on this exercise. If you are working through this book as part of a class or practicum team, pick someone from your group. Or you could ask a friend or colleague to help you. Tell your discussion partner that the purpose of this exercise is to gain more insight about how our cultural identities play out in various relationships or settings by exploring how others experience us culturally, especially in how our cultural identities are related to our experiences of power, privilege, and oppression.

We offer one word of caution when completing this exercise. It is possible that asking someone how they view your cultural identity could lead to painful feelings, especially if the cultural identity is linked to experiences of prejudice or discrimination. Thus, it is important to complete this exercise in a safe context, ideally in a relationship in which some level of openness and trust has been established.

To begin, ask your discussion partner to spend some time describing what they notices about you and your cultural identities. What cultural identities do they notice about you? These identities could be things they pick up from your physical appearance. Or they could be things you have shared with them over the course of your relationship. Or they could even be things that they have assumed to be true about you. Ask your discussion partner to say whatever cultural identities come to mind.

Then, ask your discussion partner to consider which of your cultural identities might be associated with experiences of power and privilege and which of your cultural identities might be associated with experiences of prejudice, discrimination, and oppression. Again, your discussion partner may not know these things about you, and that is OK. People make snap assumptions all the time without having the necessary information to make an informed judgment. Ask your discussion partner just to say what they think, even if it is not correct.

After you have completed this interaction, take some time to think, reflect, and journal about your experience. How did the discussion go? Was it comfortable or awkward? Did anything surprising or unexpected come up as a result of your interaction? Compare the cultural identities that you wrote down in the sociocultural identity wheel exercise with the cultural identities that your discussion partner noticed. Which cultural identities were similar? Which cultural identities were different? If there were differences, what do you make of these differences? Also, compare how you rated your experiences of power, privilege, and oppression associated with your cultural identities and how your discussion partner assumed you might experience power, privilege, and oppression on the basis of the cultural identities they identified. What was similar? What was different? If there were differences, what do you make of the differences? If you have time, complete this exercise with three different people and notice what is similar and different across relationships. If there were differences in how people experienced you, what do you make of these differences?

Conclusion

Taken together, we encourage you to think about your cultural identities and worldview and explore how these identities intersect with systems of power, privilege, and oppression. These relationships between your cultural identities and broader systems will be essential as you begin to think about how your cultural identities, as well as your client's cultural identities, intersect to affect the processes of therapy. Throughout, we have asked you to maintain an attitude of cultural humility, acknowledging the limitations in your cultural worldview, as well as the limitations we all have to understanding the cultural worldviews of those we come into contact with.

Working on Cultural Biases, Power, and Privilege

3

It is not our differences that divide us.
It is our inability to recognize, accept, and celebrate
those differences.

—*Audre Lorde*

Josh: When I began to explore my cultural identity
in more depth, including the connections or
intersections between my identity and experience
of power and privilege, the next step for me was
to think about how my cultural identities and
experiences would affect my work with clients.
What personal work could I do to more effectively
connect with my cultural identities and those of
my clients?

The first step for me was to become more
comfortable with cultural differences. When I
was growing up, I mostly surrounded myself with
friends who were similar to me and believed the
same things I did. These relationships and situations
felt comfortable, but they did not stretch me and
help me to become more effective in engaging with
people who were different from me. When I realized
this, I tried to be more proactive about developing
a wide range of relationships—not just with people
who were like me.

http://dx.doi.org/10.1037/0000037-004
Cultural Humility: Engaging Diverse Identities in Therapy, by J. N. Hook, D. Davis,
J. Owen, and C. DeBlaere

I remember developing a close friendship with a woman at my church who was African American. There were some key differences in our beliefs, values, attitudes, and how we saw the world (e.g., religion, family, racial, and economic issues). For example, I remember one night we got into a heated argument about the benefits and drawbacks of corporal punishment. The relationship was not comfortable or easy—the early stages of the friendship were filled with conflict and disagreement. But we both stuck with it. Even though we disagreed, we prioritized the relationship and were committed to trying to understand each other's perspective. Looking back, I learned that coming into contact with difference—and not running from it when it gets uncomfortable—is an important skill that is only developed through intentionality, practice, and experience.

A second step was to explore some specific areas in which I recognized I held some cultural biases. One example for me was exploring my attitudes toward people who identified as lesbian, gay, or bisexual (LGB). Growing up, I was taught in church that being gay was a sin. I did not have any friends or family members growing up who identified as LGB, so I did not have to question that belief. When I got more involved in my graduate work in counseling psychology, I started to develop stronger values related to social justice, and I struggled to figure out how these new values fit in with the beliefs I had about sexual orientation when I was growing up.

My work in this area involved a combination of reading, research, and personal experience. About halfway through graduate school, one of my best friends from church came out as gay, and I walked with him through a difficult time of trying to integrate his religious and sexual identities. Recognizing I was engaged in this discussion whether I liked it or not, I started reading as much as I could on the intersection of religion and sexual orientation, trying to figure out what I believed. I realized that there was a wide spectrum of how Christians viewed sexual orientation, and many of these viewpoints, although they were different from what I had learned growing up, had both research evidence and scriptural support for their views. This was not a quick or easy process, but eventually, I came to a position that honored my faith commitment as well as the values I was developing that prioritized social justice and equality for sexual minority individuals.

The third step for me was exploring what I thought I should do with the privilege and power I held based on my cultural identities. This was one of the most challenging journeys for me because I did not know what to do. I knew I had experienced a series of unearned advantages based on my cultural identities (e.g., White, male, heterosexual, upper-middle class), but I did not know what to do with that. I focused on trying to understand what it meant to be an ally. What would it look like to support and work for justice in my personal and professional life?

Cultural Humility and Cultural Biases, Power, and Privilege

In the previous chapter, you spent quite a bit of time exploring your cultural background and worldview. You identified the cultural identities, beliefs, and values that are important to you, you explored your motivations for engaging in cultural exploration, and you reflected on how your cultural identities are linked with experiences of power, privilege, and oppression.

In this chapter, we begin to explore how your unique set of cultural identities and particular cultural worldview set the stage for your work with clients. Your cultural identities and worldview can make connecting with certain types of clients easier or more difficult. Also, you might find it easier or more difficult to address certain cultural topics in therapy according to your cultural identities and worldview. In this chapter, we try to come up with a plan for some personal work you can do to set the stage for effective work with clients, focusing on the intersections of your and your clients' cultural identities and worldviews. Throughout this chapter, the focus is on cultural humility. What do you cherish about your cultural identity and worldview? What are the potential biases, or areas with which you are less familiar because of your cultural heritage? How can you use your strengths while also recognizing your areas for growth, with the goal of engaging in effective work with your clients who hold a variety of cultural identities and worldviews? We organize our discussion into three areas: (a) increasing comfort with cultural differences, (b) working to identify and reduce cultural biases, and (c) using your power and privilege to work toward justice.

Cultural humility is about getting in touch with your strengths and growth edges, as well as being open to cultural differences, with the ultimate goal of becoming a more effective therapist for your clients, especially when cultural differences threaten the work that is being done in therapy. This chapter builds on the previous chapter and walks you through some personal work that you can do to cultivate your cultural humility and set the stage for effective work with your clients. Increasing comfort with cultural differences will help you be open to connecting with clients from different cultural backgrounds. Identifying and reducing your cultural biases will help you work on your growth edges regarding your work with culturally diverse clients. Using your privilege to work toward justice will help you use your strengths to help your clients who hold marginalized cultural identities.

INCREASING COMFORT
WITH CULTURAL DIFFERENCES

To begin, we encourage you to think about engaging in a variety of activities that will increase your comfort with your own and other cultures. Often our natural tendency is to surround ourselves with individuals who look like us and have similar beliefs. There are a variety of reasons for this, but in general, being a part of a group provides consensual validation for what we think and believe, which increases our self-esteem and makes us feel better about ourselves (Pyszczynski, Greenberg, Solomon, Arndt, & Schimel, 2004). However, the more we insulate ourselves from others, the more difficult it will be to feel comfortable connecting with individuals who are different from us—including our clients. If we want to be effective in helping and coming alongside clients who hold a wide range of cultural identities and worldviews, we have to become comfortable with a wide range of cultural identities and worldviews. This is directly linked to one of the core pillars of developing a multicultural orientation: cultural comfort (Owen et al., 2017). So the first part of the personal work is to push yourself outside your comfort zone and engage with individuals, groups, and ideas that are different from your own.

Cultural Learning and Exploration

Part of becoming more culturally comfortable with other cultural identities and worldviews involves making it a priority to engage in cultural learning and exploration. In this exercise, we ask you to select a cultural group that you do not know much about and with whom you have had not much experience. To help select what to focus on, consider the following questions: Do you feel you have a tendency to make judgments about a particular cultural group or worldview? Do you feel any cultural group is superior or inferior to you? Do you disagree with any cultural group or worldviews?

Before you do anything, spend some time thinking, reflecting, and journaling about this aspect of culture. What do you know (or think that you know) about this culture? What do you not know about this culture? What are your personal experiences with this culture? What are you curious about? What questions do you have? These questions speak to the heart of cultural humility because we want you to identify when you are feeling less capable of developing a connection with others.

After you have spent some time reflecting on where you are at right now, do some research and find a documentary or book about this cultural group. As you watch, listen, or read, pay attention to any thoughts, feelings, or reactions that come up. To track your reactions, you may want to use the cultural comfort scale presented in Exhibit 1.3. Afterward, spend some time thinking, reflecting, and journaling about your experience. If you like to express yourself through art, draw a picture or create a work of art that reflects your experience. What did you learn about the cultural group? How has your understanding or perspective about this cultural group changed? Was anything that you saw or read surprising? Did you find that any of your previous thoughts about this group turned out to be inaccurate or untrue? What feelings came up for you as you watched the documentary or read the book (e.g., sad, angry, scared, happy, excited)? Did this experience motivate you to engage in any further learning and exploration about this cultural group?

Hopefully, this experience sparked your interest in learning about different cultural groups. We encourage you to make this cultural learning and exploration exercise a regular part of your continuing education and learning. For example, you might think about trying to watch one new documentary or read one new book about a different cultural group each month to continue your learning and growth in this area. You can continue to track your reactions with the cultural comfort scale to compare to your level of comfort across different cultural groups.

Case Example: Kate and Grace

As you engage in new cultural learning and exploration, it can be helpful to take risks and explore these issues in supervision. When the goal is to appear as competent as possible, we might be tempted to "fake it until we make it" and conceal areas in which we feel less culturally comfortable. In contrast, cultural humility leads us to accurately view and take responsibility for our limitations. The primary avenue for doing this in our field is supervision or consultation (Hook, Watkins, et al., 2016). We never function independently as therapists, but we always seek to acquire greater wisdom through seeking to balance and temper our perspectives with the perspectives of other professionals. This structure is intended to promote cultural humility systemically, but it only works if therapists are willing to take risks to let others see their work, including potential mistakes or problems.

Consider the following supervision example between Kate, a 34-year-old, White, heterosexual, cisgender, female therapist who is completing her internship at a university counseling center, and Grace, a 50-year-old, White, lesbian, cisgender, female supervisor. They discuss Kate's initial session with Brad, a 20-year-old, White, heterosexual, transgender man. The following is the dialogue between them. As you read, consider the possibilities that Kate could pursue for cultural learning and exploration about the salient cultural identities for her client.

> *Grace:* Thanks for bringing up your session with this client. How did you feel like the initial session went?

Kate: Well, I think OK. If I'm honest, I was a little nervous. I haven't seen a transgender client before in therapy, so I was kind of scared that I would mess something up. I guess I'm hoping that didn't come through to my client.

Grace: So it sounds like this is new territory for you—something you haven't had a lot of experience with, and you really wanted to help this client.

Kate: Yeah, exactly. I'm really excited to work with him, and I feel a lot of empathy for individuals who identify as transgender and what they have to go through in our society. But yeah, I feel like a newbie, like I don't really know what I'm doing.

Grace: I think it's pretty normal to feel some anxiety when you're working with a client who identifies with a cultural identity you haven't worked with before. So I want to affirm you—what you're feeling is very normal. Did you notice your anxiety coming through in any way during your session?

Kate: Well, nothing terrible happened, but I just felt like I wasn't as comfortable as I normally am. Like, for example, on the intake form, he put down two names—one female and one male. I wasn't sure what name I should use. I just asked him, which seemed to be OK, but I stumbled a bit on my words, so I wonder if he could tell I was nervous.

Grace: Well, I think you did the right thing there by asking him. Sometimes the best thing we can do when we aren't sure about something having to do with our client's cultural identity is just to ask the question. I think our clients actually appreciate this—it shows that we are humble, curious, and open to explore this aspect of culture that is important to them.

Kate: Well, thanks, that makes me feel better.

Grace: I was curious how much you know about transgender issues. One thing that might help with becoming more comfortable is learning more about transgender individuals and the issues they face in society. Have you done much reading or exploring about that?

Kate: Not a lot. I was thinking about that some after seeing the client. We touched on it a bit in my multicultural counseling course, but to be honest, I haven't done a lot of exploration in this area.

Grace: Got it. Well, since you are going to be working with this client, this might be a good opportunity to do some learning and exploration on this issue. Where do you think you can start to find information?

What did you think of this exchange between Kate and her supervisor? How do you think the supervisor handled Kate's anxiety about her first session with Brad? How did cultural humility play into Kate's first session with Brad and Grace's interactions with Kate? If you were Kate's supervisor, what additional questions might you have asked to help her in her work with Brad?

The Social Contact Hypothesis

The encouragement to increase your comfort with other cultures through learning and personal experience is based on the *social contact hypothesis*, which states that interpersonal contact with culturally different individuals can reduce prejudice and promote intergroup harmony under certain conditions (Utsey, Ponterotto, & Porter, 2008). In his book *The Nature of Prejudice*, Gordon Allport (1954) outlined several factors that were necessary for social contact to effectively reduce prejudice: (a) equal status between members of different groups, (b) common group goals, (c) emphasis on cooperation to attain group goals, and (d) support by those in a position of authority. In a review of studies that investigated the contact hypothesis, Pettigrew and Tropp (2006) found that across 525 studies, intergroup contact did work to reduce prejudice. Importantly, the effects were greater when all four of Allport's conditions were met. The social contact hypothesis has been examined with several different cultural identity groups, including groups that vary by race and ethnicity, gender, age, disability or ability status, and sexual orientation.

In your work with clients who have different cultural identities, it might be helpful to think about how you could implement some of Allport's (1954) guidelines into your work. For example, one of Allport's factors is that the members of the different groups have equal status. In therapy, there is already a power differential between the therapist and client. How might you work to decrease that power differential? A second factor is an emphasis on cooperation to attain group goals. How could you work with your client to develop a common goal for therapy or emphasize cooperation toward that goal?

In this next exercise, you will practice having an in-depth cultural conversation with a friend or colleague. Sometimes it can feel awkward to ask questions and discuss a client's cultural identities because we may not have these kinds of conversations often in our everyday lives. Discussions about cultural identities can feel deep and personal, so sometimes we avoid them unless we already have established a deep sense of intimacy. Cultural differences can also fuel division and conflict in our society (e.g., Haidt, 2012), so we might avoid engaging in cultural conversations because we are afraid of conflict. The best way to become more comfortable talking about cultural identities is to practice. As you talk through some of these questions and issues, the topics will become more natural for you, and you will, hopefully, be more comfortable engaging in these discussions with your clients.

Pick a friend or colleague who is willing to sit down for an hour or two and practice having a cultural conversation with you. If you are working through this book with a class or practicum team, it would be ideal to pair up with someone in your group. Find a place that is comfortable. Leading up to the conversation, spend some time thinking, reflecting, and journaling about your thoughts, feelings, and expectations about the conversation. Also, spend some time thinking about what kinds of questions you might want to ask your discussion partner. Prepare some questions you might want to ask, but be flexible: The conversation may lead you to ask questions that you had not planned. If you feel stuck, the following are some ideas for questions (depending on the cultural identities of you and your discussion partner, some questions may apply and some may not).

Ask questions that address your discussion partner's cultural identities and worldview (Locke & Bailey, 2013):

- What is your cultural heritage? What is the culture of your parents or primary caregivers? With what cultural group(s) do you identify?
- Which of your cultural identities are most salient to your identity? Which of your cultural identities are less salient to your identity?
- What is the cultural relevance of your name?
- What beliefs, values, and attitudes do you hold that are important to you?
- What beliefs, values, and attitudes do you hold that are consistent with the dominant culture? Which are inconsistent with the dominant culture?
- How does your cultural group view therapy? Are there alternative methods for helping and working with mental health problems that are common in your culture?
- How does your view of therapy relate to your cultural heritage?

Ask questions about experiences with various aspects of culture (Locke & Bailey, 2013):

- Degree of acculturation: bicultural (comfortable in both the dominant culture and the culture of origin), traditional (more comfortable in the culture of origin), marginal (little connection with the both the dominant culture and the culture of origin), acculturated (more comfortable in the dominant culture).

- Poverty: Examine factors such as housing, employment, unemployment, underemployment, educational opportunities, undereducation, and life expectancies.
- History of oppression: Explore actual and vicarious oppression.
- Language and the arts: bilingualism; cultural understanding of sight, sound, and movement; and nonverbal communication (e.g., tone of voice, rate of speech, pitch, volume, proxemics, smiling, greetings, farewells).
- Racism and prejudice: Ask about experiences of individual, institutional, and cultural racism and prejudice.
- Sociopolitical factors: Understand the culturally unique social factors that affect a culture.
- Child-rearing practices: Examine the kinship network, gender roles, issues of respect, assertiveness of a culture, obligations of children to parents and parents to children, issues of competition.
- Religious practices: belief system, belief in God, god, gods, supernatural others, the role of religion in the culture, how religion affects the relationships between individuals, groups, and nature.
- Family structure: How does the culture organize itself in kinship patterns, who has authority, what is the impact of marriage outside the cultural group, what is the nature of the relationships among family members, how is lineage determined?
- Values and attitudes: worldview and existential questions, time (oriented on the past, the present, or the future), human relations (are individual, collateral relationships, or lineal relationships most valued?), human activity (is the focus on doing, being, or becoming?), human nature (at birth, are people considered basically good, bad, neutral, or mixed?), supernatural (is the relationship with the supernatural one of control, subordination, or harmony?).

After finishing the conversation, spend some time thinking, reflecting, and journaling about what happened during the conversation. If you like to express yourself through art, draw a picture or create a work of art that reflects your experience. What thoughts, feelings, and reactions came up for you during the conversation? What parts of the conversation were easy or flowed naturally? What parts of the conversation were difficult or awkward? What was it like to ask questions about your discussion partner's cultural identities? What was it like for your discussion partner to ask you questions about your cultural identities? What was it like to share about your cultural identities? Were some of your cultural identities easier or more difficult to share about? Following the conversation, how do you feel toward your discussion partner? Do you feel more or less connected to them? Would you like to continue the conversation and talk more about anything that came up? Did the

conversation motivate you to talk more about culture and cultural identities in your other relationships?

WORKING TO IDENTIFY
AND REDUCE CULTURAL BIASES

In addition to becoming more comfortable with different cultural groups,
we believe that an important aspect of personal cultural work involves
becoming aware of and reducing cultural biases you might hold. Cultural
biases occur when you have an incorrect (e.g., overly positive or overly
negative) view of a particular cultural group or issue (Pedersen, 1987).
Often cultural biases take the form of *stereotypes*, which are cultural
views that are fixed, oversimplified, and overgeneralized (Ashmore &
Del Boca, 1981). Cultural biases can come from a variety of sources.
One source involves the cultural and moral beliefs and values you learned
in your family and local community (e.g., schools, sports teams, religious or spiritual communities). Often our cultural biases are "caught"
more than "taught" within the various institutions of which we are a
part. Perhaps your parents or primary caregivers held certain biases or
prejudices. Even if they did not explicitly teach you to hold those biases
or prejudices, you might have implicitly picked them up from being
around your parents or primary caregivers, internalizing their underlying thoughts and attitudes as your own. Also, you may have had
negative personal experiences with individuals or groups who hold certain cultural identities, which have influenced your expectations for
future interactions.

Identify Cultural Biases

No one is perfect. We all have certain cultural biases that we hold toward
various groups. In this next exercise, we ask you to work to identify
some of your cultural biases. The purpose of this exercise is twofold.
First, it is important to be aware of our biases, so that they do not operate
unconsciously in the therapy room. For example, if you hold a negative
bias toward a particular cultural group but are not aware of your bias,
you may struggle to form a strong working alliance with a client from
that cultural group but not understand why. Or you might lead clients
in a direction they do not wish to go because you have a negative perception of their cultural worldview, which might affect their goals for
therapy.

Also, awareness is often a helpful prerequisite for change. Ultimately,
we would like you to develop and implement a plan to reduce your cultural biases, but it is difficult to address or work on issues of which you
are not aware. So becoming aware of your cultural biases can be con-

sidered an important first step in your journey to reduce your cultural biases so you can be more effective in helping a wider range of clients.

In what follows, we lead you through a series of questions designed to identify cultural biases you might hold. The first set of questions involves powerful negative stories about cultural groups that were taught in your family when you were growing up. Your primary care-givers taught you a large amount of information during your formative years. Some of this teaching was explicit (i.e., it took the form of words and rules). Some was implicit (i.e., it was not spoken but was conveyed through their attitudes and behaviors). Part of this teaching involved how to navigate a diverse multicultural world. These cultural stories can be powerful determinants of your beliefs, values, and attitudes growing up, and they can set the stage for how you engage with people who are different from you.

Take some time and reflect on your childhood. Think about what your primary caregivers and other family members taught you about people from different cultural backgrounds. First, think about what kinds of things were taught explicitly. What did they say regarding people from different cultural backgrounds? What did they teach you about people from different racial or ethnic groups and nationalities? What did they teach you about gender and sexual orientation? What did they commu-nicate about people who were rich versus poor or people who had a dis-ability versus those who were able bodied? Pay particular attention to lessons that encouraged distance from and anxiety toward people who were different. Were any cultural groups framed as dangerous or less than dangerous? Did your primary caregivers share any powerful sto-ries or experiences about people from different cultural backgrounds? What did these stories or experiences communicate?

After reflecting on the lessons that were taught explicitly, spend some time thinking about what your primary caregivers taught you implicitly about people from different cultural backgrounds. Did any members of your family make off-handed comments about people from different cultural backgrounds that framed these individuals in a negative light? How did your primary caregivers react when you became friends with or dated individuals from different cultural backgrounds? Also, think about the types of people with whom your family socialized. Did your parents and grandparents have friends who identified with a range of cultural identities? If so, how do you think this engagement with cul-turally different groups reflected their attitudes? If not, how do you think this lack of engagement with or avoidance of culturally differ-ent groups reflected their attitudes? One approach that may help you identify implicit cultural messages from your family of origin is to spend some time looking through old family photographs or looking through photographs you have posted on social media. As you look through and reflect on these photographs, what memories come up for you about how your family thought about people from different cultural backgrounds? What cultural beliefs or biases did they hold, even if they may not have been explicitly stated?

The second set of questions involves negative past experiences with individuals from various cultural backgrounds. Write down any negative experiences that come to mind about interacting with people from various cultural groups. For example, maybe a person from a particular cultural group made fun of you or beat you up when you were growing up. Maybe you tried to fit in with a certain cultural group but were rejected, and you felt left out. Try to think back on any negative cultural experiences you may have had growing up, and write whatever comes to mind.

After you have finished thinking about the negative cultural experiences, take some time to think, reflect, and journal about this experience. If you like to express yourself through art, draw a picture or create a work of art that reflects your experience. Do you notice any themes about the negative cultural experiences you have had? With what cultural groups have you had multiple negative experiences? Were any of the negative cultural experiences especially traumatic? How do you think these negative cultural experiences influence your attitudes toward those cultural groups today? How do you think these negative cultural experiences influence your abilities to make connections with individuals from these cultural groups?

The third set of questions involves identifying whether you might have any personal cultural struggles with your cultural identities or cultural beliefs, values, and attitudes. *Countertransference* occurs when our reaction toward a client is in some way based on our history or experiences (Racker, 1982). *Cultural countertransference* occurs when we react to an aspect of a client's cultural identity because of our personal cultural issues or struggles (Foster, 1998).

Reflect on your cultural identities. Do any of these cultural identities stand out as areas in which you struggled to integrate that aspect of culture into your overall cultural identity? For example, perhaps you experienced racism and discrimination growing up, and these experiences led you to develop negative internalized messages about your cultural identity (i.e., internalized racism; Jones, 2000). Maybe it was difficult for you to feel good about yourself and your racial or ethnic group. Or perhaps you have a disability and have struggled to accept that aspect of your identity. To the extent that you have struggled to integrate various parts of your cultural background into your overall identity, you may struggle to connect with and help clients who share that cultural identity.

Also, consider whether you have experienced changes in any of your cultural identities over time. What do these changes mean? Was the change your decision, or was it forced on you? If it was your decision, why did you decide to change that part of how you identify cultur-ally? Do you have any negative reactions toward the aspect of culture that you used to identify with but is no longer important to you? For example, maybe you were religious as a child or adolescent, but you moved away from religion or changed your religious views as you got older. Perhaps you grew up in a poor neighborhood, but now you iden-tify as upper-middle class. To the extent that you experience negative reactions toward the cultural identity that shifted, you may struggle to connect with and help clients who share that cultural identity.

Spend some time thinking, reflecting, and journaling about what came up for you during this exercise. Summarize the information you gleaned from thinking about the cultural stories that were taught by your family, your negative cultural experiences, and any struggles you have with aspects of your cultural identity. What cultural biases come up for you? What feelings come up for you as you consider your cul-tural biases? Are you motivated to do anything about the cultural biases that you identified?

Positive Cultural Biases

Although most of the time we think about cultural biases as involving negative views of a particular cultural identity or group, it would be remiss not to consider the possibility of having positive biases toward certain cultural identities or groups. In the course of your work with clients, you may discover that you hold some positive cultural biases that involve fixed, overgeneralized beliefs. Although we might not view positive cultural biases as problematic (at least compared with negative cultural biases), they still can have a detrimental effect on the therapy process. For example, positive cultural biases might result in patronization (i.e., offering inappropriate or unneeded help), overidentification (i.e., denying or minimizing bias because of assumed similarity), idealization (i.e., over-estimating desirable qualities and underestimating undesirable qualities), or the failure to challenge and accept less than optimal behaviors because of one's cultural group (Constantine, 2007).

Work through the same writing prompts that you did when you identified your cultural biases, but think about how your cultural sto-ries, cultural experiences, and personal cultural identities might be related to positive cultural biases. For example, did your parents or caregivers share any powerful positive cultural stories about particular cultural identities or groups? Have you had any positive cultural expe-riences with particular cultural groups? What aspects of your cultural identity might make it difficult to maintain a neutral stance if you had a client who shared that identity? What positive cultural biases do you have to be aware of in your work with clients?

Case Example: Edward and Bill

Ideally, we assume that the primary avenue for working through cultural biases is in supervision, but it may be that the evaluative role of supervision makes it complicated to gauge whether it is safe to truly disclose your cultural biases. In some cases, it may feel more prudent to conceal one's areas of cultural bias and instead express thoughts, attitudes, and emotions that align with what one imagines the supervisor wants to see as signs of competence. Of course, this perspective makes it difficult to use supervision effectively to make meaningful progress toward reducing your cultural biases and improving your work addressing clients' cultural identities in therapy. This is one of the practical reasons why we believe it is important to shift the focus from cultural competence to cultural humility. It is important to provide a safe environment that welcomes therapists to explore and work on the cultural biases that are a normal part of growth and development.

Consider the following supervision example between Edward, a 24-year-old White, heterosexual, cisgender, male therapist, and Bill, a 49-year-old, White, heterosexual, cisgender, male supervisor. They discuss Edward's most recent session with Mushira, a 33-year-old, Pakistani, heterosexual, cisgender, female client. The following is the dialogue between them as they discussed the most recent session. As you read, think about any possible cultural biases that either the therapist or supervisor may have toward Mushira.

> *Edward:* I'd like to talk about my session with Mushira if we can.
>
> *Bill:* Sure, remind me again what you are working on.
>
> *Edward:* Well, her presenting problem was symptoms of depression, and she also has been discussing some problems she is having with her relationship with her husband.
>
> *Bill:* OK, yes, I remember now. What came up for you this past session?
>
> *Edward:* I felt like we got to a point where we were a bit stuck. We were talking about her depressive symptoms, and I was encouraging her to think about the things in her life that brought her joy, satisfaction, and meaning to see if I could get a sense of what kinds of things she might do that would bring her out of her depression.
>
> *Bill:* OK, that makes sense. What did she say?
>
> *Edward:* OK, so that's where I felt like we got stuck. She talked about things like wanting to go back to school, and write, and travel, but she was talking about them in kind of a wistful way, like they

were impossible. And then I asked her about that, and she talked about what her husband wanted for her and for their family, which struck me as really controlling.

Bill: So the husband didn't want her to go back to school?

Edward: No, he's very traditional. And she is too, but I think there is a part of her that wants something different. And her faith is part of it too—it seems like the faith kind of promotes that traditional sort of relationship between her and her husband.

Bill: So how did you react when she started talking about that traditional worldview that was associated with her faith?

Edward: Well, I tried to be respectful of her faith, but I also felt like I needed to point out the discrepancy because I think that is related to her symptoms of depression. She has these structures in place, like her husband and her religion, that prescribe one way of life for her. But it seems like her true self is wanting something different.

Bill: So how did she respond when you made that comment?

Edward: Well, she kind of nodded, like she agreed with the interpretation. But she also got kind of quiet afterwards, which made me think that maybe it wasn't the best intervention.

Bill: I see. It does sound like you have some strong feelings about her situation. What comes up for you when you think of this client, especially related to her cultural and religious background? How do you think your own perspective influences what you want for this client?

Edward: That's a good question, and I've been trying to think about that. There are definitely some differences there. I was raised in an environment that was very egalitarian. Both my parents worked, and there weren't a lot of differences in the gender roles in my home. So I grew up thinking of that as kind of normal. I'm also not very religious myself. I don't think I have anything against religion per se—I think there are some good things about it for some people—but I get really angry when I see religion causing a lot of problems for folks. Like in the case of my client—if I'm honest, I think her Muslim faith is part of what's making her depressed. I know it's important to respect her faith, but I don't really know how to do that and also acknowledge that there might be some parts of her religion that are harmful for her.

Bill: Got it. It sounds like it will be good for you to continue to check in with yourself about how you are feeling about the intersection between your client's religious background and your own.

Edward: Yes, definitely. I will keep thinking about that.

Bill: Any thoughts on how Mushira's specific racial/ethnic and religious identities might influence her presenting concerns, beyond the fact that she and her husband ascribe to traditional gender roles? For example, I'm wondering if being a part of two communities, Pakistani and Muslim, that have sometimes been placed under suspicion in this country—especially after 9/11—might influence the priority your client places on community and family.

What did you think of the exchange between Edward and his supervisor? What cultural identities were most salient in this interaction? What cultural identities were most salient for the client? What cultural biases did Edward hold toward his client? What cultural biases was Edward aware of? What cultural biases did it seem Edward had less awareness about? If you were Edward's supervisor, what additional questions might you have asked to help him in his work with Mushira?

Reducing Cultural Biases

Once you become aware of your cultural biases, the next step is to work toward reducing your biases. We encourage you to develop a plan for identifying and reducing the cultural biases you hold with a combination of intellectual, emotional, and relational interventions. Cultural biases have a variety of possible components. For example, at the intellectual level, we might have the tendency to engage cultural differences with cognitive distortions such as stereotyping, overgeneralization, and confirmation bias (Hilton & Von Hippel, 1996). At the emotional level, we might have the tendency to engage cultural differences with anger and fear (Devine, 1989). At the relational level, we might have the tendency to avoid those who are different from us (Heider, 1958). Because cultural biases have a variety of components, it can be helpful to develop a plan that is multifaceted and activates multiple parts of you. We recommend a plan that involves intellectual learning, emotional experiences, and deep relationships.

In the last exercise, you did some work to identify some of your cultural biases. This is a great first step. In this next exercise, we invite you to do some work to begin to address and hopefully reduce some of the cultural biases you hold. We walk you through a plan that involves engagement from three different angles: intellectual, emotional, and relational.

The first activity for reducing your cultural biases involves *intellectual* engagement. Often cultural biases, prejudice, and stereotypes are not based on factual information. Instead, the root of cultural biases is usually emotional experiences, and then people gather facts to support their position. In this activity, we invite you to do some research into the actual lived experiences of the cultural group toward which you have a bias. For example, if you have a cultural bias that African American men are dangerous, you might do some research into the criminal justice system and explore how police practices and judicial processes differ according to race. Likewise, if you have a cultural bias that lesbian, gay, bisexual, and transgender (LGBT) individuals should not marry or adopt children, you might read books or articles on LGBT romantic relationships or psychological outcomes for children who have LGBT parents. Knowledge from diverse ideological perspectives has a way of nuancing one's own perspective.

Pick one of the cultural biases you identified from the previous exercises. Do some research about this cultural group. Read some journal articles and research studies about the bias you hold. After you engage in this research, think, reflect, and journal about what you read. What new information did you obtain about your cultural bias? What about the new information was consistent or inconsistent with your previous cultural views or biases? Do you feel any shift or change in your cultural bias after conducting this research? If so, describe the shift or change you experienced.

The second activity for reducing your cultural biases involves *emotional* engagement. As discussed earlier, cultural biases are often grounded in emotional reactions and are based on values, rather than being rigorously grounded in facts and figures. In this next exercise, we ask you to do some work to get out your deepest thoughts and feelings about the cultural group toward which you have a bias. This exercise was originally developed by Jamie Pennebaker and colleagues, who have found that expressive writing offers a wide range of benefits (Smyth & Pennebaker, 2008).

Take out a sheet of paper. For the next 20 minutes, write about your deepest thoughts and emotions about the cultural group toward which you have a bias. You might also write about how it feels to hold a cultural bias toward this group. Try not to censor yourself—write whatever comes into your mind. In your writing, let go and explore your cultural bias and how it has affected you. You might relate your cultural bias to your childhood, your relationship with your parents or primary caregivers, your current relationships, or even your career. Try to keep writing for the entire 20 minutes. If you run out of things to write about, it is OK to repeat some of the things you have already written down. Repeat this 20-minute writing process two more times this week.

The third activity for reducing your cultural biases involves *relational* engagement. Relationships can be one of the most powerful avenues for reducing cultural bias. Often our cultural biases are maintained because we remain distant from the cultural group toward which we hold negative thoughts and feelings. Because of our distance, we do not give ourselves the opportunity for our stereotypes to be disconfirmed, and we also do not begin to accrue positive experiences to counteract our negative biases. Developing positive relationships with individuals who belong to the group that we hold a cultural bias about is a powerful antidote to our bias.

Spend some time thinking, reflecting, and journaling about the cultural group toward which you hold a bias. Do you have any personal relationships or acquaintances who identify with that cultural identity? If so, think about one step you could take to develop or deepen that relationship. Then take that step. If not, think about one step you could take to give yourself the opportunity to meet or develop a relationship with someone from that cultural identity. Then take that step. Before developing these relationships or engaging with others, we encourage you to prepare by doing more work to understand that cultural group. This could involve reading books or articles, watching documentaries, and conducting research online. It is important to put yourself in their shoes as much as possible before interpersonal engagement.

After you have completed the intellectual, emotional, and relational activities, spend some time thinking, reflecting, and journaling about your experiences. If you like to express yourself through art, draw a picture or create a work of art that reflects your experience. During the activities, did you notice any change or softening of your cultural bias? If so, what changed? Which activity (e.g., intellectual, emotional, relational) do you think helped soften or change your cultural bias the most? What are some next steps you could take to continue your work on this cultural bias? Did these activities help motivate you to continue to work on this cultural bias? Did these activities help motivate you to continue to work on your other cultural biases?

USE POWER AND PRIVILEGE TO WORK TOWARD JUSTICE

In addition to becoming more comfortable with different cultures and working to identify and reduce your cultural biases, we encourage you to begin to think and reflect on what you might hope to do with your experiences of power and privilege to work toward justice (Constantine, Hage, Kindaichi, & Bryant, 2007; Vera & Speight, 2003). In the last chapter, you spent quite a bit of time exploring how your set of cultural identities was related to your experiences of power, privilege, and oppression. Your clients will likewise bring a set of cultural identities and experiences of power, privilege, and oppression to the therapy room, and there will be an intersection between your cultural identities and those of your clients. How can you use your cultural experiences of power and privilege to connect with and work effectively with your clients?

Exploring What to Do With Power and Privilege

In this exercise, we invite you to consider what you can do with your power and privilege. To begin, pick an aspect of your cultural identity that is associated with a high degree of power and privilege. As we noted in the previous chapter, if you belong to one or more historically marginalized groups, you might have difficulty identifying a part of your cultural identity that is associated with privilege. If this is your experience, we encourage you to push yourself a bit and consider other aspects of your identities that might reflect an aspect of privilege, even if they are not salient to you. For example, perhaps you identify as cisgender or able-bodied. Perhaps you have educational or socioeconomic privilege.

First, spend some time thinking, reflecting, and journaling about what life is like normally with your experience of power and privilege. If you like to express yourself through art, draw a picture or create a work of art that reflects your experience. Where do you notice the power and privilege show up in your everyday life? What thoughts or feelings come up for you as you think about your experience of power and privilege? Are you motivated to do anything with your position of power and privilege?

One of the most common questions people ask when they become aware of their power and privilege is what they should do with it. Next, we would like you to brainstorm some possible ideas for what you could do with the power and privilege that you identified. Try not to censor yourself—just write whatever comes to mind. What came up for you during this brainstorming exercise? Was it difficult to think about what you could do with your power and privilege? Did you think of any ideas that might work for you? Do any of your ideas have their roots within one of your other cultural identities? For example, certain religions teach that those with greater resources will be held accountable for helping the poor and marginalized. The field of psychology has stressed the importance of integrating advocacy into one's professional identity in recent years.

When people begin to become aware of their power and privilege, they usually respond in one of two ways. At one end of the spectrum, some people do nothing. They may frame their response as "not picking sides" or "not wanting to be political," but when it comes to power and privilege, doing nothing is the same as maintaining the status quo. They might also engage in various defensive processes, such as shifting the focus to their experiences of marginalization in another area or reinforcing ideologies that minimize or deny privilege. What would it look like for you to maintain the status quo in the area of privilege you identified? What feelings come up for you as you think about doing nothing and maintaining the status quo?

At the other end of the spectrum, people might become allies and advocate for social justice for a group or community to increase the power of others who are currently experiencing a low amount of privilege. What would it look like for you to become an ally and advocate for social justice in the area you identified? What feelings come up for you as you think about becoming an ally?

After you have spent some time thinking through your possible responses to power and privilege, reflect on your experience. Which response reflects what you are doing currently? Which response reflects what you would like to do? Which response is consistent with cultural humility? Did this exercise motivate you to do anything different regarding your experience of power and privilege?

Becoming an Ally

As we noted in the previous exercise, often when people begin to recognize their experiences of power and privilege, they want to do something, make a change, and become an ally for justice. However, they may not know what it looks like to become an ally. Or they might look around and begin to recognize injustice everywhere and become overwhelmed, not knowing where to begin or how much is enough. In what follows, we offer some beginning steps to help get you started in the process of becoming an ally for justice. What does becoming an ally or advocate look like in your daily life?

The purpose of this exercise is to develop daily practices of an ally. This involves using your areas of power to influence the power of marginalized individuals and groups. This influence can occur at a local level (e.g., your neighborhood, workplace, or school), or it can occur at a state, national, or global level. The goal is to work toward leveling the playing field to make society more just.

Using your power and influence to be an ally for justice is incredibly important and valuable. Often individuals who have marginalized identities have been fighting for justice for a long time and sometimes see little or no change because of the unwillingness of those in power to change the status quo. This can be a draining and disheartening experience, and those with marginalized identities can benefit from the support of allies in their lives. In what follows, we offer some thoughts and suggestions for how to get involved and effect change, but it is important to note that an important foundation for becoming an ally is to offer one's presence and support. Sometimes people who claim to be allies are quiet or silent in the face of adversity or tragedy, perhaps because they are unsure of what to say or do. This silence, however, can be deafening and heartbreaking to those who are hurting. Often individuals from marginalized groups are not looking for anything profound, just an honest acknowledgment of their pain and struggle. If you are unsure of what to do, start with offering your presence; listen and acknowledge the pain that others are experiencing. This culturally humble stance provides the foundation for the daily practices of being an ally.

After setting the foundation of presence, the next step to becoming an ally is to clarify your values related to justice in a particular area. For example, you might notice that your workplace or campus building is not accessible for individuals who have a physical disability. Or you might recognize that your waiting area and bathrooms are not welcoming for transgender individuals. Pick one of your cultural identities in which you experience power and privilege. Clarify your sense of how maintaining the status quo falls short of true justice. What would it be like to be a person who identifies with a group of lower power and privilege? See whether you can imagine what it would be like to live a day in the life of this person. What are some things that would give this person more power? What has to be done to make life fairer for this person? If you do not know, you might ask a person from that cultural group what it would look like to have a community that is more fair and just.

Once you have completed that step, our main recommendation for action is to build relationships and connect with others who are already working in this area. When you are starting out, it is easier (and more effective) to join others who have already been thinking and working on these issues. For example, is there a community group or advocacy group in your city that meets to discuss working toward justice on a particular issue? If so, consider connecting with them and see where you can help. How can you apply your energy and influence to join what is already going on? How can you help or be of service? What is the connection between their needs and your gifts and talents?

When you join others who are already thinking and working on these issues, be sure to engage with humility. Do not pretend to be the expert about what has to be done; instead, spend most of your time listening to the individuals who are most affected by the issue at hand. It is OK to be active and offer ideas or suggestions, but avoid speaking over those with marginalized identities. Also, there may be some groups or community settings that are designed only to include individuals who have a particular cultural identity in order to increase safety. When in doubt, it is OK to ask whether it is appropriate for you to attend a particular gathering.

After you have made these initial connections and begun to get a sense of where you can help, the final step is to dive in and get started. Our main recommendation when getting started is to commit to being a regular volunteer for a set period (e.g., 6 months). To grow in your identity as an ally for justice, it is important to take action consistently over time. This may involve setting boundaries on your time at first, so you do not get overwhelmed and burnt out. What would it look like for you to engage in social justice efforts in a way that could be consistently maintained over time?

After you have taken action in this area, take some time to think, reflect, and journal about your experiences. If you like to express yourself through art, draw a picture or create a work of art that reflects your experience. What thoughts, feelings, and reactions came up for you as you engaged in this process? Did it motivate you to live your life differently in relation to your privilege? How does it feel to work as an ally for justice? What would it look like for "ally" to become a core part of your identity?

Case Example: Vicky and David

In addition to becoming an ally or advocate for justice in our everyday lives, it is important to think about how to be an ally and advocate for our clients during the process of therapy. Historically, many therapeutic traditions focused solely on clients' intrapsychic and interpersonal issues, ignoring how the broader society and cultural context influenced their mental health problems. This is an unfortunate omission. Clients are deeply affected by the sociopolitical context in which they live. At times, effective therapy may involve helping to empower clients to advocate for themselves, as well as assisting clients to fight against the injustice they may face outside the therapy room.

Consider the following consultation example between Vicky, a 29-year-old, White, heterosexual, cisgender, female therapist, and David, a 39-year-old, African American, heterosexual, cisgender, male therapist. They discuss Vicky's most recent session with Shauna, a 31-year-old, African American, heterosexual, cisgender, female client. In the following dialogue, they discuss the most recent session. As you read, think about how Vicky might use her experiences of power and privilege to be an ally and advocate for her client.

Vicky: I was hoping I could get your thoughts on a client that I'm working with currently.

David: Sure, I'm happy to listen and help. What have you been thinking about?

Vicky: We've been working together for about 10 weeks now, and I think we have made some progress, but sometimes it seems like her focus is on other people and situations—almost like she wants to spend the session complaining. I guess I'm struggling with it because I believe that we don't really have the power to change anyone but ourselves. So sometimes it feels like she wants to complain about things that are outside of her control. When she does that, it doesn't feel like we're making too much progress.

David: Hmm . . . What kinds of things does she complain about?

Vicky: Well, a lot of it has to do with financial problems. Her job doesn't pay that much, and she has to take care of her son pretty much by herself. She also gets frustrated with how her boss treats her at work. She needs the job, but it does seem like a pretty bad situation.

David: So, it sounds like you are experiencing a lot of the pressures she must face on a daily basis in session. It sounds like you try to redirect the conversation. How does she react when you try to do so?

Vicky: It doesn't always work. She seems to be really focused on the external stuff.

David: Do you think there's any truth in what she says?

Vicky: What do you mean?

David: Well, I guess I'm wondering about her experiences at work and in everyday life. Does she ever talk about her experiences as an African American woman? Does she ever feel like the victim of racism or discrimination?

Vicky: A little bit. I think especially at her job—her boss is a White man, so she wonders if part of their relationship struggles has to do with her racial identity.

David: How is it for you to engage with her around those discussions, since you identify as White?

Vicky: It's a little uncomfortable. I don't share her experiences around that, obviously. I mean, we connect on the gender thing, but my experience as a White woman is very different than her experience as an African American woman.

David: Yeah, so there's definitely a power differential there, both in the room with you being the professional and also with your racial differences. I wonder if there is a way to reduce that power differential or empower her in some way.

Vicky: What do you mean?

David: It sounds like a lot of her struggles have to do with how she engages within a sociopolitical system where she is commonly oppressed, discriminated against, and disenfranchised. And there's a power differential in those situations too, like her relationship with her boss. I wonder if there's a way that you could help her experience more power in her relationship with you and if that might help her experience more power in her everyday life as well.

What did you think of this exchange between Vicky and David? How did issues related to power and privilege come into play in this discussion? How did issues related to power and privilege come into play in the relationship between Vicky and Shauna? How could Vicki act as an ally for justice in her relationship with Shauna? How could a culturally humble approach from Vicki enable her to better address these concerns with Shauna? If you were consulting with Vicky on this case, what additional questions might you have asked to help her in her work with Shauna?

Conclusion

In this chapter, we focused on becoming more comfortable with different cultures and worldviews, identifying and reducing cultural biases, and using your relationship with power and privilege to become an ally for justice.

As therapists, we are not perfect. We each hold cultural biases that hold us back from doing our best work with our clients. It is important to recognize this and put together a plan to work on it. Also, it can be helpful to think about how we might use our experiences of privilege and power for good, by becoming allies for equality and justice.

CULTURAL HUMILITY IN THE THERAPY CONTEXT

II

Cultural Humility and the Process of Psychotherapy

4

The unlike is joined together, and from differences results the most beautiful harmony.
— Heraclitus, *The Fragments of the Work of Heraclitus of Ephesus on Nature* (Ingram Bywater, Trans.)

Jesse: I have always wondered how therapy works. There are so many complexities to the therapeutic process it can be daunting to consider them all. As psychotherapy researchers, we commonly try to isolate specific techniques or therapeutic processes to gauge whether they are associated with better client outcomes. This approach is common to the scientific process, in which we try to "control" certain variables so we can isolate the effect of one particular variable of interest.

Although we have learned a lot about what works in therapy over the years, I have frequently been dismayed by the field's lack of attention to the role of culture. Even when culture has been included as a topic of interest, the results often have not been satisfying. For example, at times I have found that the scientific method, when erroneously applied to culture, can promote generalizations and stereotyping (e.g., the best treatment for *X* race is *Y* treatment). This prescriptive approach to the study and practice of culture and psychotherapy just never made sense to me.

http://dx.doi.org/10.1037/0000037-005
Cultural Humility: Engaging Diverse Identities in Therapy, by J. N. Hook, D. Davis, J. Owen, and C. DeBlaere

In my practice and work with clients, I recognized that my therapeutic style is a natural expression of how I am on a daily basis. The language I use, how I sit, the metaphors and examples are all parts of me. When I train future therapists, I try to encourage them to find their voice. Theory, the use of techniques, and empirical support are important to a certain extent. However, the expression of theory, techniques, and research in the therapy room has to be real and true to the therapist. With this mind-set, I think it is important to be genuine and flexible about how we discuss and conceptualize the role of culture in therapy.

This chapter marks the beginning of the second section of this book. The remainder of the book is focused on the practice of therapy and how to engage clients with cultural humility in the therapy room. This chapter can be conceptualized as a bridge between the theory and self-awareness work presented in the first three chapters of the book and the practical application focus of the chapters to come. The purpose of this chapter is to integrate the theoretical pillars of the multicultural orientation model with several of the main tasks of therapy.

Cultural Humility, Multicultural Orientation, and Psychotherapy

In Chapter 1, we described the origins, the broad assumptions, and the three pillars of the multicultural orientation model (i.e., cultural humility, cultural opportunities, and cultural comfort). In this chapter, we build on that foundation and discuss the therapeutic mechanisms of cultural humility in psychotherapy. In other words, how does cultural humility appear in some of the main tasks of therapy? What differentiates more culturally humble therapeutic processes from less culturally humble therapeutic processes? It is these questions we hope to address in this chapter. First, we discuss how cultural humility can inform intake procedures, including intake forms, the initial interview, and creating clarity about the therapy process. Next, we discuss how cultural humility relates to case conceptualization of clients' distress, the process of diagnosis, the development of a treatment plan, and the techniques used in therapy.

Before we begin our discussion of cultural humility in the context of psychotherapy, we want to be transparent about some of our broad theoretical assumptions about how therapy works. Of course, you can agree or disagree with these tenets as you see fit, but we want to make them explicit, so you know our position. First, it is helpful for therapists to use a theoretical model or an integration of multiple theoretical models to guide their work with clients. These models can inform how you approach a client's course of treatment from start to finish (e.g., intake processes, termination). Second, the therapeutic relationship is an important mechanism of change (Horvath, Del Re, Flückiger, & Symonds, 2011), and the therapeutic relationship works in tandem with therapeutic techniques to maximize the effectiveness of therapy (e.g., Barber et al., 2006; Owen & Hilsenroth, 2011). Third, therapy is a cultural process, so there may be a wide variety of therapies and therapeutic interventions that could be helpful to clients (Wampold, 2007). For example, possible helpful interventions could include seeking healing from a religious leader or taking medication. It can be helpful to discuss the range of possible therapies with clients. Finally, therapy is a coconstructed process (by the therapist and client) that unfolds over time. That is, therapists' expression of cultural humility should invite dialogue and joining with clients. Like most relationships, there will be mutual learning about one's experiences, values, and beliefs as topics evolve over time if there is space for those conversations. However, being culturally humble does not mean that the client moves into a "teacher" role, providing lessons on their cultural identity. Rather, the client and therapist work to understand the cultural experiences in the context of clients' lives. To further explore these points, we start with the intersection of cultural humility and intake procedures.

CULTURAL HUMILITY AND INTAKE SESSION PROCEDURES

Intake procedures take place in the beginning session (or perhaps the first few sessions) with clients. There are many ways to conduct an intake session. Depending on the type of treatment facility (e.g., community mental health center, university counseling center, private practice, hospital), there may be a particular protocol requiring the therapist to obtain specific information during the intake. It is beyond the scope of this chapter to describe all the various approaches to conducting an intake session. However, we encourage readers to explore different intake approaches, such as the therapeutic model of assessment (e.g., Finn & Tonsager, 1997; Hilsenroth & Cromer, 2007).

Typical goals of the intake are to (a) develop an initial relational bond between client and therapist, (b) assess the client's presenting concerns (e.g., symptoms, characterological patterns), (c) understand background information (e.g., family history, psychiatric history, education), (d) gather information about current contexts (e.g., family, friends, social network, work or school, legal concerns), and (e) develop an initial sense of the agreed-on goals for treatment. We believe that an important additional goal of a culturally humble intake should be to obtain information about the client's salient cultural identities, how these identities intersect with the client's presenting problem, and how the client might want their cultural identities to be incorporated into the therapy process.

Although the first session sets the tone for the therapeutic relationship between therapist and client, this relationship may have started to form even earlier. Therapists can influence clients' initial impressions through factors such as (a) how they present themselves on their website or advertisements, (b) how they set up their office and waiting room, and (c) whether they use intake forms that the client views as culturally appropriate. Clients commonly complete intake forms describing their demographic information, reasons for seeking help, screening tools (e.g., depressive screening instrument), and insurance information. For instance, consider the following example, which focuses on messages that a client might receive from a therapist when completing the intake form.

Intake Form: Cultural Considerations

In Exhibit 4.1 we have copied an example of part of an initial intake form that a client might fill out before seeing a therapist for the first time. As you read the intake form, see whether you can think of how it might cause some clients to feel as if the therapist might not be culturally safe. As you read the intake form, what aspects did you think were culturally appropriate? Alternatively, were there any aspects you thought might alienate clients from certain cultural backgrounds? For example, did you notice that the gender categories assumed that individuals identify as either male or female rather than the various other types of gender

---

EXHIBIT 4.1

Intake Form Example

Name: _____
Please indicate your age: _____
Please indicate your gender: Male   Female
Please indicate your sexual orientation: _____
Please indicate your race or ethnicity: _____
Please indicate your religious affiliation: Christian   Muslim   Buddhist
    Hindu   Jewish   Atheist   Agnostic   Other: _____
Please indicate your ability or disability status: _____
Please describe your primary reason for seeking treatment: _____
_____
_____

identities (e.g., genderqueer, transgender)? Furthermore, the labels *male* and *female* refer to biological sex rather than gender (e.g., man, woman, transgender, genderqueer). How would you feel if you identified as transgender and were asked to fill out a form such as this? You might worry that the therapist does not know much about counseling trans-gender individuals or, worse, that the therapist might think something negative about you because of your transgender identity. The open response field for race and ethnicity, in contrast, allows clients to define their racial or ethnic identity without imposing a priori restrictions.

A second issue with the intake form is that none of the questions provide the therapist with any sense of which of these cultural demo-graphics are more or less salient for the client. For instance, it could be that the client's race or ethnicity is not a salient cultural identity, even if the client identifies as a racial or ethnic minority person. In contrast, it could be that their religious identity is more central to their identity and to why they are seeking help. In Chapter 2, you completed the Multigroup Ethnic Identity Measure (Phinney & Ong, 2007), which is an example of a measure that could assess the salience of a client's ethnic identity. A more thorough intake form that asks not only about various cultural identities but also about (a) the degree of salience of one's cultural identities and (b) how one's cultural identities are related to the reason for seeking help can communicate to the client that the therapist is interested in the client's cultural background and experiences (beyond a superficial level) and also values those aspects of the client's life.

Initial Contact With the Client

The therapeutic process can also be influenced by the initial greeting and therapeutic approach used during the intake session. How therapists and clients relate to one another during the intake session sets the tone for the foundation of connectedness and trust (cf. Bordin, 1979). In addition, these first impressions can help clients understand whether the therapist and therapeutic setting form a culturally safe place (Frank & Frank, 1991; Wampold & Imel, 2015). In other words, do clients feel as though their cultural identities, perspectives, background, and experiences will be respected and honored by the therapist?

If you are currently involved in clinical work, take some time and think about how the initial environment clients experience might feel more or less culturally safe to them. To do this, think about all the steps a client would take to arrive at the initial intake session. For example, if your clinical site uses advertising or has a website, do you notice any-thing about these forms of communication that might make a client feel culturally safe or unsafe? What about the intake forms? Also, consider fac-tors such as the therapy office and waiting room. Is your office accessible to people who have physical disabilities? What reading materials do you have in your waiting room? Do they represent a range of cultural identities, or do they mainly reflect your cultural identities? If you have office staff, have they been trained to engage with clients in a culturally humble manner? What other things do you notice about your therapeutic environment that might contribute to cultural safety (or lack thereof)? If you notice something you think could be improved, are you willing to bring this up and advocate for the change? Why or why not? In addition to reflecting on the degree of cultural safety yourself, it can be helpful to consult with cultural experts and have them assess the degree of cultural safety of your clinical environment. This type of consultation can assist you to identify barriers to safety of which you may not be aware.

During the intake process, clients are also evaluating the overall expertise of the therapist, as well as the degree to which they find the therapist capable of relating to their cultural story about the nature of their problem and what might be helpful in therapy. As mentioned in Chapter 1, we contend that the therapeutic relationship is coconstructed by the client and therapist. That is, we do not think it is possible for therapists to present as value neutral or as blank slates. Instead, we believe that both clients and therapists bring their cultural values and experiences to the process of therapy, and these cultural values and experiences affect the initiation and maintenance of the therapeutic relationship.

Case Example: Fredrick and Ronny

Fredrick, a 46-year-old, biracial (Mexican American and Irish American), heterosexual, cisgender man, is a therapist at a local community mental health center in New York City. Many of his clients have lower incomes and struggle with previous trauma experiences. Several of his clients also present with experiences of economic and racial oppression, resulting in complex presentations. His new client, Ronny, is a 31-year-old, biracial (African American and Italian American), heterosexual, cisgender man. Ronny is presenting for treatment after losing his job as a computer analyst. He is currently facing eviction from his house, his girlfriend of 4 years left him shortly after he lost his job, and he describes many depressive symptoms mixed with underlying symptoms of anxiety. The following is part of the dialogue from the initial intake session after Ronny described the combination of factors that are contributing to his depressive and anxious feelings:

> Fredrick: I see that you are really facing a lot of stressors all at once. I can understand how you are feeling down and overwhelmed.
>
> Ronny: Yah [*appears stoic and looks at the floor, with an occasional glance at Fredrick*].

Fredrick: I see that this is difficult for you to talk about. I am wondering why that might be.

Ronny: I don't know—just a lot, you know.

Fredrick: I can understand that, and part of therapy is for you to be open about your thoughts and feelings with me. I am wondering if you can tell me more about how this is affecting you on a daily basis.

Ronny: I guess so [*long pause*].

In this example, Fredrick attempted to empathize with Ronny and the challenges he was having in expressing his thoughts and feelings in therapy. After empathizing, Fredrick opted to provide some psychoeducation about how therapy "works" (i.e., "part of therapy is for you to be open about your thoughts and feelings with me"). When he took the conversation in this direction, Fredrick may have missed an opportunity to truly connect with Ronny. It could be that some of Ronny's reluctance to share and be open with Fredrick is due to not feeling culturally safe in this initial exchange. Imagine you were the therapist in this situation, and consider the following questions:

- What cultural beliefs and values could be contributing to Ronny's reluctance to share?
- What could the therapist have done to be more open and curious about Ronny's process?

Consider the following alternate example for the exchange between Fredrick and Ronny:

Fredrick: I see that you are really facing a lot of stressors all at once. I can understand how you are feeling down and overwhelmed.

Ronny: Yeah [*appears stoic and looks at the floor, with an occasional glance at Fredrick*].

Fredrick: I see that this is difficult for you to talk about. I can relate to how hard it can be to share these vulnerable aspects about your life.

Ronny: Yeah

Fredrick: I really want this to be a safe place for you to share whatever you feel comfortable.

Ronny: Thanks, it's just . . . it's not typical for me to share these things—just feels weird.

Fredrick: I can totally get that. We can go at whatever pace you want. No pressure here. Is there anything we can do to help now?

Ronny: Not sure, but I appreciate it. I know I need to push myself, and it is all very real right now saying it out loud, you know.

The dialogue between Fredrick and Ronny changed quite a bit from the first to the second example. Even though the client did not have a clear sense of what he needed to feel safe, the conversation provided space for Ronny to more fully recognize and explore his feelings. The second conversation also gave Fredrick an opportunity to explore cultural messages about sharing feelings, what it means for Ronny to be in therapy, and to obtain other information about Ronny's current situation. The process in the second example was much more collaborative.

In addition, from a conceptual perspective, there are several possible explanations for the client's reluctance to share openly with the therapist. For example, Ronny may be hesitant to disclose because of cultural messages he has received, for example, that men do not show weakness (Mahalik, Good, & Englar-Carlson, 2003), therapy is not a culturally sanctioned place for healing (Wampold, 2001), or therapists should not be trusted (Whaley, 2001). Alternatively, Ronny's reluctance to share could have little to do with his cultural heritage and more to do with his depressive symptoms. Or the reluctance could indicate some combination of cultural messages and his depressive symptoms. Nonetheless, we contend that by not considering the potential cultural variants to how clients present, the therapist could erroneously "blame the client" for not fully contributing in session. Indeed, Ronny's reluctance to engage in therapy could be interpreted as "resistance" or "not being ready to change."

As seen in the previous examples, the initial connection between the client and therapist can be complex and, at times, subtle. We hope as you seek to express greater cultural humility, this will lead you to reexamine the structures (e.g., intake forms) and processes that guide the intake process. More specifically, a culturally humble stance includes, in part, approaching the initial therapeutic encounters with the following questions in mind. First, are my intake structures and practices (e.g., website, forms) inclusive of my clients' cultural identities? If not, what could I do to change these structures and practices to present a more inclusive and welcoming environment? Second, how are my cultural background, beliefs, and values, as well as my clients' cultural background, beliefs, and values influencing how we are connecting in this intake session? Finally, am I providing a culturally safe environment for my clients? What specifically am I doing to provide this environment? How would I know whether my environment was not safe for clients?

Intake Process and Assumptions

Take a moment and think about the processes involved in an intake. What are the assumptions underlying these intake processes? Typically, the therapist acquires a lot of information from the client through a series of open-ended questions, semistructured questions, and clinical diagnostic instruments. For some therapists, the intention of such information gathering is to ascertain a mental health diagnosis, develop a conceptualization of clients and their presenting concerns, and create a treatment plan. In many ways, this process is therapist-centric. That is, the therapist determines the diagnosis and generates the conceptualization and treatment plan. However, how would a more collaborative and culturally humble approach to this process look?

To begin, it can be helpful to consider how clients view their presenting concerns. Frank and Frank (1991) discussed the idea of the *illness myth*, which is the set of assumptions and beliefs about the etiology of illness (broadly speaking). We all have these assumptions and beliefs about all sorts of illnesses and conditions. For example, when Jesse was growing up, his mother would tell him he should not go out in the cold with wet hair, or he would catch a cold. Jesse still believes that to this day. He is not sure whether this is supported by science, but he (and his mother) believes that one way to get a cold is to go outside in the cold with wet hair. Although this is a simple example, the point is that clients will likely have their own illness myth regarding their struggles.

Understanding the illness myths of clients is an important part of the intake process. Think for a moment about the explanations you have for why individuals struggle with depression. Is it due to environmental factors, such as the loss of a job or a car accident? How about psychological reasons, such as how individuals think about themselves or discrepancies between their actual and ideal self? Or what about medical explanations, such as changes in levels of certain neurotransmitters in the brain? Although psychologists may prefer or tend to use one type of explanation for a client's presenting concerns, many are comfortable with a biopsychosocial model of conceptualization. This model recognizes that there are multiple sources of explanation for mental and behavioral problems. However, in addition to these justifications, there may be cultural explanations for a client's presenting concern. For instance, in the earlier example, could a client's presenting concern be linked to struggles with acculturation, racial or ethnic identity development, or experiences of discrimination? Or what if a client attributed their depression to religious or spiritual factors (e.g., God is punishing me)? Counseling and psychotherapy scholars have historically given more attention to psychological, medical, and environmental rationales (e.g., biopsychosocial) than cultural rationales for clients' distress.

If you are currently seeing clients, pick one of them. If you are not currently seeing clients, pick a friend or family member who is currently experiencing a mental health problem. Respond to the following questions, and practice thinking about possible illness myths that could explain the client's problem.

Presenting problem:
Biological explanation:
Psychological explanation:
Social explanation:
Cultural explanation:

Which explanation is most consistent with your personal illness myth for this client? Which explanation is most consistent with the client's illness myth? What aspects of the illness myth are similar between you and the client? What aspects of the illness myth are different? If the client's illness myth is different from your illness myth for the client, how could you work to resolve this difference in a way that is honoring and culturally humble toward the client's illness myth?

How therapists assess and conceptualize the distress of clients guides the treatment process (Frank & Frank, 1991; Wampold, 2007; Wampold & Imel, 2015). There are multiple ways to conceptualize clients' distress; what is key is being open to how clients understand distress and healing. Just because clients are coming to therapy does not necessarily mean they view therapy as the ideal way to solve their concerns. Moreover, for some clients, the very act of going to therapy is stigmatizing, and those stigmatizing beliefs can influence the course of therapy (see Owen, Thomas, & Rodolfa, 2013). Considering clients' views in the development of the conceptualization of their concerns and then modifying therapy accordingly may enhance the effectiveness of treatment (Benish, Quintana, & Wampold, 2011).

Case Example: Ned

The differences between clients' and therapists' beliefs about illness and healing can be important to the therapy process. Consider the following example. Ned, a 38-year-old, White, heterosexual, cisgender man, attended five sessions of individual therapy. He wanted to discuss whether he should stay at his current job, as well as explore his relationship patterns because he was having difficulty staying in a long-term dating relationship. Both of these issues were causing some mild depressive symptoms. The first two sessions focused on Ned telling his story and history. By the third session, Ned was eager to get into these topics in a deeper way. However, the session stayed mostly on the surface with a discussion of his depressive symptoms, which he did not want to focus on because they were not interfering with his day-to-day life. During that session, the therapist suggested Ned try eating one pound of raw cashews. She stated that they have similar antidepressive qualities as some medications. Ned did not want medication and was puzzled by the comment.

Nonetheless, Ned returned for the fourth session. During this session, he stated that he would like to discuss his relationship concerns.

The therapist stated they could not do any meaningful work on this topic until he was in a relationship. The session refocused on his work issues. After one more session, Ned felt that the therapist did not fully understand him and was unable to develop deeper insights about his situation. Rather, she focused more on his thoughts about his depressive symptoms and how he could address those, even when Ned said he did not want to do that.

Given this description, how was Ned's therapist viewing the presenting concerns? How was Ned thinking of his presenting concerns? What was similar in their illness myths? What was different? What cultural factors could have been useful to explore? How could you have addressed Ned's concerns in a culturally humble way?

An important expression of cultural humility involves providing clients with the chance to understand and influence how their problem is understood and the approach adopted to work toward treatment goals (see Wampold, 2007). Clients' sense of clarity about their presenting problem can change over time, and some clients are more invested in understanding the therapist's perspective and buying into the treatment approach.

In this example, if Ned believed his current distress was due to religious or spiritual factors, medication might not have been a viable or effective treatment option. Other instances are more subtle. For example, a cisgender male client who views expression of vulnerable emotions as a sign of weakness might find it counterintuitive to do things that seek to increase emotional expression. We are not saying that the client's illness myth should be the ultimate guide to structuring therapy. In some cases, changing how clients understand and attempt to address their problems may be a key intervention. That said, disagreement about the goals and tasks of therapy can undermine its potential success. Thus, therapists should be open, curious, and inclusive of clients' cultural beliefs about their distress and healing process and use all their innate creativities to draw their own and the client's perspective about the goals and approach to therapy into greater alignment.

In Ned's case, it would probably have been more helpful for the therapist to engage him in a more culturally humble discussion about his beliefs about his illness myth. This would likely have involved the therapist being open and asking questions about Ned's perspective, rather than rigidly sticking to her opinion about the cause of Ned's problems. In this example, the therapist appeared to prioritize a biological explanation for Ned's problems. If the therapist had been open to Ned's thoughts and beliefs about the underlying causes of his problems, she would have discovered that Ned believed the cause of his depressive symptoms was his struggles in dating relationships, as well as his struggles in his relationship with God. Again, we are not saying that the client's illness myth should be the ultimate guide to structuring therapy, but it is important to respect and value the client's illness myth. If the therapist had respected and valued Ned's illness myth, they may have been able to work together to collaboratively develop a plan for therapy that would have prioritized more of Ned's cultural perspective about his problem.

CULTURAL HUMILITY AND DIAGNOSIS

In many settings, part of the goal of the intake process is to provide the client with a diagnostic impression. The use of diagnoses is commonplace in many treatment settings and is part of most insurance reimbursement systems. A good deal of controversy exists about diagnostic systems, such as the *Diagnostic and Statistical Manual of Mental Disorders* (5th ed., *DSM–5*; American Psychiatric Association, 2013). For instance, the National Institutes of Mental Health director stated, "The strength of each of the editions of *DSM* has been 'reliability'—each edition has ensured that clinicians use the same terms in the same ways. The weakness is its lack of validity" (Insel, 2013). In other words, the *DSM* and other classification systems can help provide a common language for professionals to communicate about clusters of symptoms. However, simply knowing a client's diagnosis or diagnoses is not a robust predictor of treatment success. This latter point is not surprising given that most diagnostic systems, including the *DSM–5*, focus on symptom profiles and do not fully account for clients' cultural experiences.

There are also concerns about how diagnoses have been applied to clients from marginalized groups. For instance, data support that therapists are more likely to diagnosis women as being depressed and as exhibiting dependent, histrionic, and borderline personality disorder traits compared with men with the same symptoms (e.g., Becker & Lamb, 1994; Caplan & Cosgrove, 2004). Therapists' biases have also resulted in less favorable views of racial and ethnic minority clients, sexual minority clients, and clients from lower socioeconomic backgrounds compared with clients with more privileged identities (Caplan & Cosgrove, 2004).

These concerns about the validity of diagnostic systems and their use (or misuse) should serve as an important reminder to therapists to consider the strengths and weaknesses of the common tools we implement (e.g., intake forms, *DSM*). At the same time, it is important to not "toss the baby out with the bathwater." The diagnostic systems are not likely to fade away from the professional landscape in the foreseeable future. Accordingly, it is important to explore how therapists can approach the diagnostic process in a culturally humble manner. Consider the following example.

Case Example: Chris and Carl

Chris, who identifies as a 64-year-old, White, heterosexual, cisgender, male therapist, finished his first session with Carl. Carl, a 34-year-old, White, gay, cisgender man, is a local politician who is a rising star in the Republican Party. Carl came to treatment to have a place for personal growth and to vent his frustrations from the day-to-day inner workings of his campaign. Carl also mentioned that some individuals (both within the gay community and the Republican Party) have a difficult time accepting the various aspects of his identity. Despite these concerns, Carl is functioning well, as noted by his success at work and his loving marriage of 6 years to Frank. Also, he is not exhibiting any significant mental health symptoms that meet criteria for a *DSM–5* diagnosis. Chris and Carl seemed to have a good first session, standard in many respects, with Chris gathering a lot of information about Carl's history and current life situation, as well as setting the foundation for a good working alliance.

The intake session ended with a brief goal-setting discussion, and Chris and Carl scheduled a follow-up appointment for the following week. During the week, Carl received notification from his insurance company that his treatment for anxiety disorder not otherwise specified was approved. Carl was shocked because this diagnosis was not discussed with him, and he felt that Chris must not have understood anything he was saying in their initial session. He was also worried what this diagnosis could mean for his political future. At the next session, Carl confronted Chris about this diagnosis. The following is a part of the dialogue:

> Carl: I received this in the mail [*pointing to the insurance letter*].
>
> Chris: Yes, on the intake forms you signed, it informs you that I will provide a diagnosis in order for us to do work together.
>
> Carl: I don't think I remember seeing that, but if you say so.
>
> Chris: Sorry, I thought you did, and it didn't seem like you had questions. What questions do you have now? I would like to clarify anything that is confusing to you.
>
> Carl: Sure, but I don't really feel that anxious. I don't think this fits for why I am here. I wanted to look at personal growth and vent a bit to someone outside of work/personal life circles—you know?
>
> Chris: Well, diagnosis is a complicated process. It is done by mental health professionals who have a unique perspective, training, and knowledge base. For instance, I heard you saying that you have internal conflict and questioning of your gay and Republican identities that you are ruminating about.
>
> Carl: I don't think I said that. I do want to explore those identities, but I am not sure about the anxiety.

What do you think about the exchange between Chris and Carl? Reflect on any reactions you had as you read this dialogue. What do you think Chris could have done to approach diagnosis in a more culturally humble manner? Do you believe that Chris acted in an ethical manner? What do you think Chris should do now?

As you can see in this example, the therapist did not fully explore or understand the client's cultural identities and how they intersected before providing a diagnosis. He also applied a label that did not seem to fit for the client without exploring and clarifying that label with the client. There are many ways in which the therapist could have approached this process differently, starting with a stance of curiosity, nonsuperiority, and openness about the client's cultural identities. The therapist must also believe in and justify the diagnosis he is using. The balancing act for the therapist is to respect the client's perspective and also be clear and cogent regarding one's diagnostic impressions. Being sure that the client and therapist are on the same page regarding diagnosis will increase the likelihood that there is greater goal alignment to begin the work of therapy.

In many work settings, the reality is that managed care requires a clinical diagnosis for therapists to be reimbursed by insurance companies for their work. How can therapists navigate the realities of managed care yet still provide culturally humble diagnostic impressions? We have three suggestions. First, be honest and forthright with your clients about your diagnostic impressions, as well as the realities of the managed care setting in which you work. These kinds of honest discussions can go a long way in reducing the likelihood of cultural misunderstandings and offenses around the diagnostic process. Second, be cognizant of including information about cultural considerations in your assessment and therapy reports and notes. There are resources available for how to incorporate cultural considerations into one's diagnostic impressions of clients (e.g., Dana, 2005). Third, be active in encouraging the profession of psychology to carefully consider issues related to cultural considerations and diagnoses, including the benefits and drawbacks of the current diagnostic system, as well as alternate ways of organizing and categorizing clients and mental health issues.

CULTURAL HUMILITY AND CASE CONCEPTUALIZATION

One of the most difficult tasks to learn as a therapist is how to use theory to conceptualize a client's presenting problem and then translate that conceptualization into a meaningful treatment plan and interventions in session. In this process, it is first important to clarify what exactly you are conceptualizing: the client's personality, the client's diagnosis and presenting concerns, and/or the therapy process? Here, we focus on general principles that can help inform your theory-driven process related to understanding the client's personality and presenting concerns. Later in this chapter, as well as in subsequent chapters, we discuss the therapy process. To be clear, we are not proposing a framework that takes the place of your theoretical orientation (e.g., cognitive behavioral, interpersonal, psychodynamic). Thus, you will have to refer to other texts to develop a theoretically based case conceptualization (see Eells, 2007). However, it is important to understand that all psychotherapy theoretical orientations have cultural assumptions. For instance, some theories, such as cognitive behavioral and psychodynamic, assume that psychological change originates from the individual (vs. others). The roles of independence and responsibility for change are paramount. Accordingly, we encourage you to consider the cultural values and assumptions inherent in various theoretical orientations. We want to demonstrate how the multicultural orientation framework in general, and cultural humility in particular, can be informative to your conceptualization process.

Connecting Culture to Conceptualization

As we mentioned in Chapter 1, the multicultural orientation framework carries an assumption that those who are more oriented toward cultural dynamics will work harder to learn about their cultural background and the cultural background of their clients. Accordingly, our first assumption is that a deep and thorough understanding of the client's salient cultural identities can contribute to a more complete conceptualization of the client's presenting concerns. It is important to assess what cultural identities are most salient to the client. Consider the demographic information presented in Table 4.1 that is commonly provided in client descriptions and reflects a deeper psychological structure. These are examples of commonly reported demographic information, along with examples of psychological processes that can aid in the conceptualization process.

For each of the concepts on the right side of the table, there are associated theories and empirical literature to explore further. Thus, in a description of a client, it might be useful to explore these keywords and integrate them into your conceptualization of the client. For instance, consider an African American, cisgender, female client who shares that she feels angry when she gets into discussions with her African American friends about racism in the United States because she does not believe they take it as seriously as she does. This could reflect a difference in racial and ethnic identity developmental stages between her and her friends. Understanding Nigrescence theory (Cross, 1995),

TABLE 4.1

Demographic Characteristic and Potential Psychological Process

Demographic	Potential psychological process
Gender (e.g., man, woman, transgender, gender nonconforming)	Gender role conformity; gender role conflict; transgender identity; experiences of sexism, discrimination, and microaggressions; privilege; power
Race or ethnicity (e.g., Asian American, African American, Latino(a), Hispanic, Euro American)	Racial identity; ethnic identity; acculturation; experiences of racism, discrimination, and microaggressions; privilege; power
Income	Perceived social class, work ethic, experiences of discrimination and microaggressions, privilege, power
Sexual orientation	Coming out processes, sexual identity, experiences of discrimination and micro-aggressions, privilege, power

a theory of African American racial and ethnic identity development, could be informative for the therapist (and potentially the client) to help normalize the client's experience and increase insight into the friendship dynamics (e.g., different stages of racial identity development). Accordingly, the interventions that could be implemented might shift according to the specific theoretical orientation of the therapist.

Connecting Cultural Identities to Beliefs and Values

The second assumption in the conceptualization process is that understanding clients' cultural identities provides a window into their beliefs and values. When clients are raised within a cultural tradition, they likely have learned a particular set of beliefs, values, behaviors, and customs and not learned others. In turn, these beliefs and values and their relative presence and absence should be integrated into the therapist's theoretical framework for conceptualization.

Case Example: Ben

Consider the following example of Ben, a 35-year-old, White, heterosexual, cisgender, male client. Due to a diving accident when he was in his mid-20s, Ben is paralyzed from the waist down. Ben describes that he was raised to value working hard and that personal happiness is secondary to the value of providing for others. However, in his current romantic relationship, his partner feels he does not care about her, and they fight frequently. He is currently experiencing some depressive symptoms because he feels he cannot connect with his partner, and his work performance is also suffering. Ben has also been struggling to accept his physical limitations, and sometimes he feels angry and sad about his physical disability.

Using a cognitive behavioral approach combined with a gender role conflict approach (see O'Neil, 2008, for a review), the client's core schemas can be seen as reflecting masculine norms such as the importance of work, independence, and strength. These core schemas then filter down to intermediate beliefs, such as "I should work hard," "My partner should value my work ethic," and "A man should be physically and emotionally strong." These intermediate beliefs then trickle down into the client's actions and viewpoints in daily interactions, which may not be consistent with these core schemas and intermediate beliefs. A therapist could try to find the balance between respecting the client's core schemas that are part of a core cultural identity on the one hand and working with the client to determine what beliefs are flexible (vs. rigid) on the other. The therapist could also attempt to identify the interpersonal skills necessary for the client to navigate his relationships with his partner and at work. The therapist could also work with the client to integrate his physical disability into his identity as a man. Without a clear recognition that part of his struggle is directly related to his gender role identity, the therapeutic process could conceptualize his way of being as pathological and dysfunctional.

Conceptualization Should Be Coconstructed

The last assumption in the conceptualization process is that the conceptualization should include the person of the therapist in the understanding of the client. As we mentioned in Chapter 1, we consider therapy to be a two-person process, coconstructed between the therapist and client. As it relates to conceptualization, this implies that the therapist's cultural values and beliefs play a role in how the client is understood. For instance, if a therapist highly values self-care, they might see a client who works 60 hours per week to be lacking in self-compassion or balance. A culturally humble approach to case conceptualization acknowledges that the therapist has a particular set of cultural values that affect the manner in which he or she views and conceptualizes the client's presenting problem. Throughout this volume, we continue to encourage you to explore and understand your cultural beliefs and values. In doing so, consider how those values are influencing your perceptions of your clients, your conceptualization of their presenting concerns, and treatment planning.

CULTURAL HUMILITY AND TREATMENT PLANNING

Like diagnoses, a variety of approaches exist related to developing treatment plans (if you develop one at all). Some treatment settings require behaviorally anchored treatment plans, such as "the client will say three nice things this week" or "the client will exercise for 30 minutes three times this week." Other treatment plans are less defined, such as "we will meet once per week to explore the links between the client's past experiences with their family and his or her current struggles with romantic partnerships." Some of the decisions regarding treatment planning will relate to the conceptualization and theoretical orientation of the therapist. For instance, a psychodynamic therapist could generate a treatment plan that is focused on identifying primary defense mechanisms and relinquishing their maladaptive use. A cognitive therapist, however, could develop a treatment plan that is focused on understanding the cognitive model, identifying automatic thoughts and core beliefs, and challenging cognitive distortions. For our purposes, we have no judgments about the specific type of treatment plan you use (if any).

In regard to how cultural humility can be integrated with the process of treatment planning, our main suggestion is that the treatment plan should be a collaborative process between the therapist and client. One difficulty we have with treatment plans as they are generally used is that designing a treatment plan may place the therapist in an overly powerful position in relation to the client. In developing the treatment plan, the therapist decides the direction and course of the therapeutic process. On the basis of our assumption that the therapy process should be coconstructed by the therapist and client, we believe that decisions about treatment plans and the direction of therapy should also be coconstructed by the therapist and client.

Case Example: Julie and Janet

Collaboratively designing the treatment plan and direction for therapy can be difficult, especially if the therapist and client have important cultural differences that influence what they believe is psychologically healthy or indicative of the "good life." Consider the following example. Julie, who identifies as a 28-year-old, single, White, heterosexual, cisgender female, nonreligious therapist is working with Janet, who identifies as a 26-year-old married, African American, heterosexual, Christian, cisgender woman in therapy. Janet presents for therapy with symptoms of depression and anxiety related to her marriage. She wants to accept a promotion at her job that would involve more money and responsibility, but her husband does not want her to do that and instead wants to start a family and begin having children. Julie, who identifies strongly as a feminist, believes that treatment should focus on helping Janet become more independent and assertive in her relationship with her husband, which Julie believes will alleviate her depressive and anxious symptoms. Janet, however, appears to be committed to her marriage and would like to focus on how to improve her relationship with her husband.

What would you do if you were the therapist in this case? What would a culturally humble treatment plan look like? Would you be able to acknowledge your cultural background, beliefs, and attitudes and perhaps let your desires for Janet take a back seat to develop a collaborative treatment plan?

CULTURAL HUMILITY AND TECHNIQUES

The role of cultural humility in the delivery of therapeutic interventions is of utmost importance. Depending on the client's cultural background and perspective, certain techniques may be more or less helpful, and some techniques may be viewed as unacceptable. Clearly, there are many ways to negotiate the tasks of therapy, and there are hundreds of interventions, and we cannot cover them all in the scope of this chapter. Rather, we intend to describe the theoretical and practical overlap of cultural humility and the implementation of techniques. Consider the following example.

Case Example: Frank and Edna

Frank, the therapist, is a 48-year-old, African American, heterosexual, cisgender man. Edna, the client, is a 24-year-old, Asian American, lesbian, cisgender woman. Edna came to therapy for difficulties in her romantic relationship with her partner, Liza, and as a result, Edna is feeling anxious most days. She has also not come out to her parents, which is a major source of conflict in her relationship with Liza. The following excerpt is from the second session.

> *Edna:* I am worried about Liza leaving me. She has not said that she is going to leave, but I am really worried about it.
>
> *Frank:* I can see that she means a lot to you.
>
> *Edna:* Yes [*tearfully*].
>
> *Frank:* So, there is the struggle between being out to your parents and not wanting to lose Liza, right?
>
> *Edna:* I guess so. I am just not ready to tell my parents; they would never understand.
>
> *Frank:* Well, I wonder what your long-term plan is for telling your parents.

> *Edna:* I'm not sure. I don't know what to do. I am just so anxious.
>
> *Frank:* I can understand how you would feel so anxious. I wonder if we should work on skills to help tell your parents, so you won't feel so anxious?

In this dialogue, Edna and Frank are trying to negotiate the tasks of therapy. Frank's conceptualization is that Edna's anxiety stems from the potential rejection and lack of love from her parents if she were to disclose her sexual orientation. In Frank's last question, he seems to suggest that disclosing this information is an important next step for Edna.

Think about what you would do in this situation if you were Frank. What information would you want to know about Edna's cultural heritage when making a decision about whether to suggest she might work on planning to disclose her sexual orientation to her parents? What other information would you want to know about Edna's relationship with Liza to help inform this negotiation? What other information about Edna's coming out process would be important to understand? What cultural opportunities did Frank miss in this dialogue?

In this example, there were many options available to the therapist to engage the multicultural orientation framework and be more culturally humble. The therapist could have taken more steps to understand Edna's goals and how her cultural background, experiences, beliefs, and values fit with them. The therapist also could have used fewer leading questions and comments. A more open stance could have been a more effective way of honoring the client's autonomy in the process.

The keys to working in a culturally humble manner in the negotiation of tasks for treatment include (a) being aware of your cultural values and how they intersect with the client's values and presenting problem, (b) taking care not to impose your cultural values onto the client during session, (c) exploring the client's cultural worldviews and beliefs about the process of psychotherapy, and (d) remaining curious and open throughout the process. We now look at a second example of the delivery of techniques, this time with a high degree of cultural humility.

Case Example: Jannie and Selma

Jannie is a 59-year-old, Irish American, upper class, heterosexual, cisgender, female therapist. She has a strong theoretical orientation toward cognitive behavior therapy. Selma is a 31-year-old, African American, middle class, heterosexual, cisgender, female client. She works as a community organizer for a local nonprofit organization that works to end violence, poverty, and discrimination in the south side of Chicago.

Selma is struggling with some interpersonal difficulties at work, which have spiraled into symptoms of self-loathing, alienation from others, and anger (mainly directed at herself). The following is a segment from their fifth session:

Jannie: You mentioned that you would like to discuss your week at work?

Selma: Yes, it was the same thing. My coworker clearly doesn't like me, and I don't know how to connect. She makes all these plans with other folks and just does not invite me, you know, on purpose.

Jannie: How does that make you feel in those situations?

Selma: I get mad, and I just start thinking of all the reasons for why she hates me.

Jannie: What are the first thoughts that run through your head when you get mad?

Selma: That I am worthless and stuff.

Jannie: Do you think you are worthless?

Selma: Well, yeah, right now, I guess. I don't know.

Jannie: What evidence do you have that you are worthless right now?

Selma: I don't know. I just don't fit in, you know? I try, but I feel like I have a sense of anger that's driving my life right now, and I don't want to be angry.

Jannie: So, I hear you saying that you might not be worthless, but you are more angry in general. How do you think those are related?

At this point, the therapist is engaging in Socratic questioning according to cognitive therapy models (e.g., Beck, 1995). The therapist is also linking feelings of worthlessness to anger. However, there are also cultural opportunities within this process. Consider the following alternate dialogue between Jannie and Selma.

Jannie: You mentioned that you would like to discuss your week at work?

Selma: Yes, it was the same thing. My coworker clearly doesn't like me, and I don't know how to connect. She makes all these plans with other folks and just does not invite me, you know, on purpose.

Jannie: How does that make you feel in those situations, especially as the only African American in your office?

Selma: I get mad, and I just start thinking of all the reasons for why she hates me.

Jannie: How do those thoughts of being mad fit with how you see yourself?

Selma: I don't want to be the angry black woman! So, that's why I feel like I am not living up to what I am supposed to be.

Jannie: What do you think you are supposed to be?

Selma: I don't know, but I just feel crazed that I don't know how to be and how to be with other folks.

Jannie: So, there is a sense that this persona "the angry black woman" is not what you want folks to see you as, and at the same time, you are angry. How do you deal with that conflict?

Selma: I don't know. I just don't know.

What reactions do you have to the two dialogues between Jannie and Selma? What differences did you notice between the first and second dialogue? How did cultural humility influence Jannie's use of techniques in the first and second dialogue? What would you do if you were the therapist in this situation? How would you respond to Selma's last statement?

In both examples, the therapist is engaging in Socratic questioning, which is a common intervention in cognitive therapy (Beck, 1995). However, in the second example, the use of cultural humility changed the nature of the Socratic questioning to focus on Selma's cultural identity. The subsequent conversation could have led to a deepening of the therapeutic relationship.

Conclusion

Cultural humility is closely linked to many important processes in psychotherapy. This chapter gave an overview of how to infuse cultural humility into various aspects of the therapy process, including intake, diagnosis, case conceptualization, treatment planning, and the use of interventions and techniques. The key principle is that therapists may come across as culturally arrogant to the extent that they are not willing to integrate the client's cultural perspective and accept influence from the client as they set the course for therapy. Imposing our assumptions about these factors can undermine effective therapy by eroding trust. Cultural humility calls therapists to authentically value their clients' perspectives and rights to influence their experience in therapy. Now that we have set the stage, in the subsequent chapters we continue to explore how therapists can express cultural humility in their work with clients.

Strengthening the Working Alliance 5

We are like islands in the sea, separate on the surface but connected in the deep.

—William James

Cirleen: My father passed away during the fall semester of my predoctoral internship. Although he died of cancer, his illness progressed rapidly, and he transitioned from surgery, to hospice care, to dying very quickly. I was shocked by his loss and knew I needed support if I was going to thrive in my internship and transition to the next phase of my professional life as something other than an emotional zombie. So I decided it was time to go to counseling—my first experience as a client.

My supervisor recommended his good friend, Dr. W, a well-respected local psychologist. When I first met Dr. W, I observed that he looked like the prototypical therapist—he was a man, he was White, and after briefly discussing his family, I learned he was married to a woman. I was aware of the differences between Dr. W and myself regarding gender and race and ethnicity, and I wasn't certain whether

http://dx.doi.org/10.1037/0000037-006
Cultural Humility: Engaging Diverse Identities in Therapy, by J. N. Hook, D. Davis, J. Owen, and C. DeBlaere

he was a lesbian-gay-bisexual-transgender ally. Although these identity differences were not explicitly named, you can be certain I noticed.

Despite my supervisor's trusting this man and recommending him to me, I was immediately wary. There were some pretty big differences between Dr. W and myself, and I wasn't confident that he would be able to understand me, my background, or where I was coming from. Therapy involves being completely open and honest with another person, and there was something inside me that just couldn't do that with Dr. W. I knew I was holding back.

Something shifted around the eighth session. I don't recall the exact topic we were discussing, but I do remember feeling disconnected from Dr. W. Again, at the time I could not put my finger on why—he was insightful, intelligent, and his psychodynamic leanings were an excellent match for my own, but still I was guarded. I think he must have felt something similar, because he said, "You don't really trust me, do you?" and I blurted out, "No, not really." That exchange was the start of a deeper and more honest connection between Dr. W and myself. I shared my doubts about his being able to understand me fully or truly empathize with me. I told him that a lot of the time I was guarded because I wanted to protect myself from the next offense. I protected myself outside the therapy room, and I felt the need to do the same inside the therapy room.

That conversation shifted the dynamic between Dr. W and me and began the process of forming a deeper, more intimate connection and working alliance. I remember that my time with Dr. W was helpful. There were a few really important insights I developed during my work with him, not the least of which was recognizing how vigilant I was for potential experiences of discrimination and bias. But when I look back, I remember that he asked; he did not make me have to be the one to bring up our struggle to connect. Also, when I shared my difficulties in trusting him or my doubts that he could understand my cultural background and experience, he didn't get defensive. He didn't discount my fears or try to reassure me in a superficial way. Instead, he created a cultural opportunity for us to connect. We didn't act like our therapy occurred in a vacuum unencumbered by social, cultural, and political influences—influences that have shaped my experience as a woman of color in the United States. That is what I remember the most. As a person who now trains other psychologists, I tell this story. I tell students not to let their fear of being vulnerable stop them from asking important questions. It is critical to developing a strong working alliance. In truth, the session when Dr. W and I had that conversation about trust was the beginning of our best work because my trust in him truly began to develop on that day.

Cultural Humility and the Working Alliance

In this chapter, we begin to consider how cultural humility can help therapists honor, respect, and fully integrate clients' cultural identities in the therapy process. The focus of the next four chapters is on developing skills that will help in different phases of psychotherapy, including (a) establishing a strong working alliance, (b) repairing the alliance after cultural ruptures or microaggressions, (c) navigating values conflicts in therapy, and (d) working within your limits. This chapter, in particular, focuses on how therapists' cultural humility can aid in the formation and maintenance of a strong working alliance.

As illustrated in Cirleen's personal story, there are many ways culture can influence the early phases of a therapy relationship and the building of a strong working alliance. A strong working alliance is marked by a sense of trust between the therapist and client, a collaborative and open relationship, and the purposeful joining to meet the needs of the client. The working alliance is made up of three parts: bond, goals, and tasks (Bordin, 1979).

- The *bond* aspect involves the development of trust and attachment between the therapist and client.
- The *goals* aspect involves an alignment between the therapist and client for what the primary aims of therapy should be.
- The *tasks* aspect involves a collaborative agreement on the therapeutic methods that are used to reach the client's goals.

Cultural humility can positively affect each aspect of the working alliance.

Close relationships require sacrifice, investment, and support to flourish (see Rusbult, 1983, for a description of the relational investment model), and our relationships with our clients grow and develop in a similar way. We develop these relationships through being unselfish, other oriented, and responsive to our clients in positive ways. Thus, cultural humility plays an integral role in helping build a strong working alliance with our clients, especially when cultural identities are salient to therapy. The importance of cultural humility in building and maintaining a strong emotional bond with your clients aligns squarely with theory and research on the benefits of humility for the development, maintenance, and repair of relationships (Davis et al., 2013; Farrell et al., 2015). The *social bonds hypothesis* states that perceptions of humility regulate the strength of a social bond (Davis et al., 2013).

A *social bond* is an affinity for a person or group that causes one to act in a relationship-oriented way—that is, to prioritize the needs of the relationship (S. L. Brown & Brown, 2006). Clients who view their therapist as culturally humble (i.e., culturally safe, other oriented, emotionally engaged, and responsive to their needs) will be more able and willing to deepen the therapeutic bond and working alliance. Indeed, cultural humility was positively correlated with working alliance for Black individuals currently in therapy (Hook, Davis, Owen, Worthington, & Utsey, 2013).

Accordingly, the purpose of this chapter is to provide therapists with practical ways of implementing positive behaviors that will strengthen the bond, goals, and tasks of the working alliance. We focus on three main areas. First, we explore how engaging clients with an interpersonal stance of cultural humility can help therapists deepen the emotional bond and connection in therapy. Second, we discuss how therapists can strengthen the therapeutic bond by identifying and prioritizing discussion of cultural opportunities in therapy. Finally, we discuss how therapists can check in with clients and get feedback regarding how clients feel about the ongoing goals and tasks of therapy.

CULTURAL HUMILITY AND DEEPENING THE EMOTIONAL BOND

Engaging clients with cultural humility can deepen the emotional bond in therapy. In this section, we look at cultural humility from two different perspectives. First, we explore how cultural humility can counteract the natural tendency to be self-focused when working with clients who have different cultural identities. Second, we talk about how the other-oriented nature of cultural humility can help therapists to be better attuned to the emotional needs of clients.

It can be challenging to have conversations with clients about their cultural identities in therapy. Therapists might feel afraid they could make a mistake or say something that might offend a client. When we feel afraid, the natural tendency is to avoid the thing we fear. This is a common practice. In many communities, there are strong norms against discussing potentially divisive topics, such as racism, religion, politics, or other emotionally charged issues. It would be natural to extend these norms to the therapy context by avoiding topics related to cultural identity and potential cultural differences.

In this book, we are asking you to do the opposite: to move toward the difficult dialogues and engage with your client in discussions about the cultural identities that are most important to them. If you want to develop a strong bond with clients and have them trust you with all parts of themselves and their experience, we believe this is necessary. Avoidance is not an effective option.

If you do engage with clients in deep discussions about their cultural identities and worldviews, it is likely you will experience some anxiety. This is normal. In therapy, as in any relationship, taking risks to deepen intimacy can be scary. When you do experience anxiety, the natural tendency is to focus on yourself, closely monitoring your reactions and interventions. When you become self-focused, it is difficult to be your real, authentic self and engage with the client in a natural, comfortable way. Cultural humility counteracts this natural tendency to focus on yourself and instead maintains an other-oriented focus. But how do we deal with the inevitable anxiety that comes up during session? The first step is to be self-aware of your internal states when this occurs.

Cultural Security and Anxiety

In this exercise, we would like you first to think of a time when you felt a strong sense of fear and anxiety about making a cultural mistake in your work with clients. If you have not begun to see clients, think about a time when you felt a strong sense of fear and anxiety about making a cultural mistake in a friendship. Take some time to journal about your experience. What was it about the situation, the client, or your perspective that contributed to the anxious feelings? What thoughts, feelings, or physiological reactions came up for you during this experience? Were you more focused on your client or more focused on yourself?

After you have completed this first part, think of a time when you recognized an important limitation in your cultural work with a client, but you felt grounded, secure, and courageous. Again, if you have not begun to see clients, think about a time when you felt grounded, secure, and courageous about a cultural issue in a friendship. Take some time to journal about your experience. What was it about the situation, the client, or your perspective that contributed to the feelings of security? What thoughts, feelings, or physiological reactions came up for you during this experience? Were you more focused on your client or more focused on yourself?

Finally, take a few minutes to contrast these two experiences. What differences did you notice in your thoughts? What differences did you notice in your feelings or emotions? What differences did you notice in your body or physical sensations? What was different about your interactions with your clients? What are the primary markers that you are aware of when you feel a high degree of cultural anxiety?

Mindfulness

Once you become aware that you are experiencing cultural anxiety or insecurity and are beginning to become self-focused, the next step is to learn to cope effectively with these feelings so that they do not under-mine your ability to attend to the client's needs and affective experience. One potentially promising strategy involves drawing on mindfulness practices to attend to and accept your experience but maintain an other-oriented stance of cultural humility. *Mindfulness* involves cultivating a nonjudgmental awareness of your mental states and has been linked to a variety of positive effects associated with self-regulation and well-being (K. W. Brown & Ryan, 2003; Carmody & Baer, 2008; Galla, 2016). When you notice cultural anxiety or insecurity in therapy, one option is to practice a nonjudgmental awareness of these states, which may help relieve self-focused defensive processes and help you to maintain an other-oriented stance with your clients.

The following activity is designed to help you practice a mental habit of mindfulness regarding cultural anxiety or insecurity in your work with clients. Find a place where you are comfortable. Feel free to sit in a com-fortable chair, or sit cross-legged on the floor with your hands resting in your lap. Soften your gaze or close your eyes. Take four deep breaths, spending about 4 seconds on the inhalation and 8 seconds on the exhala-tion. Notice the different physical sensations in your body, such as what it feels like in your chest or your nose as you are breathing. Now take about 10 minutes to reflect on your work as a therapist, particularly as it relates to engaging with culturally diverse clients. Relax your mind and see what comes up for you. Often our minds tend to gravitate toward the things we feel anxious or insecure about, such as not knowing enough or making a cultural mistake or misstep. If this happens, just observe these thoughts with curiosity. Notice the kinds of situations or experiences that seem to draw your attention.

After you have spent some time reflecting and noticing what comes up for you, repeat the same activity, but this time see whether you can cultivate a sense of compassion toward yourself for these painful experi-ences of anxiety and insecurity. Imagine yourself tensing and then relax-ing any anxious strivings like a muscle. Notice your thoughts closely, but then release them, let them go, and return to a compassionate stance toward yourself.

After you have completed the mindfulness activity, write down any insights you had. If you spend time practicing being in a mindful state, you might find it easier to return to that state in the future, especially when you are feeling anxious or stressed. If you were able to gain a sense of greater peace and security during this exercise, see whether you can link this experience with an emotional image or a phrase. The next time you are feeling culturally anxious or insecure in therapy, try to bring this image or phrase to mind to relax, accept your feelings of anxiety, and maintain a connection with your client.

Offering Care and Support

When you can regulate your anxiety and maintain an other-oriented stance through cultural humility during cultural discussions, the emotional bond between therapist and client is likely to deepen because you are better able to tune into the client and respond to their needs for care and support. Importantly, clients' needs for care and support may look different according to their cultural background, worldview, and preferences.

For example, Donnie's dad is from rural South Georgia. To connect with others in this area of the country, people have relaxed conversations on their front porch and tell lots of stories. There is an art to it. Donnie forgot how important this was to Southern, rural culture until he moved back to Clemson, South Carolina, for his predoctoral internship. Everywhere, from the post office to the dry cleaner, people engaged with each other like they had all the time in the world, just like those relaxed front-porch conversations Donnie recalled from his childhood. People from this community connected and provided care and support for one another in a specific way, and it was important to be in tune with what was needed if you wanted to develop a strong bond. In the same way, cultural humility and empathy are necessary to explore how you can best provide care and support for your client.

In this next exercise, we ask you to explore how you tend to offer care and support to those in need. First, think about what you learned growing up in your culture and family about deeply connecting with other people. How did people offer care and support to each other? Take out a sheet of paper and write down whatever thoughts come to mind. Growing up, what things did you learn are crucial when making deep connections with others? What is the pace and nature of the conversation? What kinds of behaviors indicate interest, patience, and curiosity? What kinds of behaviors indicate love, caring, and support?

Next, spend some time thinking and journaling about your natural way of expressing care and support to others. Consider a few key times you had loved ones in pain and tried to offer care and support. What behaviors did you try? What words did you say? What questions did you ask? How did you listen? What strategies seemed to work well, and what strategies did not seem to work as well? Now think about some of your clients who have been in the most pain. What did you try to do to offer relief? What did you say and do? How did you listen? What seemed to work well, and what did not seem to work as well? Do you notice any themes or commonalities across these interactions? How do these themes relate to your cultural or family upbringing? Consider and reflect on these primary strategies you use to provide care and support to others.

If you are reading through this book in a class or practicum team, pair up with another individual in your group, share the main ways you offer care and support, and have the other person do the same. Were there any categories of care and support the other person used but you did not use? If so, this could represent an unexplored or underdeveloped way of offering care and support that you could think about developing in your life and work with clients. Finally, contact (e.g., e-mail, call) several people who know you well and ask them what they see as your strengths in terms of offering support and caring to people in pain. Also, ask whether they have noticed any ways you might improve in offering care and support to others who are struggling.

Empathy is closely linked with cultural humility and involves putting ourselves in our clients' shoes and trying to understand their perspective. Empathy communicates an intention to understand and extend caring, and it is a critical step. After empathy, the next step is to try to learn how a specific client gives and receives care and support. Clients may give and receive care and support in different ways. For example, Chapman (1992) proposed that individuals have different *love languages*, or various ways people naturally give and receive love. Some people tend to give and receive love through quality time, whereas others tend to give and receive love through other "languages," such as encouraging words, physical touch, gifts, or acts of service. Similarly, we each give and receive support in a variety of ways. As we saw in the previous exercise, your ways of giving and receiving support are likely connected to your cultural identities and family upbringing. To develop a strong bond with your client, it is important to tune in and be flexible to how your client experiences care and support. As we discussed in Chapter 1, developing knowledge about various cultural groups is helpful as a starting place for developing our empathy and ability to offer care and support for our clients. However, generalized information about various cultural groups is only a starting place and requires adaptation and contextualization to the needs of the specific client sitting in front of you.

Case Example: Dell and Courtney

Consider the following therapy example between Dell, a 25-year-old, biracial (African American and White), heterosexual, cisgender, male therapist and Courtney, an 18-year-old, White, heterosexual, cisgender, female client. Courtney presented for counseling to work on struggles adjusting to college. She had been feeling sad and homesick and had difficulty making friends and finding a place for herself at her new school. The following is an excerpt from their third therapy session. As you read, think about how Dell offers care and support to Courtney, and consider whether he does so in a culturally humble way.

> *Dell:* It's good to see you, Courtney. How have things been going this week?
>
> *Courtney:* Not too good [*shaking her head*].
>
> *Dell:* Can you tell me a bit more about how you have been feeling? What hasn't been good?
>
> *Courtney:* I just hate it here. I thought I was ready to move away for school, but I don't think I am. I feel sad all the time, like I'm always about to cry. All the other people in my classes and dorm seem so confident. They're always going out, making friends. I just can't do it [*starting to cry*].
>
> *Dell:* It definitely sounds like the transition to college has been a tough adjustment for you. I wonder if it might be important to clarify your goals, so we have a better sense of what it would look like if things were better.
>
> *Courtney:* [*Beginning to cry harder*] I don't know. I just want to be happier, more confident in what I'm doing, you know? But I don't think I can do it.
>
> *Dell:* I can see that this is really tough for you. And I think those are good goals—being happy and more confident in tackling this new transition of yours. I wonder if you could imagine being in that place of happiness and confidence—what does that look like for you? What kinds of things would you be thinking about or doing?
>
> *Courtney:* [*Still crying*] I don't know, I just don't know.

What reactions do you have to the dialogue between Dell and Courtney? In what ways did Dell try to provide care and support to Courtney? Do you think he missed anything in his interaction with Courtney? What cultural identities of Dell and/or Courtney could have been relevant in this exchange? Do you think Dell engaged Courtney with cultural humility? If not, what could he have done differently?

One thing to consider about this dialogue is the degree to which Dell responded to Courtney's emotions when they came up. Instead of attending to Courtney's emotions, he preferred to focus on clarifying Courtney's goals and helping her to outline what life would look like if those goals were met. Although this may have been consistent with Dell's solution-focused approach (de Shazer, 1988), it may not have been what Courtney most needed. It may also be helpful for Dell to consider his comfort level with emotions such as sadness and how he could work to support clients in their sadness, even if that is not his natural manner of providing care and support. The following is an alternative way Dell could have responded.

Dell: It's good to see you, Courtney. How have things been going this week?

Courtney: Not too good [*shaking her head*].

Dell: Can you tell me a bit more about how you have been feeling? What hasn't been good?

Courtney: I just hate it here. I thought I was ready to move away for school, but I don't think I am. I feel sad all the time, like I'm always about to cry. All the other people in my classes and dorm seem so confident. They're always going out, making friends. I just can't do it [*starting to cry*].

Dell: I'm sorry to hear that, Courtney. It sounds like things have been pretty tough lately, and you're feeling really sad and down [*offering her the box of tissues*].

Courtney: [*Beginning to cry harder*] Thanks. Yeah, I don't know. I was so excited to come to school, but since coming here, I just haven't been myself. I miss my mom and my family, and I don't think I really fit in.

Dell: Yeah, so it sounds like there are two things going on. You miss your mom and family back home, and then it's been a challenge to feel like you fit in here. It makes sense that you would be sad. I want to be here for you—whatever you need.

Courtney: [*Still crying*] Thanks. It helps to get it out, you know? I don't really have anyone I can talk to about this.

What reactions do you have to this second dialogue between Dell and Courtney? What was the main difference between the two dialogues? In which dialogue do you think Dell was more in tune with Courtney's needs for care and support? In which dialogue do you think Dell responded to Courtney in a more culturally humble manner? Think about how can you tune into your client's needs for care and support, even if providing for those needs does not necessarily come naturally to you.

EXPLORING CULTURAL OPPORTUNITIES TO DEEPEN THE BOND

To this point, we have focused on how engaging clients with cultural humility can deepen the emotional bond in therapy. Now, we focus on when and how to explore cultural opportunities that arise in therapy. Exploring cultural opportunities is essential to the process of deepening the bond between therapist and client, especially when the client has particular cultural identities that are salient to the client's sense of self. Developing a strong bond with a client is usually a process that involves a progression of deepening intimacy over time. Intimacy often grows and develops through self-disclosure (Finkenauer & Buyukcan-Tetik, 2015)—over time, clients share deeper and deeper parts of themselves. Through this process of progressive sharing, a greater trust in and attachment toward the therapist develops. This deeper sense of trust often results in even more self-disclosure and increased vulnerability, and the bond between therapist and client is further enhanced. For many clients, their cultural identities are important and salient aspects of who they are as people. If culture is not an integral part of the therapeutic discussion or if the therapist does not seem open or interested in learning about and understanding the client's cultural identities, a critical opportunity to deepen the bond between therapist and client may be missed.

Practice Cultural Disclosure

In this next exercise, we ask you to practice having a discussion with a friend or colleague about an important aspect of your cultural identity and see what effect this has on your relationship with that person. The next time you are having a conversation with a friend or colleague, spend some time discussing one of your cultural identities that is important to you. Take a risk and be a bit more vulnerable about your cultural identity than you usually would. Notice any thoughts, feelings, and physiological reactions that come up for you during the conversation.

After the dialogue, spend some thinking, reflecting, and journaling about what happened. How did your friend or colleague respond to your sharing? Was their response culturally humble? Was there anything about the person's response that was not culturally humble? How did your disclosure about your cultural identity affect the conversation or your relationship with that person? After sharing, do you feel more close to this person, less close, or about the same? What lessons about cultural humility or the importance of exploring the cultural identities of your clients can you take with you as a result of this exercise?

As therapy progresses, there may be times when therapists can get caught up in a focus on symptom reduction or adherence to a particular treatment plan and forget that discussions about cultural identities may be helpful or important in developing a strong bond with the client and, ultimately, in the success of therapy. To maintain a strong bond, therapists have to identify and strategically evaluate opportunities to explore a client's cultural identity with other aspects of therapy.

This theme dovetails with questions about whether explicitly discussing identity issues in therapy leads to better outcomes. For example, one possible intervention might involve directly noting racial differences in the first session. Currently, research on these questions lacks theoretical and practical nuance (e.g., Hayes, McAleavey, Castonguay, & Locke, 2016). There are many reasons therapists might decide to focus on cultural identities in session, and some strategies are more likely to help contribute positively to the therapeutic bond than others. On one end of the spectrum, it is probably not helpful for therapists to engage in a discussion about race or culture if the impetus for doing so is their own insecurity. On the other end of the spectrum, it can be helpful (or at least it usually does not hurt) to ask clients about how their family or culture views a particular presenting problem or focus of therapy (e.g., grief) and how their personal view is similar to or different from the view of their family or culture. The context is important when deciding whether to explore cultural dynamics within the therapy relationship.

Case Example: Jane and Mateo

Consider the following therapy example between Jane, a 25-year-old, White, heterosexual, cisgender, female therapist, and Mateo, a 65-year-old, Mexican American, heterosexual, cisgender, male client. Mateo sought help to work through issues related to grief and depression following the death of his wife. The following is an excerpt from Jane and Mateo's eighth session.

Jane: So how have you been feeling this week?

Mateo: OK, I guess.

Jane: Can you tell me a bit more about how you are feeling?

Mateo: I'm not feeling quite as down as before, but still not great, you know?

Jane: Yes, I understand—it can be a slow process. How would you rate your depression this week on a 1-to-10 scale?

Mateo: I'd say about a 6. It's just tough, you know? Lisa was my life. Everything revolved around our family and community. And now it's just gone. I mean, people still invite me to things, and my kids still call me, but it's not the same. I feel like they're reaching out because they pity me, not because they really want to see me. Family was everything to me, and now I've lost it.

Jane: Yeah, that does sound really tough. I'm wondering if we could talk a bit more about what you think about how people around you are acting. It sounds like some of your friends and family are reaching out to you, but you're thinking of those actions as reflecting pity, that they don't really want to see you. It sounds like there's an automatic thought coming up for you when that happens that might be important for us to explore.

What is your reaction to the dialogue between Jane and Mateo? Did you notice any cultural opportunities in what Mateo shared? How did Jane respond to those cultural opportunities? If you were Mateo's therapist, how might you have responded in a way that could have communicated to Mateo that his cultural identities were important to explore in therapy?

One thing Jane could have done was explore Mateo's feelings about his family in greater depth and how his experience of family, as well as his wife's death, related to his cultural background as a Mexican American. Instead of taking advantage of this cultural opportunity, Jane decided to focus on Mateo's automatic thoughts about the motivations of his friends and family members who were reaching out to him. This may have been an important aspect of Mateo's therapy, but Jane may have missed a cultural opportunity as well as an opportunity to deepen their bond by not asking about Mateo's cultural experiences related to the loss of his wife. Consider the following alternate dialogue between Jane and Mateo.

Jane: So how have you been feeling this week?

Mateo: OK, I guess.

Jane: Can you tell me a bit more about how you are feeling?

Mateo: I'm not feeling quite as down as before, but still not great, you know?

Jane: Yes, I understand, it can be a slow process. How would you rate your depression this week on a 1-to-10 scale?

Mateo: I'd say about a 6. It's just tough, you know? Lisa was my life. Everything revolved around our family and community. And now it's just gone. I mean, people still invite me to things, and my kids still call me, but it's not the same. I feel like they're reaching out because they pity me, not because they really want to see me. Family was everything to me, and now I've lost it.

Jane: Yeah, that does sound really tough. It seems like one of the things that is especially tough about losing Lisa is that your marriage was something that was so very important to you and felt like a link to your family and community, and now it's hard to figure out where to go next. I'm curious about how those values of marriage, family, and community might be related to your cultural background. Would you like to talk a bit more about that?

What do you think about Jane's response to what Mateo shared? Notice how she asked a question about Mateo's cultural background and invited him to explore that if he wanted to. We want to stress that as a therapist, you will have several decisions about which direction to take in the therapy process. In both examples, Jane chose a certain direction, and the chosen direction could have led to great work by the client. However, we believe that the second example exhibited higher levels of cultural humility and may be more likely to lead to a deeper bond between therapist and client, especially if the cultural identity is particularly important or salient to the client.

Bringing up Cultural Opportunities

It can help to use smooth transitions when we act on cultural opportunities. Sometimes clients might explicitly mention an aspect of their cultural identity during a therapy session. For example, a client may disclose having a sexual experience with someone of the same gender. Or a client who usually does not discuss their religious identity might disclose feeling abandoned by and distant from God. When clients make disclosures about an aspect of their cultural identity, expressing curiosity and interest reinforces the disclosure and likely strengthens the bond. Alternatively, not expressing interest may punish the disclosure and send an implicit message that the topic is off-limits. Thus, our clients may engage in cultural "tests" in which they gauge trust and get a sense of what topics are more or less welcome within the therapeutic relationship.

Other times, we may want to initiate conversations by capitalizing on cultural opportunities related to our client's salient cultural identities or experiences. These interventions have the potential to backfire when they involve abrupt transitions that come across as unnatural and/or forced. A general principle of therapy, which applies here, is that smooth transitions provide clients with a sense of security and trust (Sullivan, 1954). Especially for clients in acute distress, shifting directions quickly can feel unsettling or even stressful. When we do plan to shift directions, we can acknowledge the shift and perhaps provide a rationale (e.g., "This seems important—your disappointment this week with your brother. It reminds me of something you said earlier that seemed really important."). We can use similar techniques to explore cultural opportunities. There are often opportunities to link the current topic of conversation to what you know about the client's salient cultural identities. Even if the client does not have much energy in response to these interventions, their strategic use does signal to the client your general willingness to incorporate cultural themes into therapy and, as trust develops, clients may initiate links between the current themes of therapy and their salient cultural identities at a later time.

Before you see each of your clients this week, spend 5 minutes and think about the various cultural identities of your clients. List the cultural identities that you know about for each client. Then, make a commitment to take advantage of at least one cultural opportunity that arises during the session. Keep it simple. If the client mentions something during session about one of their cultural identities, keep track of it, and when there is a break in the conversation, ask whether the client might want to explore that aspect of their cultural identity in more depth. In particular, see whether you can link the discussion of the client's cultural identity to what is happening in therapy—either the client's presenting problem, their values, or how the client is working toward their goals. Do not force the conversation, just mention it and see whether the client wants to discuss it in further depth.

After each session, spend some time thinking and reflecting on what happened. Did you notice any cultural opportunities that arose? Did it help to "prime yourself" by thinking about the client's cultural identities before the session? How was it to ask an intentional question about the client's cultural identity? Did it feel comfortable? Did it feel like a normal part of the conversation? Do you think you asked the question in a culturally humble manner? How did the client respond? Did the client want to talk about their cultural identities in more depth? If so, do you feel as if the cultural conversation deepened your bond? How could you work on recognizing cultural opportunities more in your work with clients?

Given the centrality of cultural identities, every session likely has some opportunities to explore connections between a client's cultural identity and what is happening in therapy. These interventions do not have to be clunky or awkward. For example, a therapist might simply ask, "What did your family think when you did that?" In other cases, you may have reason to risk bringing up more explicit cultural themes, such as naming a cultural difference between you and your client. The bottom line is that regularly taking such risks to explore cultural opportunities sends the message that you care about the client's salient cultural identities, which strengthens the quality of the bond.

Connecting Issues to Cultural Identities

In this exercise, we list several topics that might be a focus in therapy. For each one, think about the various cultural identities you have learned about, either in your life, your classes, or your work with clients. Consider cultural identities that might be relevant for each topic. Also, think about how you might ask a question about culture if one of your clients brought up the topic.

Topic: Bereavement, Death, and Dying

- What cultural identities might be relevant for this topic? _____

- How could you ask a question about culture if a client brought up this topic? _____

Topic: Job Loss

- What cultural identities might be relevant for this topic? _____

- How could you ask a question about culture if a client brought up this topic? _____

Topic: Sexual Harassment or Sexual Assault

- What cultural identities might be relevant for this topic? _____

- How could you ask a question about culture if a client brought up this topic? _____

Topic: Marital Discord or Family Conflict

- What cultural identities might be relevant for this topic? _____

- How could you ask a question about culture if a client brought up this topic? _____

MONITORING ALIGNMENT OF THE GOALS AND TASKS OF THERAPY

Now that we have discussed engaging with cultural humility and bringing up cultural opportunities to strengthen the relationship bond, the final portion of this chapter focuses on ways of monitoring the goals and tasks of therapy (the other two aspects of the working alliance). This section builds on what you learned in Chapter 4 about negotiating the tasks and goals of therapy in intake, diagnosis, conceptualization, and treatment planning. We recognize that such negotiation is an ongoing process that evolves throughout the course of therapy. Consequently, it is likely helpful to routinely check with clients about how they perceive therapy to be progressing and to confirm that they continue to agree with the therapy goals and approach.

Case Example: Peter and Georgia

Consider the following therapy example between Peter, a 30-year-old White, gay, cisgender male therapist, and Georgia, a 19-year-old South Korean, heterosexual, cisgender female client. Georgia attended counseling to help her to navigate the transition to college. The following excerpt is from Peter and Georgia's fifth session.

Peter: Before we get started today, I'd like to check in with you about how you feel counseling has been going. When we started, we identified our main goal as working on your transition to college, specifically navigating your classes and making friends. I like to check in periodically just to see if those are still the main goals, or if we want to have a different focus. What do you think?

Georgia: Thanks for asking. I would say that some of my goals are the same as before and that some are different now. I think at first I was just really overwhelmed with my schoolwork, and counseling has been really helpful in helping me to get organized and having a plan for myself. So maybe we don't need to talk about that as much anymore. But the friends thing has still been kind of tough. I still feel really lonely here, like I don't fit in.

Peter: OK, yeah, so it sounds like we have seen some good progress on the transition to school and the academic stuff, but we still want to work on getting connected socially.

Georgia: Yeah, that's right.

Peter: Any new goals or things you want to add that we haven't talked about?

Georgia: Well, one thing that has been a little tough is my family. I really miss them, and they miss me too, so we talk a lot, and I have gone home to see them quite a bit this semester, but sometimes I feel like maybe I should be pushing myself to stay on campus and make friends where I'm at—you know? But when I don't have anything to do on the weekend, it's hard to stay.

Peter: OK, so it sounds like one of the things you'd like to talk about is your relationship with your family. It sounds like you value those relationships quite a bit, but you wonder if spending a lot of time with your family might be working against your goals of connecting here. Is that right?

Georgia: Yeah, that's right! And it's tough because my family is really close, so I don't want to lose that or disappoint my parents. But I need to be here too. It's just tough.

Peter: Yeah, it sounds like, on the one hand, you have a strong value related to wanting to stay connected with your family, and then, on the other hand, you are wanting to make friends here at school. Would it be helpful to talk about how to navigate that?

Georgia: Yes, definitely!

What is your reaction to the dialogue between Peter and Georgia? How do you feel about the way in which Peter checked in with Georgia about her goals for therapy? Do you think you could do something similar with your clients? Think about how you might phrase a check-in about the goals for therapy with your clients. Also, what is your reaction to the way in which Peter addressed Georgia's cultural identities during this discussion? If you were Georgia's therapist, would you have done anything differently?

Checking in About Tasks

Related to the importance of checking in regularly with clients about the goals for therapy is that cultural humility is integral to maintaining agreement on the tasks of therapy. The tasks involve the specific interventions that the therapist and client engage in that hopefully move the client toward the therapeutic goal. Several factors influence the tasks that are implemented in therapy, including the theoretical orientation of the therapist. However, it is important to check in periodically assess how the client is feeling about the primary tasks of therapy, as well as the extent to which the tasks of therapy are consistent with their cultural worldview.

Before you see each of your clients this week, spend 5 minutes and think about the primary tasks you have used in therapy with each client. The tasks might be related to your theoretical orientation. For example, if you are a cognitive behavioral therapist, your primary tasks may have been reviewing homework, Socratic questioning, and working through the cognitive model with your client, emphasizing the connection between thoughts, emotions, and behaviors. If you are an interpersonal therapist, your primary tasks may have been discussing the client's relational patterns and perhaps connecting these relational patterns with the client's family of origin and the client's therapeutic relationship with you.

Brainstorm how you might check in with your client about how she or he is feeling about the tasks of therapy. For example, you might start by conducting a general check-in and asking about how your client feels therapy is progressing. You might review some of the main tasks of therapy and ask which tasks the client has found more or less helpful. You might ask the client how the tasks of therapy are congruent with (or not) with the client's cultural values.

Once you have brainstormed some ideas for how to check in with your client, do the check-in. Pay attention to any thoughts or feelings that come up for you as you do this. Do not force a long conversation if the client does not seem interested in talking about it, but ask the question and see where it goes. After you have finished your session, take some time and think, reflect, and journal about how the check-in went. Did you learn anything new about the client? Did the client view any of the tasks you were doing in therapy to be unhelpful? If so, are you willing to adjust your approach to be more in line with the client's wants? How can you work with your client in a culturally humble manner to collaborate on the most helpful tasks for therapy?

It is reassuring when we ask our clients how things are going and they confirm the direction of therapy, but sometimes they may provide feedback that requires us to change course. Even if not explicitly mentioned, these course changes can often involve aspects of the client's cultural identity. As therapists, we are highly trained (or are becoming so) in various theoretical languages, which give us the tools to dismiss or explain away any feedback we might receive from clients. Sometimes viewing their feedback through a theoretical lens (e.g., viewing feedback as resistance) is precisely what is needed. At the same time, we encourage you to carefully weigh the possibility that our clients are "right" because they are experts on their needs and inner experience. The *American Psychological Association (APA) Guidelines for Multicultural Education and Training, Research, and Practice in Psychology* specifically note the unique capacity of therapists to explore and understand their impact on their clients in therapy as a tool of promoting "racial equity and social justice" (APA, 2003, p. 382). We always observe indirectly what they observe through more direct experience. Thus, it can be culturally arrogant to minimize or dismiss client feedback.

Case Example: Dave and Jeff

Consider the following example of Jeff (the client) and Dave (the therapist). Jeff, a 41-year-old, White, heterosexual, married, cisgender man, presented for therapy to discuss struggles in his relationship with his wife of 12 years. In the first session, Dave, a 55-year-old, White, heterosexual, cisgender male marriage and family therapist, listened to Jeff's story and noticed he appeared to have difficulty expressing his emotions. Dave thinks that emotional expression and connection could be a useful thing to work on during therapy. However, Jeff shared that he would like to spend his time in therapy learning specific skills, such as problem-solving and communication skills, so he can better navigate arguments with his partner, Judy. The following is an excerpt from the dialogue between Dave and Jeff.

Jeff: Yeah, so Judy and I just fight all the time. I think the main thing that I am hoping to do in therapy is to learn how to talk things through better when she and I disagree.

Dave: That makes really good sense, and it seems like you're hoping to improve your connection with Judy—is that right?

Jeff: Yeah, I think that's right. I didn't think of it that way. I was thinking I was just tired of fighting, but feeling more connected would be good.

Dave: I noticed when you were describing your relationship that you tended to talk about the fights and arguments but not much about how you were feeling. How is it for you to discuss feelings?

Jeff: I don't really talk about them at all. That's just not how I was raised. Guys don't do that. I tend to get quiet when things get overwhelming and go into problem-solving mode.

Dave: Similar to what is happening now?

Jeff: Ha, I guess so, yeah.

Dave: I wonder if discussing both your emotions and ways of communicating more effectively with Judy could be an important use of our time here in therapy. What do you think?

Jeff: I am not sure I totally see the point just yet, but we can see.

Dave: Sounds good. Let's talk about that next time.

What was your reaction to the dialogue between Jeff and Dave? Did you notice any differences or disconnect between how each was approaching therapy? In this example, Dave was beginning to hypothesize that Jeff's upbringing was rooted in more traditional White, male gender norms (e.g., valuing being strong and independent, controlling emotional expression; see Mahalik, Good, & Englar-Carlson, 2003), which might explain Jeff's perspective on the problem (i.e., poor communication and desire to decrease arguments) and possible solutions (i.e., learning new communication and problem-solving skills). As a therapist strongly committed to feminist theories, Dave began to hypothesize that Jeff's lack of emotional expression could be contributing to his marital issues.

This conceptualization may be valid (i.e., working on emotional expression may help Jeff to improve his marriage); however, if Dave fails to recognize that Jeff may have different ideas for how therapy should progress and these ideas may be related to Jeff's cultural background, the two might struggle to build and maintain a strong working alliance. Jeff might even drop out of therapy and feel like Dave does not understand him (or his cultural background, whether or not this is explicitly stated). Asking the client for feedback may open the door to a collaborative discussion about how therapy is progressing and also provide an opportunity to discuss the cultural identities that are important to Jeff. Consider the revised dialogue between Jeff and Dave.

Jeff: Yeah, so Judy and I just fight all the time. I think the main thing that I am hoping to do in therapy is to learn how to talk things through better when she and I disagree.

Dave: That makes really good sense, and it seems like you're hoping to improve your connection with Judy, is that right?

Jeff: Yeah, I think that's right. I didn't think of it that way. I was thinking I was just tired of fighting, but feeling more connected would be good.

Dave: I noticed when you were describing your relationship that you tended to talk about the fights and arguments, but not much about how you were feeling. How is it for you to discuss feelings?

Jeff: I don't really talk about them at all. That's just not how I was raised. Guys don't do that. I tend to get quiet when things get overwhelming and go into problem-solving mode.

Dave: Similar to what is happening now?

Jeff: Ha, I guess so, yeah.

Dave: I wonder if discussing both your emotions and ways of communicating more effectively with Judy could be an important use of our time in therapy. What do you think?

Jeff: I am not sure I totally see the point just yet, but we can see.

Dave: Let me pause for a second and check in with you. It seemed like when I suggested delving into your emotions more as part of the work here, it didn't quite connect with you. I think for me, it has been helpful to work with clients on emotion because I think

Jeff: that's one of the ways we can connect with others who are close to us. But I don't want to put that on you if that isn't what you are wanting right now. Any thoughts about that?

Jeff: Well, it just seems to me like Judy and I are in crisis right now—like if something doesn't change, I'm not sure if the marriage is going to last. Trying to work on sharing my emotions seems really different to me, like it might take a long time for me to change that. I'm not sure my relationship with Judy has that kind of time. I understand what you're saying, and I am willing to talk about that part if you think it's important, but I want to make sure I'm getting help with the day-to-day stuff too, so I can save my marriage.

Dave: Got it. So what I'm hearing you say is that you're feeling like your marriage is in crisis because of all the arguments and fighting. You're open to exploring the emotional stuff but also want to make sure we spend adequate time on trying to deal with the arguments and fighting. I'm definitely on board with that—I want to spend this time on the things that are most important for saving your marriage.

What did you think of this second exchange between Dave and Jeff? How did Dave obtain feedback from Jeff about the course of therapy? What did you think of how Dave asked for feedback? Did it feel natural or unnatural to you? If you were to ask a client for feedback, would you do so in a similar manner, or would you try something different? If you were Dave, how would you incorporate the feedback from Jeff?

Developing a Plan for Feedback

Some therapists may navigate the task of obtaining client feedback in subtle and nonstructured ways through cultivating the kind of relationship in which clients feel comfortable voicing their concerns about the direction of therapy. However, there are some advantages to providing a more formal structure for feedback. A structured process normalizes feedback and makes it routine. In addition, a structured process communicates a systemic commitment to valuing client perspectives and acknowledging that therapists can (and probably will) make mistakes and not always "get it right."

In this next exercise, we give you an opportunity to explicitly develop a plan for inviting feedback from clients. Take some time and design a plan for evaluating whether your interventions and approach to therapy are working for your client. Will you directly broach the topic or try to get feedback indirectly? If you do plan to directly introduce the topic, how often do you plan to check in with the client? Do you plan on using a survey, or will you simply ask? If you plan to be less direct in soliciting or encouraging feedback, how do you imagine this process happening? After you have spent some time thinking and brainstorming about how you will ask your client for feedback, role play a discussion with a colleague or classmate in which you ask your discussion partner for feedback about how the treatment process is going. Take notice of any thoughts, feelings, or reactions that come up for you before, during, or after the discussion.

Take some time to reflect and journal about your experience. How was it to engage in a role-play discussion within which you asked for feedback about how the therapy process was going? Was the feedback mostly positive, mostly negative, or a mix? Did it feel comfortable or uncomfortable? Did it feel vulnerable? Did it bring up any fears or insecurities about your abilities as a therapist? Did anything come up during the discussion or feedback that might influence your therapy process in the future? Did you feel more close or less close to your discussion partner following the feedback? Do you think you could have a similar discussion with one of your clients? What barriers do you see to having a discussion such as this?

Conclusion

Building, developing, and strengthening the working alliance is a critical component of effective therapy. As noted in this chapter, it is essential to think about and reflect on how the cultural identities of your client, as well as your cultural identities, intersect to affect the development of the working alliance. In this chapter, we discussed how cultural humility can play an integral role in helping build the working alliance with clients, especially when cultural identities are salient to the therapy work (which we believe is always the case). In the next chapter, we discuss situations in which ruptures occur in the working alliance and how cultural humility can play a role in recovering from cultural ruptures when they occur in therapy.

Repairing the Relationship After Cultural Ruptures

6

In this country American means white. Everybody else has to hyphenate.

—Toni Morrison, *The Guardian* (1992)

Cirleen: Early in my practicum training, I saw Lakshmi, a Muslim, heterosexual woman, at a community mental health center. She was 23 years old and her family had emigrated from India when she was five. Lakshmi came to therapy because she had been feeling depressed for several months and it was impacting her motivation at work and her marriage. On multiple occasions, Lakshmi mentioned that she was just "too different." We explored this idea. When did she start to feel this way? How did these feelings develop over time? Lakshmi slowly began to recollect a number of pivotal experiences. She recalled being in school, the only student of color in her class, fasting for Ramadan, and being directed by a teacher to sit in a classroom alone during the lunch hour every day of that month so as not to subject the other students to her religious practice. She talked about how she hated that her father was a "walking stereotype" because he owned a Dunkin

http://dx.doi.org/10.1037/0000037-007
Cultural Humility: Engaging Diverse Identities in Therapy, by J. N. Hook, D. Davis, J. Owen, and C. DeBlaere

Donuts. She hated the racist things that people would say to her and her mother when they worked shifts at the store, or just the raised voices of people who assumed that she didn't speak English. Lakshmi wanted to be "normal."

At the time, I was a doctoral student learning concepts and language that helped me better understand and express my experiences growing up as a biracial Asian American woman in a predominately White community—concepts such as internalized racism, benevolent sexism, marginalization, and intersectionality. For me, learning about oppression and acquiring the language to talk about it was empowering. Do not get me wrong—it can also be demoralizing at times to sit with the understanding of systemic oppression. However, with the knowledge I was gaining as a graduate student, I was obtaining tools, and I intended to use these tools to combat oppression—both in my life and in the lives of my clients.

Given that background and context, you may not be surprised to hear that I wanted to share this knowledge with Lakshmi. In our fifth session, I decided to include some psychoeducation in our work together. I explained the concept of internalized racism and how it could apply to her experience. I told her there was nothing wrong with her, that it was society that was flawed, not her. Lakshmi nodded, but was quiet in response. As I was writing my case note after the session, I felt good about our interaction and believed that it would really help Lakshmi to understand that experiencing racism and discrimination wasn't her fault. Looking back, I thought I could rescue Lakshmi from her pain. I wanted to do that. In retrospect, I can identify my own projection and countertransference. After a lot of supervision and introspection, I saw I didn't meet my client where she was. I thought about what I would need or want in that situation, and assumed that my client needed or wanted the same thing. Unfortunately, Lakshmi never returned to therapy after that session and I never had the opportunity to work through the rupture with her.

Although the outcome of our therapy work was not as positive as I had hoped it would be, I did learn an important lesson. When we are more self-focused than client-focused, we are vulnerable to a variety of cultural ruptures (e.g., microaggressions, countertransference due to overidentification). It is important to note that the message of this story is not to avoid conversations about culture, oppression, and privilege in therapy. It is quite the opposite. In considering my work with Lakshmi, I wish I had asked more questions about her culture, her identity development, and her understanding of her identities. Even if I think I understand a client's cultural background and experiences, each client is unique. As we discussed in Chapter 5, a better understanding of these aspects of Lakshmi's experience would have allowed me to intervene in a way that would have fit with where she was. It takes cultural humility to be patient, meet clients where they are, and admit my limitations as a therapist.

Cultural Humility and Identifying and Repairing Cultural Ruptures

The topics we covered in the last chapter set the stage for developing a strong working alliance that can withstand the work of therapy. However, as much as we might try to be as humble and respectful as possible toward our clients' cultural identities, it is likely that we will sometimes make a mistake or misstep regarding our clients' cultural identities or how we engage in a discussion about culture in the therapy room. When these cultural strains or ruptures in the therapeutic relationship occur, it is important to repair the break in trust, attachment, and connectedness. In this chapter, we focus on two primary aspects of this process. First, we discuss how to identify when a cultural rupture may have occurred in therapy. Second, we discuss how to repair a cultural rupture after it has occurred.

IDENTIFYING CULTURAL RUPTURES

There has been quite a lot of research on general alliance ruptures, which involve tension or breakdown in the collaborative relationship between the therapist and client (Safran & Muran, 2006). This body of work indicates that the first major challenge is noticing that a rupture has occurred. Unfortunately, many therapists overlook the subtle signs that indicate a rupture has taken place (Binder & Strupp, 1997), and most clients do not directly address a rupture until it may be too late and they are already strongly considering termination. The following activity is intended to help you begin to identify characteristics of ruptures in general to inform your ability to identify ruptures in therapy.

Noticing Offenses in Everyday Life

We would like you to consider a situation in which a conflict occurred in your everyday life. For this exercise, it does not have to be an example from a therapy session—it can be any example of a conflict that comes to mind. It could be an argument you had with a romantic partner, a disagreement with a friend, or something that happened with a client. Once you have a conflict in mind, write a few sentences describing it and what happened. Then reflect and journal about the following questions, which are designed to provide you with a context for understanding how a conflict might be identified, as well as the steps you could take to attempt to repair a conflict, if you choose to do so.

When the situation occurred, how did you know you were in the midst of a conflict? What were the signs and signals that indicated a conflict was happening? Did you notice anything happening in the other person or yourself? Were you aware of any physiological reactions happening in your body? What thoughts and feelings came up for you? What was your immediate and default reaction? Did you attempt to try and resolve the conflict? Why or why not? How did the conflict resolution process go? What parts of the process were effective, and what parts were not effective? Were you able to resolve the conflict? Why or why not?

Next, we would like you to reflect and journal about some questions designed to increase your humility about the situation and the conflict. First, write a few sentences describing the conflict from the point of view of the other person. Now take some time and compare and contrast (a) your description of the conflict and (b) the description of the conflict from the point of view of the other person. What was similar about the two descriptions? What was different? What was it like to consider the other person's point of view?

It may have been difficult to write a thorough description from the point of view of the other person. We have greater access to our experience—especially painful feelings—than we do to the other person's experience. Often, we might make up a story about what the other person is thinking or feeling or what their motivations may have been. Our story may or may not be true. Think back to the conflict. What information about the other person's point of view would have been helpful for you to know when dealing with the conflict? What questions would you have liked to ask? Is there anything about your interactions with the person that may have conveyed a sense of arrogance on your part? If you had the chance to do it over, how could you have engaged in a more humble manner?

Cultural Ruptures and Microaggressions

Many ruptures have cultural underpinnings. We refer to these cultural misunderstandings or hurts as *cultural ruptures,* and they have the potential to disrupt the working alliance if they are not addressed and worked through. A cultural rupture occurs when clients perceive that an aspect of their cultural identity was targeted or implicated in an offense. A type of cultural rupture that has received a great deal of scholarly attention involves microaggressions (Hook, Farrell, et al., 2016; D. W. Sue et al., 2007). *Microaggressions* are offenses that are often largely invisible to the people that commit them but that occur regularly within society due to the prevalence of stereotypes and cultural norms that form "normal" prejudice and discrimination. Microaggressions in therapy occur when tensions, strains, and ruptures that occur in the relationship between therapist and client are related to cultural messages conveyed by the therapist (Owen, Imel, et al., 2011). Microaggressions negatively affect clients' perceptions of their therapists' level of cultural humility (Hook, Farrell, et al., 2016) and therapy outcomes (Owen, Tao, & Rodolfa, 2010).

The next exercise provides concrete examples of the kinds of behaviors that clients may experience as racial microaggressions. In Table 6.1, we present examples of racial microaggressions in Column 1 and possible interpretations of those statements in Column 2 (examples from D. W. Sue et al., 2007). For example, if a therapist asks a question such as "How long have you lived in this country?" a client could interpret it to mean that the therapist does not think the client is a United States citizen. This is an example of a statement that many Asian Americans hear regularly, and it reflects a stereotype of Asian Americans as perpetual foreigners. Read through the table and consider how seemingly innocuous statements can signal an underlying prejudice or bias.

Take some time to reflect and journal about your experiences reading through the statements. What did you think of the list of statements

TABLE 6.1

Microaggression Examples

Column 1: Microaggression	Column 2: Possible interpretation
"Where were you born?"	You are a foreigner.
"You are a credit to your race."	It is unusual for someone of your race to be intelligent.
"When I look at you, I don't see color."	Denying a person of color's racial or ethnic experiences.
A White woman or man clutching their purse or checking their wallet as a Black or Latino man approaches or passes.	You are a criminal.
"I'm not racist. I have several Black friends."	I am immune to racism because I have friends of color.
"Everyone can succeed in this society if they work hard enough."	People of color are lazy and/or incompetent and should work harder.
Asking a Black person, "Why do you have to be so loud and animated? Just calm down."	Assimilate to the dominant culture.
Being ignored at a store counter as attention is given to the White customer behind you.	Whites are more valued customers than people of color.
A college or university with buildings that are all named after White heterosexual upper class males.	You do not belong. You will not succeed here. There is only so far you can go.

Note. Adapted from "Racial Microaggressions in Everyday Life: Implications for Clinical Practice," by D. W. Sue et al., 2007, *American Psychologist*, 62, pp. 276–277. Copyright 2007 by the American Psychological Association.

that could be interpreted as microaggressions? Did you have any reactions while reading them? Were you surprised by any of the statements on the list? Have you made any of the statements on this list (or statements like them) to your clients? If so, your motivation may not have been to offend, but can you see how certain statements—when heard over and over again across relationships and contexts—could make someone feel increasingly invalidated or marginalized?

D. W. Sue et al. (2007) described three types of microaggressions. *Microassaults* involve explicit and intentional acts of racism, prejudice, or discrimination (e.g., referring to someone as "colored"). *Microinsults* are more subtle, often unconscious messages that put down an individual's cultural group (e.g., asking a person of color, "How did you get this job?"). *Microinvalidations* are messages that deny the experience of a cultural group (e.g., claiming to be "colorblind," which denies the racial experience of people of color). Of the three forms of microaggressions, clients are most likely to perceive microinvalidations and microinsults their therapists express in the form of dismissive messages about their cultural heritage or through culturally inappropriate interventions (Burkard & Knox, 2004; Neville, Lilly, Duran, Lee, & Browne, 2000; Salvatore & Shelton, 2007; Shelton & Delgado-Romero, 2011).

As therapists, we can engage with the scientific literature on microaggressions to increase our sensitivity to the repeated slights individuals from marginalized groups experience within society, which can increase our awareness of and responsiveness to clients. We might not expect it, but microaggressions do occur in therapy. For example, in a college student sample of racial and ethnic minority students seeking counseling at a college counseling center, 53% of clients reported they had experienced at least one microaggression over the course of their therapy experience (Owen, Tao, Imel, Wampold, & Rodolfa, 2014). In a community sample of racial and ethnic minority adult clients, 81% of clients reported they had experienced at least one microaggression over the course of their therapy experience (Hook, Farrell, et al., 2016).

The purpose of the next exercise is to help you think about and understand how microaggressions might show up in therapy. On the basis of data from focus groups looking at the experience of African American clients in therapy, Constantine (2007) identified 12 categories of racial microaggressions that might occur in therapy. We list each category, along with its definition and an example, in Table 6.2.

What do you think of the categories of racial microaggression that can occur in therapy? Looking back on your work with clients, have you committed any of the microaggressions on the list? Which microaggressions do you think you are most likely to commit in therapy? Why do you think you are more likely to commit certain microaggressions than others?

TABLE 6.2

Examples of Racial Microaggressions in Therapy

Microaggression	Definition	Example
Colorblindness	Denying racial–cultural differences	"I don't see you as Black; I just see you as a regular person."
Overidentification	Denying or minimizing individual racial bias because of assumed similarity	"As a gay person, I know just what it's like to be discriminated against because of race."
Denial of personal or individual racism	Professing presumed freedom from or immunization to racism	"I'm not racist because some of my best friends are Black."
Minimization of racial–cultural issues	Minimizing or dismissing the importance of racial–cultural issues to a person of color	"I'm not sure we need to focus on race or culture to understand your depression."
Assigning unique or special status on the basis of race or ethnicity	Assuming that a positive behavior or characteristic is atypically present in a person on the basis of race or ethnicity	"You're not like other Blacks; you're a credit to your race" and "You're a very articulate African American."
Stereotypic assumptions about members of a racial or ethnic group	Assuming that a behavior, norm, or characteristic exists on the basis of a person's race or ethnicity	"I know that Black people are very religious" and "Did you grow up in the inner city?"
Accused hypersensitivity regarding racial or cultural issues	Assuming that a person of color is hypersensitive during a discussion of racial or cultural issues	"Don't be too sensitive about the racial stuff. I didn't mean anything bad or offensive."
Meritocracy myth	Ignoring the responsibility of individual perpetrators and sociopolitical systems for perpetuating racism	"If Black people just worked harder, they could be successful like other people."
Culturally insensitive treatment considerations or recommendations	Displaying cultural insensitivity in the context of understanding or treating clients' concerns	"You should disengage or separate from your family of origin if they are causing you problems."
Acceptance of less than optimal behaviors on the basis of racial–cultural group membership	Accepting or normalizing potentially dysfunctional behaviors on the basis of a person's racial or cultural group	"It might be OK for some people to cope by drinking alcohol because their cultural norms sanction this behavior."
Idealization	Overestimating the desirable qualities and underestimating the limitations of a person on the basis of racial or ethnic group membership	"I'm sure you can cope with this problem as a strong Black woman" and "Black people are so cool."
Dysfunctional helping or patronization	Offering help that is unneeded or inappropriate on the basis of racial or ethnic group membership	"I don't usually do this, but I can waive your fees if you can't afford to pay for counseling."

Note. Reprinted from "Racial Microaggressions Against African American Clients in Cross-Racial Counseling Relationships," by M. G. Constantine, 2007, *Journal of Counseling Psychology*, *54*, p. 5. Copyright 2007 by the American Psychological Association.

The microaggressions described in Table 6.2 focus on race, but people also experience microaggressions for other cultural identities (e.g., gender, sexual orientation, disability or ability status, religion) and their intersection with each other (e.g., women of color). One way to start to learning more about the different types of microaggressions is by examining the professional literature on microaggressions for various cultural identities. On the basis of conversations happening in professional communities, authors have given examples of more commonly occurring offensive behaviors. For example, Shelton and Delgado-Romero (2011) interviewed lesbian, gay, bisexual, and queer (LGBQ) individuals who experienced microaggressions in therapy and identified seven themes: (a) assuming that sexual orientation is the cause of all presenting issues, (b) avoiding and minimizing sexual orientation, (c) attempting to overidentify with LGBQ clients, (d) making stereotypical assumptions about LGBQ clients, (e) expressing heteronormative bias, (f) assuming that LGBQ individuals need psychotherapeutic treatment, and (g) warning about the dangers of identifying as LGBQ. Gender microaggressions against women in therapy have also been described (e.g., encouraging women to be less assertive; Owen et al., 2010). However, some microaggressions are highly contextual and can change over time. Looking at Table 6.2, can you think about common slights you have observed regarding other cultural identities?

Becoming more aware of microaggressions is a process that involves caring about other people and learning to think accurately about and empathize with their experience. For example, last year, Donnie had a Jewish colleague tell him what it was like to raise his son within a predominately Christian culture. This was not new information per se, but Donnie experienced the next December and the focus on the Christmas holiday in a whole new way. The colleague's description of his experience echoed in Donnie's mind as he entered various spaces. He thought about what it would be like for his family. Donnie remembered stories his colleague told him about his son feeling left out. Conversations about inclusive language regarding religious holidays had a different kind of traction in Donnie's heart and mind.

If cultural ruptures are not effectively repaired, they can undermine the working alliance and lead to poor outcomes with clients. For example, when clients experienced more microaggressions in therapy, they reported a weaker working alliance with their therapist (Constantine, 2007; Morton, 2012; Owen, Imel, et al., 2011; Owen, Tao, et al., 2014). Clients experiencing more microaggressions in therapy also reported lower levels of psychological well-being (Owen, Imel, et al., 2011) and less satisfaction with therapy (Constantine, 2007). Experiencing microaggressions in therapy even sets the stage for more negative therapeutic interactions in the future. For example, clients who reported more microaggressions in therapy said they were less likely to seek therapy in the future (Crawford, 2011).

Case Example: Juan and Jessi

In this next exercise, we consider a case example of a cultural rupture or microaggression that might occur in therapy. This example is intended to help you consider some ways you might improve your ability to detect cultural ruptures or microaggressions within the therapy context.

Juan identifies as a 20-year-old gay, Latino, cisgender man. He is currently in his third year as an undergraduate student at a large university in the northeastern United States. Juan grew up in a devoutly Roman Catholic household and a relatively conservative community. Consequently, Juan has only disclosed his sexual orientation identity to his friends and select family members. In addition, Juan has only recently begun to date men. Before college, he had one relationship with a man, but this relationship was not disclosed to others.

Now that Juan is living in a more metropolitan area that is more affirming of his sexual orientation, he is beginning to explore his sexuality. Although Juan is excited about dating, he also struggles with his own internalized homophobia and a fear of rejection. To help address these concerns, Juan decided to attend counseling. Early in therapy, Juan's therapist, Jessi, who identifies as a nonreligious, White, cisgender woman, disclosed to Juan that she identifies as lesbian.

After a few months of therapy, Juan and his therapist have been able to explore his trepidations about dating, and he is feeling more and more comfortable exploring his dating prospects in the city. However, Juan also began to share an additional perceived challenge about dating, namely, racism. He shared with his therapist that he sometimes feels uncomfortable at gay bars and restaurants because he is often the only Latino man present and sometimes the only visible person of color. These feelings of discomfort have sometimes led Juan to avoid going out.

When Juan broached the topic with his therapist, Jessi replied, "Come on, don't play the race card. You know you just need to get out there." Juan did not directly respond to his therapist's comment, and the session continued, seemingly without incident. However, Juan was deeply hurt and angry with his therapist. He talked little for the remainder of the session and "just wanted to get out of there." There is some evidence that microaggressions that occur in the context of a therapy relationship where there is an identity match—in this case both Juan and Jessi identify as sexual minorities—may be more impactful to clients (Hook, Farrell, et al., 2016). Juan returned to therapy the following week and the subsequent week before not showing up two additional times and eventually terminating with his therapist. He never told her exactly what happened.

This scenario clearly depicts a microaggression (i.e., invalidation of Juan's race or ethnicity). Furthermore, Juan's therapist never addressed the incident with him, and he did not feel comfortable bringing up the topic with her. Spend some time thinking and reflecting on this case example. What was your initial reaction to the therapist's comment? Although Juan never confronted his therapist, what indications did he provide to his therapist that a rupture had occurred? What do you think the therapist could have done in this situation to address the microaggression?

This example illustrates why it is important to show interest in and discuss clients' cultural identities throughout the course of therapy. Perhaps if Juan's therapist had explored all of Juan's salient cultural identities early in the therapy process, the issue of ethnicity could have been more fully explored and validated. This may have created an environment in which this particular microaggression could have been avoided altogether. At the very least, asking about Juan's ethnicity would have acknowledged Juan's multiple cultural identities in ways that would have made them more present and understood by the therapist.

Perhaps with a stronger foundation of trust, Juan would have felt more comfortable challenging his therapist's statement or sharing his feelings about the microaggression. That being said, this is not by any means Juan's responsibility. It is our responsibility as therapists to develop a strong working alliance, to do our best to avoid committing cultural ruptures, and to address them if and when they do occur. In this instance, Juan's silence and subsequent no-shows were strong indicators that something was amiss. These also could have been opportunities for his therapist to intervene.

REPAIRING CULTURAL RUPTURES

Now that we have discussed some strategies for identifying cultural ruptures in therapy, we want to discuss how to repair them when they do occur. Although cultural ruptures are likely to undermine the working alliance if left unaddressed, taking steps to repair the rupture has the potential to rebuild the working alliance, perhaps even resulting in a stronger alliance and a deeper bond than before the rupture occurred. Next, we discuss four aspects of repairing cultural ruptures: (a) dealing with defensiveness, (b) cultivating an environment in which the client can disclose cultural ruptures, (c) getting client feedback about cultural ruptures, and (d) putting together a cultural rupture repair action plan.

Dealing With Defensiveness

First, by definition, microaggressions are subtle and ambiguous statements that typically result in confusion, discomfort, and frustration.

Accordingly, it can be difficult for therapists to recognize they have committed a microaggression. If they do recognize the offense, it can be difficult to accept that one has perpetrated such an offense. Defensiveness is a common and expected reaction. It is important, then, to anticipate this possible reaction and consider ways we might respond differently. One thing that is difficult about perpetrating microaggressions is that there are always several perspectives of the offense. Microaggressions usually evoke a dynamic in which the offended person feels devalued or invalidated by some aspect of the interaction, but the perpetrator sees the behavior as innocuous or benign. If the offended person does confront the event, the perpetrator's response is often to clarify, justify, or defend their behavior and perspective.

Granted, it might be easier to own one's responsibility for committing a microaggression if the offended person always communicated about offenses using "I language," excellent emotion regulation, and positive engagement. This might be a legitimate request to make of a romantic partner, asking them to learn to address conflict in ways that make a productive conversation about conflict most likely. However, as therapists, we should aspire to practice interpersonal skills that will help us respond to microaggressions effectively even when the client's response leads us to feel highly defensive and insecure. It is not the client's job to take care of our feelings; however, it is (literally) our job to attend to theirs. The purpose of the next exercise is to provide a microaggression self-talk plan that can help you plan for and quickly reduce defensiveness when it arises.

Think of an example of a microaggression you have committed with a client. If you cannot think of a specific offense, think about a microaggression from Table 6.2 that would likely make you feel defensive if you were accused of committing it. Also, think of some of the contextual factors that might make it particularly difficult to respond in an open and nondefensive manner, such as how the confrontation occurred, your relationship with the offended person, the cultural identity of the client, or your personal state of mind (e.g., high stress).

Under high strain, it is difficult to reduce defensiveness, but we would like you to develop a plan for self-talk that will help you to reduce defensiveness in the midst of a conflict situation. Write two or three phrases that might help you shift gears, engage with cultural humility, and put clients' needs first, rather than attending to your own needs to justify yourself. For example, what could you say to yourself to validate and honor your experience of the event without needing to invalidate the client's experience of the offense? What are some things you could say to yourself that would remind you to explore and honor the client's perspective and experience?

Cultivating an Environment in Which the Client Can Disclose Cultural Ruptures

As noted in the example of Juan, sometimes clients do not choose to disclose when they have experienced a microaggression in therapy. Thus, it is important to cultivate an environment in which clients feel safe to bring up offenses. In the previous chapters, we discussed several strategies that therapists can use to help make the therapy room a safe place where clients are more likely to feel comfortable bringing up cultural offenses if they occur.

It would obviously be great if we never committed an offense that would cause a cultural rupture with our clients, and we believe that none of us would want to do that intentionally. At the same time, worrying too much about committing a cultural offense or microaggression within a therapy session is not likely to be helpful. Being too self-focused and worried about making mistakes likely distracts and detracts from other positive behaviors that can strengthen the bond between therapist and client. A better strategy may be to direct one's energy toward establishing a supportive and trusting working alliance and making it a regular practice to check in with clients about how they are experiencing the relationship, including any possible offenses or ruptures. Mistakes are a normal part of life, and it is likely that you will make some cultural mistakes with your clients because you are an imperfect human who is learning and growing in your development as a therapist. If you have done the personal and relational work with your client to make the therapy room a culturally safe place before the offense occurs, you will likely be able to hear your client's feedback and respond effectively.

One of the most difficult aspects of repairing cultural ruptures and microaggressions is that we are unlikely to receive accurate feedback from our clients unless we cultivate the kind of environment in which they are willing to take substantial risks to repair the relationship. In this exercise, we would like you to consider some of your personal relationships and the degree to which you feel comfortable addressing conflict with different individuals with whom you are in relationship.

First, in what kinds of relationships are you least likely to confront minor to moderate offenses when they occur? What are some of the qualities of these relationships that make it more difficult for you to think that it is worth confronting hurts? Next, think of the relationships in which you are most willing and able to address hurts and offenses when they occur. What qualities of that person or relationship make it easier or more likely for you to disclose when moderate or minor shifts occur in the relationship? After reflecting on these questions, write down 10 qualities of a therapeutic environment or relationship you think would facilitate client disclosure of a cultural rupture or microaggression.

Getting Client Feedback About Cultural Ruptures

Now that you have a better sense of the type of environment you would like to create to enable client feedback about cultural ruptures and micro-aggressions, we turn to how you might go about actually obtaining feedback after a cultural rupture has occurred. In the previous chapter, we discussed several strategies for obtaining formal and informal feedback on how clients think therapy is going. These strategies are important because they communicate your interest in investing in the relationship, as well as your openness to being responsive if there is something that would improve the client's experience.

One strategy some of us have implemented in the clinics where we have worked is to have clients fill out a brief weekly measure of their therapy experience, including their perceptions of the working alliance during that week's session. The therapist can look at these data and see a graph of the working alliance with each client each week. One simple strategy for identifying cultural ruptures is to examine the alliance scores each week and look for dips in ratings of the working alliance. A dip in working alliance could indicate a cultural rupture or strain in the relationship. If this does occur, therapists can think about whether they may have done something to contribute to it, or they could check in with clients to see whether anything happened in the previous session that may have caused distance or strain in the relationship.

If your clinical setting measures working alliance on a regular basis, spend some time and review the alliance ratings for all your clients each week. Do you notice any dips in the working alliance ratings for any of your clients? If so, did anything happen the previous week that may have contributed to a strain in your relationship? If nothing comes to mind, it might be a good idea to check in about this with your client the next week.

Perhaps you do not work in a clinical setting that regularly keeps track of client ratings of the working alliance. How might you check in with your clients during a session to get feedback on how they are feeling about therapy or whether any cultural ruptures have occurred? The following are some examples of in-session language that could be helpful here. For example, during the initial session, you might say something such as the following:

- "I want to be sure we are on the same page throughout this process, so if there is anything that arises that does not seem to fit for you or you find off, I hope you can share those concerns with me, and I might just check in about that from time to time, if that's OK."
- "I want this place to be a safe place where you can talk about your beliefs and values, and if there are any moments when you feel that might not be the case, please let me know."

The following are some examples to get feedback from clients in ongoing sessions. For example, near the end of a session, you might say:

- "I just wanted to check in with you about how things are going in our sessions."
- "Are we on the right path here for addressing your goals?"
- "Has there been anything we have discussed that isn't sitting right with you?"
- "I know we have been discussing important issues over the past session, and we talked about [a specific cultural issue]. I wonder how you felt that conversation went?"

Get together with a friend or colleague and practice asking some questions to get feedback about the working alliance, cultural misunderstandings, and cultural ruptures. As you are practicing, take note of what kind of language feels natural to you. Check in with your discussion partner and get feedback about how you came across. Did you feel comfortable asking for feedback? Did you come across as defensive in any way? What could you adjust, either in your body language, tone of voice, or choice of words, to present as more culturally humble?

Cultural Rupture Repair Action Plan

Finally, because culturally humble therapists acknowledge their limitations and understand they have the proclivity to make cultural mistakes (and that making such mistakes is a normal part of the therapeutic process), they ought to respond to cultural ruptures and microaggressions in therapy in such a way as to increase the likelihood of forgiveness, compassion, and reconciliation. For example, culturally humble therapists are likely to make more effective other-oriented apologies than therapists who are not culturally humble, which is likely to lead to higher levels of forgiveness and reconciliation. Many of you know intuitively how to do this, but some ways of dealing with ruptures are more effective than others. Next, we discuss a plan—based on research on forgiveness and reconciliation—that can help you clarify the important elements of an effective response to cultural ruptures.

In this exercise, we walk you through how to develop an action plan when a cultural rupture has occurred in therapy. To make this plan more concrete, we return to the example of Juan introduced earlier in the chapter. Juan's therapist did not address the incident and may not have even been aware that a rupture had occurred at all, but for the purposes of this exercise, let us suppose she became aware she had committed a microaggression toward Juan. What could she do if she wanted to acknowledge the microaggression and attempt to repair the cultural rupture? What steps would she take? The following plan of action integrates what we have discussed in this chapter.

- Step 1: Check in with yourself. How are you feeling about the cultural rupture? When you think about what happened, do you feel sad, scared, or angry? What feelings come up when you think about addressing the cultural rupture with your client? What are you feeling toward the client right now?

- Step 2: Consider your client's perspective. Put yourself in your client's shoes. How do you think the client is feeling about you, your relationship, or the therapy process? What do you think your client would want regarding the resolution of the cultural rupture? What action would be in their best interests? One strategy to help take your client's perspective is to think of a situation in which a person who held a position of power in their interaction with you said or did something that was invalidating of your experience. How did that feel? What steps could they have taken to repair the rupture? Did they do anything to exacerbate the problem?

- Step 3: Clarify your motivations. What could be the reasons for addressing the cultural rupture? How do you think addressing the rupture could help you and the client reconnect? An important consideration is to remember that, as therapists, it can be tempting to explain how what we said was "right" and defensible—we might even be able to put a theoretical conceptualization behind our comments. If you feel a pull to do this, it might be a good time to stop, assess, check in, and explore your need to be "right," rather than empathic. However, if your motivation is to help you and your client reconnect and restore the working alliance, your motivations may be in a better place. Remember, the focus here is on your therapeutic mistake or misstep. As therapists, we are in the position to honor our clients' cultural heritage.

- Step 4: Consult. Sometimes if we are struggling to decide whether and how to address a cultural rupture in therapy, it is a good idea to consult with a supervisor or colleague. Take some time to talk through what happened, as well as your proposed course of action. Be open to feedback.

- Step 5: Acknowledge the incident or rupture. When acknowledging the cultural rupture, use "I" statements, take responsibility, and clearly state your interpretation of the rupture. For example, in the case of Juan's therapist, she could have said, "I think I just said something that was hurtful and invalidating of your experience."

- Step 6: Invite your client to share their perspective and feelings. It is important to create a safe space for your client to share their perspective of the cultural rupture. Also, remember that a client may not feel comfortable doing this immediately. As with any conflict, it can take time to process an incident and clarify one's thoughts and feelings. Thus, be patient and leave the door open for future dialogue. You may also ask for permission to revisit the issue in the not-too-distant future.

▮ Step 7: Apologize. Apologizing for a cultural rupture is critical and requires the very focus of this book—cultural humility. Apologizing requires vulnerability and a willingness to admit you made a mistake. Apologizing is a means of honestly owning and taking responsibility for our actions. When a rupture has occurred, we have to acknowledge our role in the rupture. An effective apology involves more than just saying, "I'm sorry." Good apologies involve certain ingredients, including (a) making a statement of the apology, (b) naming the rupture, (c) taking responsibility for the rupture, (d) expressing your feelings and emotions about what happened, (e) addressing the emotions of your client, and (f) making a commitment to do things differently in the future (Kirchhoff, Strack, & Jager, 2009).

Think about a current or past client with whom you committed a cultural rupture or microaggression. Spend some time putting together a rupture repair action plan. Think, reflect, and journal about each step. If this is an issue you are having with a current client, try working through the last three steps with the client. Take notice of what worked well and what things you could improve on in the future. If this was an issue with a past client with whom you no longer have a relationship, get together with a friend or colleague and practice working through the last three steps with them. As you are practicing, take notice of what worked well and what things you could improve on in the future. Check in with your discussion partner and get feedback about how you came across. Did you feel comfortable bringing up the cultural rupture and making an apology? Did you come across as defensive in any way? What could you adjust, either in your body language, tone of voice, or choice of words, to present as more culturally humble?

Ineffective and Effective Apologies

The final step of the rupture repair action plan, making an effective apology, is so critical for facilitating relationship repair that we would like to spend some additional time providing science-informed training on the elements of a good apology. Remember the main components of a good apology described in the previous section (Kirchhoff et al., 2009). In the following exercise, you have the opportunity to apply this information to some apology examples.

Next, we provide three examples of ineffective apologies. Now that you understand the ingredients of a good apology, see whether you can (a) identify what was wrong with the ineffective apology and (b) turn these ineffective apologies into effective apologies that are likely to generate empathy and willingness to risk relationship repair on the part of your client.

Ineffective apology: "I'm sorry, but I think maybe you're being a little too sensitive."

- What was wrong? _____
- Effective apology: _____

Ineffective apology: "I don't know what I did to upset you, but I'm sorry."

- What was wrong? _____
- Effective apology: _____

Ineffective apology: "I'm sorry you took it that way. It's not what I meant."

- What was wrong? _____
- Effective apology: _____

Case Example: Deanne and Mary

To make the information on rupture repair and apology more concrete, we consider another example of a microaggression in therapy, as well as the therapist's attempt to apologize and repair the cultural rupture. Consider the following therapy example between Deanne, a 48-year-old, White, heterosexual, cisgender female therapist, and Mary, a 30-year-old, White, heterosexual, cisgender female client. Mary sought therapy to address her depressive and anxious symptoms after her partner's recent extramarital affair. Therapy initially went well. Mary felt a strong connection with Deanne, and she was able to process the feelings of loss, anger, and hurt that she experienced following the affair.

During the 10th session, Mary shared with Deanne that she was feeling angry with God and not feeling connected at church anymore. Instead of exploring the topic, Deanne moved on, missing something Mary viewed as an important disclosure. Mary did not address what happened at the time, but she felt unsettled with Deanne after that. Mary had questions about what happened. Was Deanne religious and offended that she felt upset at God? Was faith not that important to Deanne, so she just did not understand it or want to talk about it? Mary felt herself shutting down.

Deanne did not know what exactly was happening between her and Mary. But she did notice a shift in their relationship during that session. For example, Deanne noticed that Mary seemed a bit short and guarded with her responses. Mary seemed more irritable and sad than usual. Deanne tried a few open-ended questions to get things moving, but the therapy remained stuck, and she started to feel anxious and unsettled too. Something was off in their relationship, but she did not know what to do. Deanne decided that in their next session, she would try to address what was happening with Mary, with the hope of gaining insight and repairing the relationship if necessary.

Deanne: Mary, I've noticed that something seemed different the last time we met and also today. In prior sessions, you shared things on your mind freely, but now you seem more cautious.

Mary: Yeah, I guess so.

Deanne: [*Sitting in silence, but expressing interest and caring.*]

Mary: Well, I've been thinking a lot about last session. I felt like maybe you didn't understand where I was coming from.

Deanne: [*Feeling anxious, with her mind racing, so she reminds herself to stay engaged and nondefensive, even though she feels like pulling back.*] Something happened last week that is related to how you feel today. Can you tell me what happened?

Mary: Well, I was talking about how terrible everything has been. Most of the session felt fine, but then I started talking about some of the struggles I have had lately with my religion. You know, feeling angry at God.

Deanne: Ah, yes, I remember that. Yes, something did seem to shift. What was going on with you then? I can tell this is a hard conversation, but I'm so glad you are willing to have it with me.

Mary: Well, you just seemed uncomfortable, and I didn't know what that meant. All of the sudden, I felt very self-conscious. I realized I didn't know anything about your faith background, or even if it's OK to ask. I wasn't sure if I offended you, or you just didn't see how important this was to me, but I just wanted to curl up into a ball and hide.

Deanne: Ah, Mary, I think I am starting to see. You didn't quite know what it meant, but what you shared about your spiritual life was really important, and I didn't seem to get it. Worse than that, you didn't know how to interpret the fact that I just moved on to something else. I am so sorry, Mary. I see now that was very painful. I could tell this was really important to you, and there was a lot of pain behind your statement. To be honest, I wasn't quite sure what you needed from me. I realize now you may have needed more support and engagement. Is that right?

Mary: Yes! I had no idea how to put words to all that I was feeling. I wanted you to help me untangle the complex feelings I was having. Instead, we just moved on [*starting to cry*]. I felt so alone.

Deanne: Mary, I wish last week had gone so differently, but I am so glad to have another chance to revisit this issue. We can absolutely talk about your spirituality. Would you like to talk more about how you are feeling about God and your church now?

What is your initial reaction to this dialogue? How did Deanne know that a rupture had taken place? What steps did she take to invite feedback from Mary about the rupture? Do you consider what happened to be a microaggression? When Mary shared what had happened and how she felt, how did Deanne respond? How did Deanne acknowledge the rupture? How did Deanne invite Mary to share her perspective and experience about the rupture? How did Deanne apologize for the rupture? Did Deanne incorporate all the elements of a good apology? If you were the therapist in this situation, how would you have responded to Mary?

Conclusion

Building and maintaining a strong working alliance is essential for effective therapy. However, we are not perfect, and sometimes we make mistakes. These missteps can sometimes take the form of microaggressions or cultural offenses or ruptures. It is essential to try to minimize committing cultural offenses in our work with clients, but we also need to also create an environment in which clients feel safe to address cultural ruptures when they do occur. If we can have open and honest discussions with clients about cultural ruptures, we may be able to work to repair the relationship when a rupture occurs. In the next chapter, we discuss difficult situations in which therapists experience cultural value conflicts in their work with clients.

Navigating Value Differences and Conflicts 7

We hang on to our values, even if they seem at times
tarnished and worn. . . . What else is there to guide us?
—Barack Obama, *The Audacity of Hope:*
Thoughts on Reclaiming the American Dream

Josh: When I met with Sharon for the first time, I
noticed right away there were some differences in
our cultural identities. She was a 46-year-old, African
American, cisgender woman, working two part-time
jobs to make ends meet. She was a single parent with
four children between the ages of 12 and 25 and two
small grandchildren, all of whom lived with her in
government-subsidized housing. I was a mid-20s,
White, cisgender, male graduate student. I was an
only child who grew up in a suburb of Chicago, and I
was single with no children.

She was in treatment for alcohol dependence.
Therapy seemed to progress reasonably, but at times
we struggled to connect with each other, and some
of our struggle had to do with the value differences
and conflicts between us. For example, Sharon placed
a high value on her family. She valued her children
and grandchildren over almost anything. At the time,
I struggled to fully support this value. I thought that
many of Sharon's stressors were linked to her family

http://dx.doi.org/10.1037/0000037-008
Cultural Humility: Engaging Diverse Identities in Therapy, by J. N. Hook, D. Davis,
J. Owen, and C. DeBlaere

members, some of whom I judged were making poor decisions and taking advantage of her financially.

But I had to come to terms with the fact that I held a different set of values than Sharon. They were not completely different. Family was important to me as well, but other values, such as independence, education, and self-actualization, sometimes took precedence. For example, I was OK with moving far away from my family to attend graduate school. When deciding on schools, I got accepted to a school close to my home, but I almost viewed the proximity as a negative because I wanted to move away and explore something new.

I could tell these value differences sometimes got in the way of our therapy work together. I could feel myself wanting Sharon to be more independent and set better boundaries with her children, especially the ones who were adults themselves. I thought that some of these relationships were part of the stress that was leading Sharon to drink. Sharon agreed that her family was causing her stress. She knew her older children were making bad decisions that were negatively affecting her health and well-being. But she was not willing to draw a hard line or boundary with them (e.g., tell them they either had to pay rent or leave). Maintaining her family relationships and taking care of her children and grandchildren were her highest priorities, and because I was coming from a different place and had a different set of values, I had a difficult time understanding her perspective. For our therapy to be effective, I would have to recognize the value differences between us but honor and prioritize her values. I had to see whether there was a way forward in treatment that worked within her value framework.

Cultural Humility and Navigating Value Differences and Conflicts

The purpose of this chapter is to explore ways to navigate situations in which you experience strong value differences or conflicts between yourself and your client. One of the more challenging aspects of effectively engaging with cultural identities in therapy occurs when our personal values conflict with the values of the client we are trying to help. We each have a set of values—the things we consider to be "good," "right," or "desirable." Values are important to therapy because they help frame our ideas of what positive mental health and well-being look like. These values help frame the collaborative goals that we develop with our client. What does the client hope to gain from therapy? What does the client want their life to look like as a result of therapy? These therapy goals are all affected by one's values about what it means to have "good" mental health. In this chapter, we cover three important aspects of working with value differences and conflicts: (a) exploring your values, (b) recognizing when a value difference or conflict occurs, and (c) addressing the value difference or conflict in therapy.

EXPLORING YOUR VALUES

What is it about values that makes it difficult to engage with someone who has a different set of values? According to Graham and Haidt (2010), core values bind people together into close-knit groups, but they also lead to conflict and tension with other individuals and groups who may not share our core values. When we share our core values with others, it provides a sort of "glue" for our relationships. Think about your closest friends and family members. Think about the groups to which you are strongly committed. It is likely you share at least some core values. Perhaps shared values are what brought you together in the first place. However, even though core values draw people together, they can also lead individuals and groups to have negative reactions toward outgroup members who do not share their cherished values. To the extent that we use core values to identify who is on "our team," it is similarly easy to view others who do not share our core values as the "other," outside of our care and concern.

Jonathan Haidt and colleagues presented a model for organizing values based on five moral foundations (Graham et al., 2011; Haidt, 2013). The model is not a comprehensive list of values or virtues but rather attempts to describe some of the foundational considerations people use to evaluate what is right and wrong. First, some individuals place a high value on *harm* and make moral decisions based on whether a person or other living thing is hurt. Second, some individuals prioritize *fairness* and make moral decisions based on equality and justice. Third, some individuals stress *loyalty* and make moral decisions based on a commitment to one's team, tribe, or group. Fourth, some individuals place a high value on *authority* and make moral decisions based on the ordered, hierarchical system of which they are a part. Finally, some individuals prioritize *purity* and make moral decisions based on avoiding pathogens and contaminants. In general, liberal individuals have profiles that prioritize the moral foundations of harm and fairness, with a lower emphasis on loyalty, authority, and purity. In contrast, conservatives tend to prioritize all five moral foundations equally (Graham, Haidt, & Nosek, 2009).

To successfully navigate value differences and conflicts, you must first understand and acknowledge how you judge right from wrong, which is closely linked to your cultural background and worldview. Having an accurate sense of yourself culturally (including your values) is a core aspect of cultural humility (Hook, Davis, Owen, Worthington, & Utsey, 2013). One important way to get a sense of the value differences or conflicts you might experience in therapy is to complete a measure that can help give you insight into your core values.

Next, we provide a measure of values: Exhibit 7.1, the Moral Foundations Questionnaire (MFQ; Graham et al., 2011). The MFQ is based on the theory we described earlier in this chapter; namely, there are five moral foundations that people use to make decisions about right and wrong (i.e., harm, fairness, loyalty, authority, and purity). For our purposes, this model provides a language for beginning to think and

---

EXHIBIT 7.1

Moral Foundations Questionnaire

Part 1. When you decide whether something is right or wrong, to what extent are the following considerations relevant to your thinking? Please rate each statement using this scale:

0 = not at all relevant (This consideration has nothing to do with my judgments of right and wrong)
1 = not very relevant
2 = slightly relevant
3 = somewhat relevant
4 = very relevant
5 = extremely relevant (This is one of the most important factors when I judge right and wrong)

_____ 1. Whether or not someone suffered emotionally
_____ 2. Whether or not some people were treated differently than others
_____ 3. Whether or not someone's action showed love for his or her country
_____ 4. Whether or not someone showed a lack of respect for authority
_____ 5. Whether or not someone violated standards of purity and decency
_____ 6. Whether or not someone was good at math
_____ 7. Whether or not someone cared for someone weak or vulnerable
_____ 8. Whether or not someone acted unfairly
_____ 9. Whether or not someone did something to betray his or her group
_____10. Whether or not someone conformed to the traditions of society
_____11. Whether or not someone did something disgusting
_____12. Whether or not someone was cruel
_____13. Whether or not someone was denied his or her rights
_____14. Whether or not someone showed a lack of loyalty
_____15. Whether or not an action caused chaos or disorder
_____16. Whether or not someone acted in a way that God would approve of

Part 2. Please read the following sentences and indicate your agreement or disagreement:

0 = Strongly disagree
1 = Moderately disagree
2 = Slightly disagree
3 = Slightly agree
4 = Moderately agree
5 = Strongly agree

_____17. Compassion for those who are suffering is the most crucial virtue.
_____18. When the government makes laws, the number one principle should be ensuring that everyone is treated fairly.

EXHIBIT 7.1 (*Continued*)

Moral Foundations Questionnaire

_____19. I am proud of my country's history.

_____20. Respect for authority is something all children need to learn.

_____21. People should not do things that are disgusting, even if no one is harmed.

_____22. It is better to do good than to do bad.

_____23. One of the worst things a person could do is hurt a defenseless animal.

_____24. Justice is the most important requirement for a society.

_____25. People should be loyal to their family members, even when they have done something wrong.

_____26. Men and women each have different roles to play in society.

_____27. I would call some acts wrong on the grounds that they are unnatural.

_____28. It can never be right to kill a human being.

_____29. I think it's morally wrong that rich children inherit a lot of money while poor children inherit nothing.

_____30. It is more important to be a team player than to express oneself.

_____31. If I were a soldier and disagreed with my commanding officer's orders, I would obey anyway because that is my duty.

_____32. Chastity is an important and valuable virtue.

Note. To score the MFQ yourself, you can copy your answers into the grid in Figure 7.1. Then add up the six numbers in each of the five columns and write each total in the box at the bottom of the column. The box then shows your score on each of five psychological "foundations" of morality. Scores run from 0 to 30 for each foundation. (Questions 6 and 22 are just used to catch people who are not paying attention. They do not count toward your scores.) The average politically moderate American's scores are 20.2 in Harm/Care, 20.5 in Fairness/Reciprocity, 16.0 in In-group/Loyalty, 16.5 in Authority/Respect, and 12.6 in Purity/Sanctity. Liberals score a bit higher than that on Harm/Care and Fairness/Reciprocity and much lower than that on the other three foundations. Conservatives show the opposite pattern. For more information about moral foundations theory, scoring this form, or interpreting your scores, see this version of the original tool at http://www.MoralFoundations.org. To take this scale online and see how you compare with others, go to http://www.YourMorals.org. Adapted from "Mapping the Moral Domain," by J. Graham, B. A. Nosek, J. Haidt, R. Iyer, S. Koleva, and P. H. Ditto, 2011, *Journal of Personality and Social Psychology, 101*, p. 385. Copyright 2011 by the American Psychological Association.

talk about your core values, as well as what types of value conflicts you might expect to experience in your work with clients.

Complete the MFQ. After you finish, calculate your results using the grid in Figure 7.1 (scoring instructions are provided with the MFQ). What foundational values are most important to you? What values are less important to you? Do the results of this questionnaire "ring true" for you? Do you think the results of this questionnaire accurately describe the things you rely on to judge right and wrong? When you think about the other things that are most important to you, can you organize them according to these five foundational values or would the model need expansion to describe your moral system? On the basis of the results of this questionnaire, what types of clients and issues might you expect to bring up difficulties about value differences or conflicts in your therapy work?

FIGURE 7.1

Question #	Your Response	Question #	Your Response	Question #	Your Response	Question #	Your Response	Question #	Your Response	Question #	Your Response
1		2		3		4		5		6	
7		8		9		10		11			
12		13		14		15		16			
17		18		19		20		21		22	
23		24		25		26		27			
28		29		30		31		32			

Harm / Care	Fairness / Reciprocity	In-group/ Loyalty	Authority / Respect	Purity / Sanctity

Scoring sheet for the Moral Foundations Questionnaire.

RECOGNIZING A VALUE DIFFERENCE OR CONFLICT

In some of your therapeutic relationships, your values will likely line up (for the most part) with those of your client. For example, the client might be depressed and want to reduce the depression and become more satisfied with their life (perhaps falling under the harm/care domain). You might value life satisfaction as well, and thus therapy moves forward without a deep consideration of your values. Your values are congruent with those of your client, and thus therapeutic goals are easily set, and therapy moves forward with relatively few incidents.

But in other therapeutic relationships, you might get the sense that there are some value differences or conflicts between you and your client. We started this chapter with one such example. Josh's client strongly valued family and connection, whereas Josh strongly valued independence and boundaries. There was a difference here (perhaps a smaller emphasis on loyalty and respect for authority), and it was a bit of a struggle for Josh to find a way to support the client and her values. But there are other examples as well. Maybe you strongly value equal rights for lesbian, gay, bisexual, and transgender (LGBT) individuals but have a religious client who is struggling with guilt and shame associated with her same-sex attraction. You believe that part of the reason for her guilt and shame is due to involvement in a religious community that labels her sexual attractions as bad and sinful, and you would like her to become more free and open with her sexuality. But your client places a high priority on her religious values regarding sexuality and would like you to help her adjust her behavior to be consistent with those values. This represents a value conflict. How do you move forward in a way that honors and respects your client's values?

Or perhaps you strongly value independence and pursuing your personal goals and dreams. Your client is attending school in the United States but grew up in a family with strong collectivistic family values. Your client's parents have several specific goals for your client—make straight *A*s, get into medical school, become a doctor, get married and have children to carry on the family name, and so forth. Your client is struggling because she strongly values her family and wants to make them proud but is not sure she even wants to be a doctor. She feels conflict between her wants and desires and the desires of her family. Because you strongly value independence and pursuing your goals, you want the same for your client, and you find yourself encouraging her in this direction. But in doing so, are you respecting your client's values or pushing your agenda for her?

Examples of Value Differences and Conflicts

To begin thinking about value differences and conflicts, we describe some hypothetical scenarios that might elicit a reaction from you on the basis of your personal set of values. For each hypothetical scenario, imagine you are the therapist for each of the clients described. Think about what values you hold that apply to this particular client situation. Think about whether there might be a value difference or conflict between you and the client. Read each of the following brief client descriptions and then answer the subsequent questions designed to help you clarify your values and reactions to the conflict:

> Case 1. Sid is a 45-year-old, White, heterosexual, cisgender father of two. His daughters are aged 16 and 20. He is a widower. Recently, Sid was charged with sexually abusing his daughters. The abuse allegedly began a year after his wife's death, when the girls were 12 and 16. Sid has been court ordered to attend counseling.

What personal values do you hold that apply to this client situation?

Do you foresee any value differences or conflicts that might come up between you and this client? If so, briefly describe the value difference or conflict.

> Case 2. Eliza is a 33-year-old, White, cisgender woman who has recently begun a lesbian relationship with her neighbor, Kathy. This is Eliza's first relationship with a woman. She has always been attracted to women, but she married her husband, John, immediately after high school. They have a son. Eliza is still married to John, but she intends to ask for a divorce and move out of state with Kathy to begin a new life. Eliza decided to attend therapy to help her get up the nerve to carry out her plan.

What personal values do you hold that apply to this client situation?

Do you foresee any value differences or conflicts that might come up between you and this client? If so, briefly describe the value difference or conflict.

Case 3. Frankie is a 27-year-old, White, heterosexual, cisgender man in a relationship of 4 years. He came to therapy to address issues of substance use. In his fifth session with you, Frankie discloses that he has contracted a sexually transmitted infection (STI) and has not told his girlfriend. He states that he is not totally surprised about his STI status given that he has unprotected sex with other women every few weeks. He shares that he thinks these other sexual contacts prevent his relationship with his girlfriend from feeling dull and monotonous. Frankie does not feel that this topic is relevant to his work in therapy and would like to keep the focus on his desire to be less dependent on alcohol and other drugs.

What personal values do you hold that apply to this client situation?

Do you foresee any value differences or conflicts that might come up between you and this client? If so, briefly describe the value difference or conflict.

Case 4. You are working with a family that recently emigrated from India. The family was referred to therapy by child services because the parents refused medical treatment for their daughter's seizures. Emergency room doctors have become familiar with the family because of the daughter's multiple emergency admissions. The hospital contacted child services because the little girl's condition is worsening and will continue to do so unless she receives medical care. Through an interpreter, you can glean that the reason the family is refusing medical treatment is religious.

What personal values do you hold that apply to this client situation?

Do you foresee any value differences or conflicts that might come up between you and these clients? If so, briefly describe the value difference or conflict.

Take some time to think and reflect on your responses to each of the hypothetical scenarios. Of the four, which one elicited the strongest reaction from you? Which scenario tapped into your values the most? For which scenario did you foresee the greatest chance of a value difference or conflict between you and the client? Which scenario do you imagine being the most difficult for you to work with? As you consider this challenging scenario, what feelings come up for you (e.g., sad, angry, scared, happy, excited)?

Describing Value Differences and Conflicts

When we are working with clients, we might sometimes experience a value difference or conflict but struggle to put words to our experience. It is important to be able to talk about value differences and conflicts so we can process them, either individually or with a colleague or supervisor. In the following exercise, you have an opportunity to describe the value difference or conflict you experienced in the previous exercise.

Think back to the previous scenario that you felt represented the strongest value difference or conflict for you. Think about the strong feelings that the conflict evoked in you, such as confusion, anger, or sadness. Take 5 minutes and journal about your feelings regarding this value difference or conflict. Just write whatever comes to mind, without trying to censor. Try to focus on your deepest thoughts and feelings about the value difference and conflict. What is it about this value difference or conflict that brings up strong feelings in you? What feelings are triggered by this case? If you run out of things to write about, that's OK—just keep writing whatever comes to mind. After you finish writing, read back through your journaling and make a note of what values seem to be at stake for you. See whether you can describe at least two values that are at odds with you as a result of considering work with this case.

Emotions in Value Differences and Conflicts

The process of recognizing value differences and conflicts can be difficult to navigate and may involve strong emotional reactions. Emotions play an important role in navigating value differences and conflicts. According to Haidt (2013), we do not primarily process morals or values with the analytical part of us. Instead, we have a tendency to make gut-level decisions about morals or emotions and then search for evidence to support our gut-level decisions. In other words, we may have an initial reaction of "good" or "bad" and then try to figure out why we react in this way. Because they play such a powerful role in morals and values, it is important to be able to put words to the emotions you are experiencing. According to *emotion-focused theory* (Greenberg, 2004; Pascual-Leone, Andreescu, & Greenberg, 2016), the process of verbalizing emotions is a key strategy for enhancing self-regulation and the ability to respond effectively to real-life situations.

Exhibit 7.2 lists some key moral emotions. Take a look at the list and think back to your experience when you read the scenario in which you expected to have a large value difference or conflict with the client. What are the key emotions that came up for you as you read the scenario? What emotions do you think you might have to work through to work successfully with this kind of client?

After thinking about the scenario in which you had a value conflict and identifying the underlying emotions, discuss this scenario with a colleague you trust. First, listen and ask questions to see how the other person thinks about the different values that are in tension. If you decide to share your perspective on the scenario, try to create a collaborative tone that makes it easier for you and your colleague to connect at a deeper, more vulnerable level.

EXHIBIT 7.2

Moral Emotion Examples

Admiration	Gratitude
Anger	Guilt
Awe	Happiness
Compassion	Inspiration
Contempt	Joy
Contentment	Love
Disgust	Pride
Embarrassment	Relief
Empathy	Respect
Envy	Sadness
Excitement	Sympathy
Fear	

Experiencing value differences and conflicts in your role as therapist is inevitable. Sometimes these value differences will be small, and it will be easy to negotiate and get on the same page as your clients. Other times, however, the value differences will be large, and it will seem impossible for you and your client to get on the same page. It may feel like you are between a rock and a hard place. One course of action seems to violate your values; another course of action seems to violate the client's values. Even the most mature and healthy therapist will experience value differences or conflicts with their clients. A core part of every person's cultural identity is their sense of right and wrong— and therapists are no different. Thus, we will not pretend that it would be possible or desirable for therapists to avoid completely ever having value differences or conflicts with their clients. Instead, we want to help you develop practical guidelines and strategies for managing situations in which your most cherished values are different or conflict with the values and expectations of the client.

Case Example: Paula and Robert

Consider the following therapy example between Paula, a 51-year-old, Puerto Rican, bisexual, cisgender, female therapist, and Robert, a 50-year-old, African American, heterosexual, cisgender, male client. Robert is attending therapy to get help with his drinking problems. In the last year, he was fired from his job for showing up to work drunk, and he was convicted of driving under the influence. Robert also believes his drinking problems contributed to his divorce several years ago and his estrangement from his two adult children. Paula, an experienced addictions therapist, has begun to work with Robert using an eight-session cognitive behavioral protocol focused on developing more adaptive ways of coping with stress other than drugs and alcohol. The following is an excerpt from their fourth session.

Paula: OK, let's begin by checking in about the previous week. How many drinking days did you have and how many drinks per drinking day?

Robert: Honestly, it was kind of a tough week. I think I drank 3 days. Two days weren't so bad—about four beers each day. But Friday night I kind of lost it— I drank most of a 12-pack.

Paula: OK, so 3 drinking days and about 20 drinks in total. That's actually quite a bit of improvement from when we started, so I want to honor you for that. What do you think went well?

Robert: Well, I still had those 3 days, so I'm not feeling as good about those days. But I would say I'm feeling more hopeful than before, you know, that I could actually quit for good. Between my sessions with you and my AA meetings, I feel like I'm doing a lot of work, so that feels good.

Paula: So it sounds like you're feeling more hopeful, and you're putting forth quite a bit of energy on your counseling. And maybe there's the support piece too—through your counseling and your meetings?

Robert: Yeah, that's right. Support is key for me. A lot of times when I've tried to quit in the past, I've been pretty much on my own.

Paula: We haven't talked about your AA meetings before. What are those like for you?

Robert: It's just nice to be around a bunch of people who are trying for the same goal, you know? I'm trying to quit, and they are too. So there's kind of this environment of accountability. Not like they look down on you if you had a drink, but there's some people who have been sober for years—it's pretty inspiring. And then there's the higher power aspect of it as well. I haven't been able to give up drinking before, and I've been trying for the last 20 years. So I do think I'm powerless to change on my own, like they say.

Paula: OK, well, I'm glad you have people to support you besides what you are getting in therapy. The main topic for the session today is developing a plan to deal with relapse when it occurs.

Did you have any reactions as you read the dialogue between Paula and Robert? Did you notice any clues that a value difference or conflict was occurring? If you did notice anything, what made you think a value difference or conflict might be occurring? If you were Paula, how might you have addressed this with Robert?

Next, let us assume that Paula is committed to a harm-reduction model of working with clients who struggle with substance abuse problems. Suppose that she believes that the AA model, with its focus on abstinence and submitting to a higher power, is problematic and inconsistent with what she is trying to do in therapy with Robert. If you were Paula in this situation, how might you address this value difference or conflict with Robert? And how would you do so in a culturally humble way?

Regulating emotions that arise when discussing value differences and conflicts takes practice, so once again, see whether you can find a colleague whom you trust but who might have a different perspective on this case example. It is a simple behavior—but ask for a different perspective. Listen more than you talk. If you share, practice what we call a *movement intervention*. State what your initial reaction was. Then share with the other person that their perspective has changed how you understand things and explain how. Then see whether they offer an additional reaction. Most likely, you will not be able to resolve completely your ambivalence or dissonance and reach complete agreement, which is OK. You are two different people, and it is natural to have different perspectives and points of view. You could practice communicating about the difference, but see whether you can do this in the most disarming way possible, showing that the relationship is more important to you than being right. For example, one idea is to share the part of you that is still thinking or struggling. Share with your colleague that you will continue to explore other perspectives—or at least learn to sit better with the dissonance. Perhaps acknowledge impatience or other feelings you have related to ambiguity. Conflict does not have to create distance. If two people remain vulnerable and seek to build emotional trust, these interactions can deepen a relationship.

ADDRESSING THE VALUE DIFFERENCE OR CONFLICT IN THERAPY

Some scholars have discussed ways in which therapists might engage clients about values and value differences. For instance, Worthington (1988) developed a model for how therapists might engage with clients about religious values. Worthington posited that religious clients were likely to hold values associated with the authority of religious individuals, the authority of scripture, and ingroup norms (note the similarity to the binding foundations within moral foundations theory, including authority, loyalty, and purity). Outside clients' specific value positions they had a *zone of toleration* in which they could comfortably engage with individuals who held values that were different from theirs. Some clients had zones of toleration that were quite narrow, whereas others had zones of toleration that were quite large. Therapists likewise held religious values associated with the authority of religious individuals, scripture, and ingroup norms, as well a zone of toleration in which they could comfortably engage with individuals who held values that were different from theirs. Worthington theorized that clients and therapists could develop a strong therapeutic relationship if their particular value positions were within the others' zone of toleration.

Although Worthington (1988) focused on religious values, we believe this model can be extended and applied to any value conflict you might experience with a client. Clients have a range of value positions on various topics. For example, one client may be strongly committed to values such as conservative politics, opposition to abortion and gay marriage, commitment to family, and patriarchal gender values. Another client may be strongly committed to values such as liberal politics, immigration reform, Catholic religious beliefs, and criminal justice reform. A third client might be strongly committed to values such as equal rights for LGBT individuals, collectivism, and egalitarian gender roles. Each client is likely to have a zone of toleration for these values. Likewise, therapists have their value positions and zones of toleration. Effective therapy occurs at the overlap of the client's and therapist's zones of toleration. Cultural humility is critical for therapists to expand their zone of toleration (Woodruff, Van Tongeren, McElroy, Davis, & Hook, 2014).

There are several possible steps to intervention when you recognize a value difference or conflict between you and your client. Cultural humility involves prioritizing the cultural perspective and worldview of your clients, and this includes their values (Hook et al., 2013). We believe clients have the right to self-determination, even if their values, goals, or view of what "mental health" looks like differ from your own. So ultimately, when value differences or conflicts occur, the values that should take precedence are those of the client. Cultural humility will help you navigate this process and deal with your internal reactions to these differences.

Empathy and the Empty Chair Technique

To understand and prioritize your clients' values, you have to be able to truly empathize with your clients, their experience, and their worldview. You might experience the following with a client: You notice a value difference or conflict, and you know that you should be experiencing empathy for the client's perspective, but try as you might, the empathy just is not there. The *empty chair technique*, with roots in gestalt therapy (Perls, Hefferline, & Goodman, 1951), is a powerful intervention for helping individuals work through ambivalence and gain deeper levels of cognitive and affective empathy. The intervention is designed to help you develop greater awareness of the perspective of another person.

In the typical empty chair intervention, the individual sits in one chair and talks to another person (or perspective, such as a part of oneself) who sits in an "empty chair." The person then switches seats and talks from the other person's perspective. The individual alternates back and forth between perspectives. Then, after the activity, the facilitator often helps the individual process what the experience was like and consolidate any insights gained. We use this technique in the next exercise. (Ideally, you would complete this activity with a colleague or supervisor observing.)

If you are currently seeing clients, choose a current client with whom you are experiencing a value difference or conflict. If you are not currently seeing clients, choose a past client or one of the hypothetical scenarios described earlier in the chapter. Use the empty chair to talk to yourself from the vantage point of the client. Try to consider potential aspects of your client's cultural or family history that may have contributed to their way of being and value position. Also, consider any current extenuating circumstances in your client's life that might be at play.

Take some time to think and reflect on the empty chair exercise. Did anything come up for you? Did you experience any insights about your client's behavior or values? If you completed this activity with another person, discuss what your experience was like and any insights gained.

If you allowed yourself to participate fully in the exercise, you might have noticed some resistance on your part to truly being willing to understand and prioritize your client's values relative to your own. Try to notice these feelings of resistance, honor them, and then see whether you can set them aside. The goal of this exercise is to understand that if we can move past our judgments of a person, we may be able to identify points of understanding, which can lead to additional points of connection. This is empathy. We are trying to walk in another person's shoes with less judgment. It is through empathy that we can begin to bridge our value difference or conflict. We do not need to agree with the behavior, actions, or values of the other person, but it is important to mitigate our tendency to link behavior we view as objectionable with our view of the person's character and value.

Adapted Empty Chair Technique

Next, we adapt the empty chair technique to take advantage of your colleagues who may have a better sense of what your client may be experiencing. When therapy involves substantial cultural differences, you may need additional support to engage clients and their values with empathy.

Recruit a colleague or supervisor to help you with this exercise. Discuss with your discussion partner the client with whom you are working. Also, tell your discussion partner about the value difference or conflict you are experiencing with your client. Now, instead of you speaking from the other perspective (as you did in the empty chair technique), invite your discussion partner to speak from the client's perspective. If you can, complete this activity with two or three colleagues to gain a variety of perspectives.

Spend some time reflecting on your experiences. Did anything stick out to you as important regarding your cultural exchanges with your colleagues? Did your colleagues offer any perspectives on your clients and their values that you had not thought about previously? Did they offer any perspectives on the value difference or conflict that you had not thought about previously? Did you experience more empathy or less empathy for your client following these cultural exchanges? Do you feel more or less able to prioritize your client's values relative to your values following these cultural exchanges?

Addressing Value Difference or Conflict in Therapy

Although it is an important first step to understanding and prioritizing your client's values throughout the therapy process, there may be times when it is a good idea to address the value difference or conflict in therapy. For example, you might have a discussion about your value difference with your client. This kind of discussion may lead therapy in a new direction or help the client consider other options or goals. Also, there may be times when you feel the value difference between you and your client is too large, and you feel unable to support the client in their values and goals. If this occurs, referral may be an option. However, as you become a more culturally humble therapist, our hope is that you would be able to work with and support a wide range of clients (and their accompanying sets of values).

The following are some practical steps for increasing your cultural humility about value differences and conflicts. First, you can work to identify your core values, like you did at the beginning of this chapter. Second, you can gain self-awareness for what it feels like when you are faced with a value difference or conflict. This involves learning and gaining insight into your areas of cultural countertransference, which occurs when you have personal reactions to clients based on your cultural history, values, or experiences. Cultural countertransference can occur with clients both within (i.e., intraethnic countertransference) or outside (i.e., interethnic countertransference) your cultural group (Roysircar, 2004). Third, you can develop self-regulation skills and engage in the challenging work of cultivating a more secure belief that you can explore different values without losing a sense of integrity. Fourth, you can develop habits of daily life that regularly require you to continue to learn and grow from individuals and groups who hold values that are different values from yours.

When thinking about how to address value differences and conflicts in therapy, an important first step is to have a general sense of some of the different ways therapists may try to address or cope with value differences or conflicts during a therapy session. Some of these strategies are more effective than others. However, gaining a basic understanding of the possible strategies and outcomes can provide you with a language for describing how you engage with value differences and conflicts when they occur in therapy.

The following are possible strategies for dealing with value differences and conflicts when they arise in therapy:

- *Immobilization*. The therapist becomes fixated on the value difference or conflict and associated emotions (e.g., anger, anxiety) and is unable to progress with the client in therapy or seek help.
- *Antagonism*. The therapist and client become at odds regarding the value difference or conflict, and/or the therapist in the position of power imposes their values on the client.
- *Distraction*. The therapist engages in self-distraction to avoid the value difference or conflict and also redirects the client from the source of the value difference or conflict.
- *Ethical bracketing*. The therapist attempts to bracket their values, empathize with the client, and provide ethical and effective therapy.
- *Collaborative discussion*. The therapist can have an open and honest discussion with the client about the value difference or conflict they are experiencing, with the goal of moving forward in a mutually agreed-on direction.
- *Referral*. The therapist and client cannot bridge the value difference or conflict in a way that leads to effective work, and they collaboratively decide that it is in the best interest of the client to work with a therapist who can provide better support for the client's values.

Take some time and reflect on your experiences thus far in therapy. When you have experienced a value difference or conflict with a client, what is your typical way of responding? How would you like to respond when you experience a value difference or conflict with a client? Which responses reflect a high level of cultural humility? Which responses reflect a low level of cultural humility?

Develop a Value Hierarchy

We discuss ethical bracketing and collaborative discussion in more depth later. First, however, we want to highlight that it may be helpful to learn the skills of this chapter while focusing on more manageable value differences and conflicts before moving on to your most difficult and possibly even traumatic value differences and conflicts (e.g., working with sexual violence perpetrators if you have experienced sexual harassment or violence yourself). This concept is called *scaffolding* (Wood, Bruner, & Ross, 1976)—working within your current abilities before trying to expand them.

According to the *zone of proximal development* (Vygotsky, 1978), people tend to learn best when they work on new skills that are appropriately challenging but not too far outside their current abilities. Applied to the work of navigating value differences and conflicts, some value differences or conflicts may feel too difficult to work through at that moment. That is OK. It can be helpful to work on a more moderate value difference or conflict first to learn and practice the necessary skills. Then, once you get more comfortable with the skills involved, you can move on to addressing more challenging value differences and conflicts. In this next exercise, we help you identify a value difference or conflict that may represent a manageable place to begin.

Make a list of at least three of the most salient value differences and conflicts you have experienced in your work thus far. If you cannot think of a good example from your clinical work, think about an example from a close relationship (e.g., friends or family). Put these topics in order from most difficult to least difficult. This is a value hierarchy of value differences and conflicts you have experienced. Identify the third most difficult item on your value hierarchy sheet. Work through the following activities with this value difference or conflict. If you feel up to it, you can work through the process again with your second most difficult item and your most difficult item.

1. Describe the value difference or conflict using value language.
2. Identify the moral emotions you are having in the midst of the value difference or conflict.
3. Use the empty chair technique to cultivate empathy.
4. Use the adaptive empty chair technique to obtain additional perspective from others.

Ethical Bracketing

In this section we discuss ethical bracketing and collaborative discussion in more detail. It is important to note that in some cases, it may not be possible for a beginning therapist to engage in these techniques, and more immediate action (e.g., referral) may be required to protect the client's welfare when a major value difference or conflict occurs. We each have limits in our ability to navigate value differences and conflicts. If there is a client who holds a value position that is truly outside your zone of toleration, it is important to recognize this and seek to refer the client to a therapist who is better able to support the client and the client's values. There is a balance here. It is important to recognize that there are situations in which a referral is the best option, both for the therapist and client. However, it is also important to be willing to push yourself to work with clients who may be outside your comfort zone because this is the best way to grow and develop into a therapist who can be effective working with a wide range of clients.

When considering issues of referral due to value differences and conflicts, supervision and consultation are of utmost importance. A defining feature of value differences and conflicts is that the feelings that come up are often negative, and without some resolution, the value difference or conflict will likely make productive therapy difficult. So, what do we do? How do we work with the feelings that come up? The first step is to consult, whether that is in the context of supervision or with a trusted colleague. This step is crucial. It allows you to process what you are thinking and feeling with a trusted third party and get a second opinion about whether you should try to push yourself to address this value difference or conflict or whether referral is in the best interests of the client.

Now, we return to the strategy of ethical bracketing. Kocet and Herlihy (2014) defined *ethical bracketing* as

> the intentional separating of a counselor's personal values from his or her professional values or the intentional setting aside of the counselor's personal values in order to provide ethical and appropriate counseling to all clients, especially those whose worldviews, values, belief systems, and decisions differ significantly from those of the counselor. (p. 182)

Ethical bracketing can provide an initial stance that protects therapist from imposing their values too strongly on the therapy process; however, therapists who use ethical bracketing may sometimes experience a lack of integrity unless they can achieve a greater level of emotional integration. As we discussed earlier, value differences and conflicts are associated with intense emotional responses. Consequently, it is important to consider exercises that can help you attend to your emotions and cultivate empathy during ethical bracketing.

The following model provides a cognitively based set of strategies for helping therapists (a) consider how their personal values may influence their clients and (b) ethically manage this potential for harm or coercion (Kocet & Herlihy, 2014). The intention is to gain cognitive perspective to be able to tolerate the ambiguity and potential distress that can result from dissonance between your personal values and those of the client. The approach delineates five steps, which involve engaging increasing levels of professional support:

1. *Immersion.* Therapists immerse themselves in self-reflection about the value difference or conflict they are experiencing.
2. *Education.* Therapists educate themselves on the nature of the value difference or conflict.
3. *Consultation.* Therapists consult their professional ethical codes and literature on best practices.
4. *Supervision.* Therapists obtain supervision and consistent consultation when applying ethical bracketing to the value difference or conflict.
5. *Personal therapy.* Therapists can consider personal therapy to identify their barriers and biases to working with a particular client or presenting concern.

Spend some time thinking and reflecting on the strategy of ethical bracketing. Have you ever used this strategy in your work with clients? Was it possible for you to separate your personal values from your professional values when navigating a value difference or conflict? What about this was most difficult for you? When you were engaged in ethical bracketing, were you able to get the outside support (e.g., consultation, supervision, personal therapy) you needed? How did this outside support help you in your ethical bracketing process?

Collaborative Discussion About Values

In addition to ethical bracketing, sometimes it can be helpful to have a discussion about value differences or conflict with your client. Admittedly, the appropriateness of these kinds of discussions may depend on your theoretical orientation. The four of us have been influenced by *interpersonal theory* (e.g., Teyber & McClure, 2011), which views the interpersonal dynamics and interactions between therapist and client as an important source of both conceptualization and intervention. Thus, we tend to be relatively more willing to self-disclose our feelings and reactions and talk about what is happening in the therapy room.

Case Example: Barbara and Alex

Consider the following example of Alex, an 18-year-old, Latino, heterosexual, cisgender man attending his first semester of college. He decided to go to therapy to address various depressive symptoms and difficulty adjusting to college. At this point, he had seen his therapist, Barbara, a 26-year-old, White, heterosexual, cisgender woman, for two sessions

at the university counseling center. Alex, who was raised in a devoutly
Catholic family, recently had sex while under the influence of alcohol.
Alex feels a great deal of shame and guilt related to this recent behavior. Barbara, who identifies as spiritual but not religious, is struggling
to support Alex's beliefs and even finds them problematic. Specifically,
she is concerned that his feelings of shame and guilt are potentially
damaging to him. After consulting with her supervisor, Barbara decided
to look for opportunities to have a collaborative discussion with Alex
about their values in the next session.

> *Alex:* I still feel so ashamed for what happened. If my
> family knew what I did, they would be so dis-
> appointed in me.
>
> *Barbara:* It sounds like there is a very clear rule that you
> broke related to sexuality.
>
> *Alex:* Yes, I was supposed to wait until I was married
> to have sex. Instead of doing that, I waited until
> my first time getting drunk and woke up next
> to some stranger. I was so stupid. I don't even
> remember what happened, but I don't think we
> used protection. I feel so dirty.
>
> *Barbara:* I'm noticing that you are saying some very harsh
> things to yourself: "stupid," "dirty." In addition to
> your family, I also get the sense that this affected
> your spirituality. Is that true?
>
> *Alex:* Yes, it did. I went to church last week, but I felt
> numb. I felt like an outsider, like I no longer fully
> belonged. It was so painful. I tried to pray, but it
> felt like I was just talking to myself. I have no idea
> what to do next. I wish I could turn back time, but
> I'll never be able to get my innocence back.
>
> *Barbara:* Alex, as we discussed in our first session when
> you asked, I am not a religious person. But I'd
> really like to understand your values around reli-
> gion and sexuality, so I can better support you. It
> sounds like you have a strong sense that you have
> done something very wrong. Is that right?
>
> *Alex:* My feelings certainly say so. My family and church
> have always had very clear rules about sex. I just
> wish the pain would go away. If I could change
> my values, I would. I've tried before, but anytime
> I push the limits, it feels like my conscience is right
> there. I feel so worthless and sinful. I've confessed
> to my priest, but I still feel terrible inside. That's
> part of the reason I came here.

Barbara: Alex, I can tell you are dealing with a lot. Your religious identity is very important to you but also changing. And what you did last week felt like it changed you too, and you're not quite sure how to move forward from here.

What is your reaction to the dialogue between Barbara and Alex? What value differences or conflicts did you notice during the dialogue? Do you think it was a good idea for Barbara to bring up the value difference she noticed between her and Alex? In your view, was Barbara able to affirm Alex in his values about religion and sexuality, even though she held a different set of values? How do you think you would have navigated this value difference if you were Alex's therapist?

The goal when having a collaborative discussion about value differences and conflicts is to explore the difference or conflict, learn from it, and find a way forward to work collaboratively toward the client's goals. The collaborative discussion involves naming and exploring the value difference or conflict with the client. The client and therapist can discuss the value difference or conflict and the ways in which it may affect the therapy relationship and process.

It is important for therapists to engage with cultural humility throughout this process. This involves, first, listening to clients and trying to understand their perspective. There may be some important information the client can offer regarding the value difference or conflict that could move the conversation forward in an important way. It is also important for the therapist to prioritize the client's values and perspective. Ultimately, clients have a right to hold the values they prioritize, and it is not our job to change their perspective. However, just as we might learn new information from the client's perspective, it is possible that clients may benefit from hearing our perspective on the value difference or conflict.

Finally, therapists should be open about possible ways forward. Your theoretical orientation may provide some guidance in understanding the nature of this dynamic and the degree to which engaging the value difference or conflict in therapy is likely to lead to positive outcomes. It may be that, following the discussion, the client may decide that they would be best served by a referral to a different therapist. More likely, however, you will be able to find a way forward that honors and respects the client's values and perspective. It also is likely that both the therapist and client may benefit from having an open and honest discussion about the value difference or conflict.

If you are currently seeing clients, choose a current client with whom you are experiencing a value difference or conflict. If you are not currently seeing clients, choose a past client or one of the hypothetical scenarios at the beginning of the chapter. Recruit a colleague or supervisor to help you with this exercise. Have them play the role of your client. Practice having a collaborative discussion about the value difference or conflict you are experiencing. It is OK if this conversation feels a bit awkward at first—you will feel more comfortable with practice. After the discussion, check in with your discussion partner and ask for feedback. Did they feel as if their cultural perspective and values were honored and respected, even though the discussion centered on the value difference? How could you have engaged differently in order to lead a more productive conversation about the value difference or conflict? What was the end result of your conversation?

Value Hierarchy Revisited

Return to your value hierarchy. Previously, you worked through a series of steps from describing the value conflict to participating in an adapted empty chair technique. Now we would like you to revisit your value hierarchy and incorporate the more recent activities.

Again, list your values conflicts from most to least challenging. Identify the third most difficult item on your value hierarchy sheet. Work through the following activities with this value difference or conflict. If you feel up to it, you can work through the process again with your second most difficult item and your most difficult item.

1. Consult with a colleague or supervisor about this value difference or conflict.
2. Practice ethical bracketing.
3. Practice having a collaborative discussion about the value difference or conflict.

Conclusion

Navigating value differences and conflicts with clients can be a difficult process. This may be especially true if these value differences and conflicts involve cherished values that are core to your personal cultural identity. Navigating these value differences and conflicts also has the potential to change who you are as a person because you must learn to clarify and integrate conflicting values in a novel way. Although the process can be difficult, it can also lead to tremendous growth. Confronting and navigating value differences and conflicts forces us to examine (and perhaps change) our most strongly held values. Our encouragement is to engage in these situations with hope and expectation. You will likely come away from these interactions changed and enriched.

Working Within Your Limits 8

It is unwise to be too sure of one's own wisdom. It is
healthy to be reminded that the strongest might
weaken and the wisest might err.

—Mahatma Gandhi

Donnie: We each are likely to run into clinical situations
or have certain clients that bring us face to face with
our limits. I remember seeing a 29-year-old White
cisgender male veteran named Tom in therapy,
who used to be part of an elite Special Forces group
until an injury abruptly ended this career track.
By the time Tom made it to my office, he had been
struggling for several years with severe posttraumatic
stress disorder symptoms, and he also had developed
alcohol dependence. Tom had returned to college to
try to put his life back together, but he was having
trouble just making it through the day. He saw
some terrible things during combat, including some
brutal scenes of how his comrades treated enemy
combatants and their remains. At first, I focused on
building a strong working alliance, and I thought that
process was going well. We had a good relationship.
I think Tom trusted me, and he was relying heavily
on my support. But at the same time, I felt like I was
in way over my head. I certainly talked about my
experiences in supervision, and I got some helpful

http://dx.doi.org/10.1037/0000037-009
Cultural Humility: Engaging Diverse Identities in Therapy, by J. N. Hook, D. Davis,
J. Owen, and C. DeBlaere

resources, but it did not feel like it was anywhere near enough. I was definitely running up against a limit.

There were some cultural factors that were at play in the therapy room. Gender, specifically the idea of masculinity and what it meant to be a strong man, seemed to be pretty important. Tom wanted to be a good man. Before the injury, a lot of Tom's identity was connected to being in the military, including his physical and mental prowess. Experiencing his injury made Tom weaker, and he was struggling to figure out how to deal with that. There was the physical component (e.g., pain, not being able to engage in the same activities as before), which was difficult for Tom to deal with, but there was also the emotional component. Tom's experiences at war broke something inside him. He had no idea what to do with his feelings. Tom sometimes felt intense rage that seemed to come out of nowhere, and he had trouble regulating those feelings. I had not served in the military, so I felt limitations in my abilities to understand where Tom was coming from. I was able to ask questions about his experience, and I had an outsider's understanding of military culture, but I could tell there was a divide between us. I could not fully know what it was like for him to experience war at such a young age.

Age had an interesting impact on our work together as well. We were about the same age, which under some circumstances might have helped connect us. In my work with Tom, however, I felt like our similarity in age accentuated the sense of a divide between us. Here we were, two men of similar age. Someone seeing us in the hallway might view us similarly. However, I was about to finish my doctorate in psychology. I felt positive and optimistic about the future. Tom, however, was struggling. He was a man with a head full of painful memories, broken dreams, and a sense of inner chaos that made it hard for him to make it through a single day without major doses of alcohol to numb the pain. In my work with Tom, I had come face to face with a limit, and I was struggling to figure out how to navigate that.

Cultural Humility and Working Within Your Limits

As you can see from this clinical example, sometimes during therapy we come face to face with our limits. One problem with effective therapy regarding cultural identities is that we sometimes have little awareness about our limits. Sometimes the more limited we are, the less likely we are even to recognize our limits. This problem is called the *Dunning-Kruger effect* (e.g., Kruger & Dunning, 1999), and it has been documented across a variety of areas of knowledge. For example, the less intelligent a person is, the more prone they are to inaccurately estimate their intelligence. Likewise, the less expertise one has, the more likely one is to misunderstand one's degree of expertise.

Applied to work with culturally diverse clients, the less experience you have working with a particular cultural issue, the more likely you may be to inaccurately perceive the level of help you need. Consequently, we have to think about systematic ways to help avoid making this mistake because overestimating your ability to work with cultural issues can quickly cause problems in your work with clients. This is not just something that "other people do"; we are all prone to minimize and deny our limitations. This tendency is precisely why our profession relies so heavily on supervision within our training model (Tracey, Wampold, Lichtenberg, & Goodyear, 2014).

Sometimes therapists can become so removed from seeing their limitations that they become almost entirely insulated from client feedback. Our tendency to overlook our limitations raises another issue—we often want other people to see us as more competent than we are. This goal to be viewed well often takes precedence over the more aspirational goal of developing expertise. In fact, for this and other reasons, psychotherapy is, unfortunately, a field in which experience does not necessarily contribute to greater expertise (Tracey et al., 2014). Furthermore, a robust literature has explored why trainees conceal their limitations in supervision (e.g., Mehr, Ladany, & Caskie, 2010).

When therapists fail to recognize the limitations in their clinical work, it may be difficult for them to respond effectively to their clients' needs. These issues, which pertain directly to cultural humility, have led some psychologists to explore ways to systematically embed client feedback into the formal structure of therapy (Lambert & Shimokawa, 2011). For example, in some clinical settings, clients automatically fill out a short questionnaire after each session rating their assessment of the working alliance. Therapists can review these ratings and can proactively bring up and address issues with clients if they observe possible issues or problems reflected in the client feedback ratings. Thus, one of the pragmatic issues we try to address in this chapter is how to recognize when you have to actively seek assistance to address limitations in your ability to work with a client.

In your work with clients, you may not feel you have the sufficient time and stamina to expand your skills unless the limitation is affecting your competence or expertise in an obvious or blatant way. Because of this, it is important to have a plan for what to do when you are faced with your limits and determine you need additional help or resources. Regardless of your career stage or level of experience, you likely have professional structures in place that are designed to provide support and additional training as you encounter new and challenging cultural situations or issues. However, it is important to identify how you will know when you need more than these typical support structures and what resources are at your disposal when this need arises.

In this chapter, we aim to help you anticipate and put together a plan for what you will do when you inevitably encounter your limitations as a therapist. This awareness of your limits might come up when you are working with a client who presents with a cultural identity (or intersection of identities) with which you have little or no experience. Or an awareness of your limits might occur when you are forced to address a particularly salient value conflict. When you are first learning how to do therapy, there are specific methods of obtaining new knowledge and skills, such as reading books and journal articles, watching therapy skills videos, or visiting online discussion boards. Although these methods may provide a starting point for building knowledge and addressing limitations for working with cultural diversity, there is a different set of skills that are needed to put yourself in a good position to notice and respond effectively to your limitations in working with clients' cultural identities. In helping you to respond effectively to your limitations, we focus on two primary areas: (a) learning to recognize limits in your clinical work and (b) developing a strategy to address limits when they occur.

LEARNING TO RECOGNIZE LIMITS IN YOUR CLINICAL WORK

A core aspect of cultural humility is being able to acknowledge and own your limitations (Hook, Davis, Owen, Worthington, & Utsey, 2013). In Chapter 3, we discussed how to identify your cultural biases, so you have already done some work on identifying some of the limits you might expect to face in therapy according to your personal cultural identities, background, and experiences. In this chapter, we shift the focus to the therapy room. How can you recognize when you are running into a limit during a therapy session? When you do come face to face with a limit, what steps can you take to get the help and support you need? We first address the issue of learning to identify your limits.

Limits and the Johari Window

Before you get started addressing and working on your limits, the first step is to become more aware of your professional limits and take the time to consider the boundaries of your competence. Again, we all have limits—areas we either do not know much about or with which we struggle to engage. Others may not necessarily see them. We may not necessarily see them. The *Johari window* (Luft, 1969), presented in Table 8.1, is a model that was created to categorize the kinds of

TABLE 8.1

Personal Limits and the Johari Window

	Things I know about myself	Things I do not know about myself
Things others know about me	Quadrant 1: Limitations are clear and open. I am aware of these limits, and other people know about them also.	Quadrant 2: Limitations are observable. I don't know about these limits, but other people can observe them in me.
Things others do not know about me	Quadrant 3: Limitations are hidden. I am aware of these limits, but other people do not know about them.	Quadrant 4: Limitations are unknown. I do not know about these limits, and other people do not know about them either.

information that are known (or unknown) to the self, as well as the kinds of information that are known (or unknown) to others. It can be a helpful heuristic as you begin to think about your personal and professional limits.

Quadrant 1 involves limitations that are clear and open. You are aware of these limits, and other people (e.g., client, supervisor, colleague) know about them also. This could be because you have already addressed a similar issue with another client or, in the course of your training, you recognized this limit as an area for growth and took action to address the concern.

Quadrant 2 involves observable limitations. You don't know about these limits yet, but other people (e.g., client, supervisor, colleague) can observe them in your behavior. If another person gives you feedback about this limit, it can move from Quadrant 2 to Quadrant 1.

Quadrant 3 involves limitations that are hidden. You may know about this limit, or perhaps you suspect you may have this limit, but others (e.g., client, supervisor, colleague) may not be aware of it. This quadrant could represent cultural identities or issues you recognize you may struggle with (e.g., ability status concerns, sexual orientation), but you have not yet addressed or shared this struggle with others for one reason or another. Also, if these issues got triggered in your work, you have not let others in on your process, and they have gone unnoticed by your clients, supervisor, and colleagues.

Quadrant 4 involves limitations that are unknown. These limits are completely out of your awareness as a therapist, and they have not yet been noticed by others (e.g., client, supervisor, colleague). These limits may be related to lack of contact, knowledge, or experience with various types of individuals or presenting concerns.

Take some time and think, reflect, and journal about the limitations in your work with clients of which you are aware. These limits may be related to the cultural biases you identified in Chapter 3, or they may be other issues that have come up in your work with clients. In what areas are you aware that you have limitations in your ability to work with particular types of clients or cultural identities? What thoughts, feelings, or reactions come up for you when you think about your limits?

Gain Insight Into Limits That Are Observable

As we saw from the Johari window exercise, sometimes we have limits that are observable to others but not to ourselves. We may not know about them, but others may be able to get a sense of our limits from our behaviors or interactions. In this next exercise, you will do some work to get feedback about some of your observable limits from others who are familiar with your professional work. Set up a meeting with two or three people who are familiar with your clinical work. A supervisor would be a great choice, as would be a colleague who is in your group supervision class or someone with whom you consult and discuss your cases. Tell them you are doing an exercise in which you are trying to get a sense of some of your professional and personal limits, even those about which you might not be aware. Ask whether they would be willing to share with you two to three strengths that they see in you as a clinician and two to three weaknesses or limits. As they share the limits observed in you, try to listen non-defensively and see what you can learn from the observation. Remember that it is normal to have limits—even experienced therapists struggle with certain types of clients and issues.

After your meeting, take some time to think, reflect, and journal about your experiences. What came up for you during the discussion? What thoughts, feelings, or reactions were present? What did you think about the feedback you received? Did any part of the feedback ring true for you? Was any part surprising? Did you disagree with any part of the feedback? Revisit your journal a couple of weeks later. Did any other thoughts, feelings, or reactions come up for you as you have sat with the feedback for a while?

Sharing Limits That Are Hidden

Other times we have limits that are hidden. We know about them, but our clients, supervisors, and colleagues are not aware of the limit. There are several reasons we might keep a limit hidden. Maybe we are embarrassed, or we feel a great deal of shame about the limit. Perhaps we are worried there might be negative consequences if we were open about our limit. Whatever the reason, we might keep the limit to ourselves, not letting other people in on our process.

There are a few difficult things about keeping limits hidden. One problem is that it does not always work. We can try our best to keep a limit hidden, but often the things we try to hide, repress, and deny come out sideways (Johnson, 1991). It is stressful to keep something hidden. Sometimes the very act of trying to hide a limit might negatively affect our work with clients because we are less likely to be able to connect in a genuine, real way. Sometimes we might think we are hiding a limitation, but the people around us can get a sense that something is up.

A second problem about hiding limits is that it takes a lot of energy. When we try to hide something, there is a part of us that is always monitoring ourselves, the situation, and the reactions of others: How am I doing at hiding this limit? What will happen if I am found out? I hope they do not know that I am struggling with this issue. To the extent that you are hiding and monitoring your limits, you may find it difficult to be present and engage with your clients.

A final problem is that hiding our limits makes it less likely that we will make progress on addressing and working on them. It's tough to figure out and work through an issue all by ourselves. Usually, we need the help and support of others in our lives to work through and make progress on our limitations. If we are not open about our limitations, we do not give ourselves the opportunity to get the help and support we need. The next exercise involves sharing one of your hidden limits with someone you trust.

Pick a supervisor or colleague whom you trust and with whom you feel safe. Ask whether you could process something with them. Then take a risk and be open with them about the limit you are experiencing. It may be something that you have not shared with anyone before. We recognize that this is scary, but try to remember that we ask our clients to be similarly vulnerable every session.

After the discussion, take some time to think, reflect, and journal about your experiences. What was it like to be open and share one of your hidden limits? What thoughts or feelings came up for you before, during, and after the interaction? How did the person you shared with respond to your disclosure? Has anything changed about how you approach or engage with the limit in your life or work with clients? Was the person you shared with helpful in any way?

ADDRESSING LIMITS IN THERAPY

In this section, we suggest a practical strategy that can help you address the limits you may face in the therapy room. The model involves (a) an underlying attitude of cultural humility, (b) an attunement to feedback (both from yourself and the client), (c) obtaining feedback about limits from clients, and (d) a step-by-step process to address limits when they occur.

Underlying Attitude of Cultural Humility

First, it is important to have an underlying attitude of cultural humility when thinking about limits (Hook et al., 2013). What this means is that limitations, as a normal part of the therapy process, are to be leaned into rather than avoided. Check professional arrogance at the door. No one needs a therapist who is overly confident and hides insecurity through thinking they can competently treat all clients of various cultural backgrounds. An attitude of cultural humility acknowledges that running into your limitations is part of what it means to learn and grow as a therapist. It is something that is to be expected, rather than something to be anxious about or avoid.

Case Example: Richard and Margaret

Consider the following supervision example between Margaret, a 50-year-old, White, heterosexual, cisgender female supervisor and Richard, a 32-year-old, White, heterosexual, cisgender male therapist. They discuss Richard's clinical work with Nora, a 30-year-old biracial (Latino and White), heterosexual, cisgender female client. Nora is attending therapy to lose weight. The current dialogue occurred after her second session. As you read, pay attention to how Margaret and Richard discuss Richard's possible limits. Think about whether he has an underlying attitude of cultural humility.

> *Margaret:* Let's stop the tape for a minute. Any thoughts or reactions to how Nora is presenting this week?
>
> *Richard:* Well, I thought it was a pretty good session. I felt like she really opened up, especially about some of her past struggles and emotional issues that seem related to her difficulties with losing weight. I also think we have a pretty good plan in place for moving forward with the diet and weight loss goals.
>
> *Margaret:* Yes, it does seem like you and Nora started to get to a deeper place this session, which was neat to see. I guess I was having a bit of a reaction to how quickly you were moving toward implementing a plan of action. I'm not sure we have a clear understanding yet about all the factors that are contributing to her struggles with her weight.
>
> *Richard:* OK, so maybe I could have slowed it down a bit. But she was pretty clear that she wanted to lose weight. I thought it might help to get her started on some things.
>
> *Margaret:* I get that, but it just seems like there's a lot going on. She seems to feel a lot of shame about her weight,

and we do live in a society that gives women very clear messages that they need to look a certain way. I guess I wonder how much you are considering those factors in your treatment.

Richard: I understand that society gives all of us messages about weight and appearance, but for her, it seems to be more of a health issue.

What reactions do you have to the supervision dialogue between Margaret and Richard? Did it seem as though Richard was culturally humble and open to considering a limitation? What cultural identities were relevant in this discussion? What cultural identities did Margaret and Richard discuss during the dialogue? What cultural identities might they have missed?

In this example, Richard did not seem open to discussing the importance of gender and the sociocultural context that is likely connected with Nora's goal of losing weight. He also did not respond in a culturally humble manner when his supervisor attempted to point out some of his limits. Also, there were other cultural identities that were not discussed during the dialogue that may be important to consider to effectively treat this client (e.g., race or ethnicity). Finally, it is worth considering whether losing weight is an appropriate goal for Nora. A discussion about size as a cultural identity, as well as considering alternate perspectives on dieting and weight loss (e.g., Health at Every Size; Bacon, 2010), may also be helpful for this client. Consider the following alternate dialogue between Margaret (the supervisor) and Richard (the therapist):

Margaret: Let's stop the tape for a minute. Any thoughts or reactions to how Nora is presenting this week?

Richard: Well, I thought it was a pretty good session. I felt like she really opened up, especially about some of her past struggles and emotional issues that seem related to her difficulties with losing weight. I also think we have a pretty good plan in place for moving forward with the diet and weight loss goals.

Margaret: Yes, it does seem like you and Nora started to get to a deeper place this session, which was neat to see. I guess I was having a bit of a reaction to how quickly you were moving toward implementing a plan of action. I'm not sure we have a clear understanding yet about all the factors that are contributing to her struggles with her weight.

Richard: OK, so maybe I could have slowed it down a bit. But she was pretty clear that she wanted to lose weight. I thought it might help to get her started on some things.

Margaret: I get that, but it just seems like there's a lot going on. She seems to feel a lot of shame about her weight, and we do live in a society that gives women very clear messages that they need to look a certain way. I guess I wonder how much you are considering those factors in your treatment.

Richard: Hmm, yeah, you know, I think you make a really good point. I think I was being action oriented and just trying to solve the problem. But you're right; there are things about our society that probably make this issue really tough for Nora. And I'm not sure I always understand that as a man. I probably need to look into this a bit more.

Margaret: I appreciate you acknowledging what you don't know in this situation—that's really important to be aware of. What do you think are some ways you could get more information?

What did you think about this second dialogue between Margaret and Richard? What was different about Richard's attitude and reactions in the two dialogues? In which dialogue was Richard more culturally humble? What behaviors did you notice that were markers of cultural humility?

Attunement to Feedback

In addition to engaging with an attitude of cultural humility, it is essential to be attuned to feedback about limits, both from yourself and from the client (Hook, Watkins, Davis, & Owen, 2015). Feedback from yourself involves being curious about situations in therapy in which you experience discomfort, anxiety, or distress, especially when these feelings accompany discussion that involves a client's cultural identities. The discomfort could be a signal that you may be in a situation in which you are confronting one of your limits.

Case Example: Karla, Julia, and Jeff

Consider the following therapy example of Julia, a 58-year-old, Latina, heterosexual, cisgender woman, and her husband, Jeff, a 62-year-old, White, heterosexual, cisgender man who presented for couples therapy. The impetus for seeking therapy was that after 30 years of marriage, Julia wanted a divorce. The couple has one child, a son, currently in graduate school. Karla, a 24-year-old, Asian American, heterosexual, cisgender woman is their therapist. She is in the second month of her first practicum at a community mental health center. The following excerpt is from the couple's first session.

Jeff: We want to work on our marriage.

Julia: "We" do not want to work on our marriage. I have not been happy with Jeff for a long time but stayed because of his diagnosis.

Karla: What diagnosis is that? I didn't see anything about a medical or mental health condition on the intake form.

Julia: Yeah, Jeff doesn't like to list it, but he was diagnosed with early onset Alzheimer's disease 5 years ago. He's getting worse all the time.

Karla: I am so sorry to hear that.

Jeff: I don't like it any more than Julia does, but I need Julia to take care of me. Can you believe she would want to leave me knowing that I am getting worse? She should stay and take care of me. I mean, we said the vows. For better or worse. In sickness and in health.

Julia: Honestly, the guilt of leaving is what has kept me in the marriage for the last few years. I just don't think I can do it anymore.

Toward the end of the first session, Karla asked how the couple felt about the session.

Karla: Well, I really appreciated getting to know you both a bit better today. I think I have an initial sense of the issues you two are facing. It seems like the first issue may be to agree on a goal for therapy. Does that sound right to you two?

Jeff: I guess so.

Julia: I suppose.

Karla: How did you feel about today? Do you have any questions for me?

Jeff: Yeah, how old are you?

Karla: I'm 24.

Julia: You have got to be kidding. My son is about your age. What can you possibly know about working on a 30-year marriage?

Do you have any reactions to the dialogue between Karla, Julia, and Jeff? How would you feel if you were the therapist in this situation? How would you respond to the question about your age and the client's comments about your lack of experience? What might this exchange say to you about some of your possible limits in seeing these clients?

After the session, Karla felt overwhelmed for a number of reasons. First, she had never conducted therapy with a couple before now. Second, she had not previously had a client with a disability. Finally, the couple had hit on one of Karla's main insecurities as a therapist—her young age and feelings of inexperience.

Obtaining Feedback About Limits From Clients

In addition to being attuned to your own feedback, it is important to obtain regular feedback from your clients about how they are feeling about therapy. Sometimes asking for feedback from clients about how therapy is going can be scary, because it can be difficult to hear that there may be some negative aspects of your work or how you are engaging with clients. This can be particularly true considering topics related to culture and diversity because therapists tend to like to view themselves as culturally competent and can be defensive about the idea that they are not respecting cultural differences in therapy. If therapists can sit with the anxiety that comes with obtaining feedback from clients, however, this can be a good source of information about situations in which you may have come into contact with a limit. Earlier in the book, we discussed one idea for obtaining structured feedback from clients: Have clients fill out consistent ratings of their perceptions of the working alliance. Spend some time thinking about your current clinical work and setting. Do you have any structures in place for receiving consistent feedback from clients about your limits? If so, how are you using this feedback? If not, how would you feel if this kind of structure were implemented? What do you see as the positives or negatives that could come from this kind of system?

It is also possible to obtain unstructured feedback about limits from your clients. Do you ever check in with clients about how they feel the therapy process is going? What about checking in about how clients feel about how their cultural identities are addressed in therapy? Sometimes we accidentally send messages that we are not that interested in or open to feedback. It is possible clients may not share negative feedback with you because of the power differential between therapist and client, but by asking for feedback, you give them the opportunity. If you have done a good job building trust in the relationship, clients may be more willing to be open and honest about how they are feeling about the therapy process, as well as their relationship with you. If difficulties or problems are present, it may give you an opportunity to address these issues.

If you are currently seeing clients, pick a client from whom you will obtain some unstructured feedback about how the therapy process is going. If you are not currently seeing clients, pick a friend or colleague to check in about your relationship with them. The next time you see the client, ask if you could check in with them about how therapy is going. How are they feeling like you are connecting during the therapy hour? How do they feel like they are doing in progressing toward their therapy goals? How do they feel like their cultural identities are being addressed in therapy? Is there anything about therapy or how you are connecting that they would like to shift or change?

After you have a discussion with a client to obtain feedback, check in with yourself about how the experience went. What thoughts or feelings came up for you before, during, and after the interaction? Did anything about your relationship with the client shift or change as a result of asking for feedback? Are there any changes you would like to make regarding asking clients for feedback?

Plan for Addressing Limits

What do you do when you become aware that you have reached one of your limits? In what follows, we describe a structured process that can be helpful for addressing the limits you might face with a potential client. The process involves five possible steps: (a) identify limitations; (b) acknowledge existing strengths, skills, and resources; (c) access education and professional resources; (d) identify sources of support; and (e) have a dialogue with the client about your limit. In the next activity, you will walk through these steps with a hypothetical case. Once you get familiar with the process, the following exercises involve applying the steps with one of your current clients.

Read the following case example and imagine that you have been assigned the following client. Marena is a 30-year-old, heterosexual, transgender Latina woman who moved to the United States from Ecuador. Though she possesses male external genitalia, Marena's voice never deepened at puberty, she does not have facial hair, and her physical frame is petite. Marena has felt she was female since she was a young child. Marena was bullied throughout school by her peers, and she describes her childhood as socially isolating and full of shame. Marena's parents would not allow her to identify openly as female, so she attended college far away from home so she could pursue hormone therapy and live freely as a woman. She presents for therapy because she is pursuing gender-affirming surgery, and therapy is required before having the surgical intervention.

Step 1: Identify Your Limitations

Take some time and consider what some of your limits might be for working with Marena. What limitations are you aware of currently?

Using the Johari window, in what quadrant would you place your limits? Do you think you might have any limits of which you are not aware? If you are struggling to identify your limitations, the following are some questions to ask yourself.

Have you worked with a transgender client before? If so, how many? What is your level of familiarity with gender-affirming surgery and what it entails? What documents will you be required to provide, if any? How much do you know about transgender identity? What is your gender identity, and how might your identity be related to gender and sex privilege? What is transphobia and internalized transphobia? How might these concepts affect your therapy relationship and your conceptualization of Marena? How might the intersection of Marena's identities (e.g., race, ethnicity, gender) affect your therapy relationship and your conceptualization of her presenting concerns? Are you aware of local transgender-affirming organizations and resources? How do you feel about working with Marena? What thoughts, feelings, and expectations come up for you as you think about beginning therapy? How might those feelings inform your understanding of your limitations?

These questions represent only the beginning of the introspective process necessary to better identify your potential limitations for working with Marena. You might also consider completing an inventory on transgender issues to more specifically identify gaps in your knowledge or particular biases you may possess. As you think about beginning therapy with this client, generate at least three additional questions you feel are important to consider as you work with Marena.

Step 2: Acknowledge Existing Strengths, Skills, and Resources

In addition to thinking about your limitations, it is also important to acknowledge the strengths and skills you already possess that would be applicable to your client. Not only will your existing strengths and skills be helpful as you begin therapy, but they may also help you to work on addressing your limits with this client. For instance, the ability to provide unconditional positive regard and basic counseling skills remain functional skills that can be applied to different types of clients. As you work to develop the awareness and knowledge necessary to conduct therapy most effectively with Marena, these skills will allow you to be of service to her. Take some time to think about your existing strengths, skills, and resources for working with Marena. If you are struggling to identify your current strengths, skills, and resources, the following are some examples of questions to ask yourself.

What specific strengths and skills do you think you could bring to bear with this client? These could include basic counseling skills such as effective use of open-ended questions, rapport building, or affirming

Marena's strengths. Or you might have had some specific training for working with transgender clients. Maybe you have struggled with your gender identity in the past, and you have a high level of empathy for clients who present with a similar struggle. What resources are already at your disposal? For example, perhaps there is a local lesbian–gay–bisexual–transgender–queer community center you could connect with.

Step 3: Access Opportunities for Education and Professional Resources

If you know you are in a situation in which you are faced with a limit, an important next step is to identify and access opportunities for education, training, and other professional resources. For example, you could attend training sessions for continuing education or conference presentations. You could access books or articles on the cultural identity you know little about. The American Psychological Association (http://www.apa.org/practice/guidelines/) and American Counseling Association (https://www.counseling.org/knowledge-center/competencies) have published a number of guidelines for ethical practice with various populations. These guidelines integrate evidence-based practices into their recommendations and can be a particularly effective place to begin your search.

Take some time and think about beginning therapy with Marena. What opportunities for education or professional resources might be available in your area? Try to find at least one training course and one reading that would be a helpful first step. If you are struggling to think about what opportunities for education or resources might be available, the following are some examples of things to think about.

Depending on your limitations (e.g., use of appropriate terminology, gender-affirming surgery procedures), you might seek out books, journal articles, documentaries, and websites related to transgender concerns. You might also review psychological research on the experiences of transgender people. Importantly, in this search for resources, Marena's multiple marginalized identities would have to be considered. Issues of culture and Marena's unique location at the nexus of her gender and ethnic identities, as well as other identities you would assess (e.g., sexual orientation, social class), will directly affect her experience.

Step 4: Identify People Who Can Support You

In addition to obtaining opportunities for education and resources, seeking supervision and consultation is likely warranted in this case. It is important to obtain support and guidance when you are operating in a situation in which you have reached a limit in your knowledge and skills. Also, trainees often experience anxiety and threats to their sense of self-efficacy when presented with a client or client issue that represents a limit. Supervision and support from colleagues can normalize this process and reinforce existing strengths, skills, and resources. If your limits involve negative biases or countertransference issues, it might also be worth considering discussing your issues in personal therapy. Take some time and think about your work with Marena. Who could support you in this process? If you are having difficulty identifying people, here are some examples to think about.

As an initial contact, it is probably a good idea to connect with your supervisor about your work with Marena. Or, if you are not a trainee, you might think about setting up a time to consult with a colleague. Before working with this client, it would be helpful to identify any biases you might have about Marena and explore potential value conflicts you may have in working with her. If you experience a strong amount of countertransference in your work with Marena, it might be useful to process these reactions in your own therapy work.

Step 5: Consider Having a Dialogue With the Client About Your Limits

This next step may not be appropriate for all clients, but one option when you experience a limit in your work with clients is to explore the issue with the client. Your willingness to do so demonstrates vulnerability, openness, and a willingness to learn. This kind of dialogue could also lead to deeper discussions about cultural issues because the client may feel that the therapist is interested and wants to know more about the client's cultural identities. Whether you actually implement this intervention requires careful consideration of a variety of factors. Talking with your clients about your limits may feel unsettling for some clients. This kind of intervention works best when it openly names an area in which the client clearly possesses greater cultural knowledge and expertise, and you communicate a desire to learn. Engaging in this process with a supervisor will likely help you make a good decision about how to strike the right balance of remaining professional while also sending a clear message that you are interested and open to learning more about your client's cultural identities.

Take some time to think and reflect on your work with Marena. Do you think it would be appropriate to engage in a dialogue with her about some of your limits? Why or why not? If you engaged in this type of dialogue, what would you share with Marena? What would be the purpose of your dialogue?

If you do decide to have a dialogue with Marena about your limits, it can be helpful to practice this type of dialogue with a supervisor or colleague. Take some time to think and reflect on the limitations you experience with Marena. Next, recruit a supervisor or colleague to help you practice. Give them a bit of background about Marena and this exercise. Then practice having a conversation about the limits you experience in your work as a therapist. Be honest—acknowledge when you feel as though you are struggling to understand your client. Be positive—share your heart and desire to understand and connect with your client in a deeper way. Be curious and seek to understand—ask how you could better support the client and the cultural identities that are important to your client.

Once you have completed the practice dialogue, ask your supervisor or colleague for feedback. Did the supervisor or colleague feel respected and supported? Did they feel you were being genuine? Did the conversation feel more connecting or more distancing? See whether you can incorporate the feedback as you think about having these kinds of dialogues with your clients.

Practice may not make us perfect—but it does help us grow. In fact, one of the key behaviors associated with cultural humility involves consistently being willing to acknowledge, own, and take appropriate steps to address one's limitations (Hook et al., 2013). This can become part of the rhythm of one's development and growth as a therapist.

Case Examples

The key to learning a new skill is consistent practice, so in this next exercise we would like you to use the following four case examples, which involve complex cultural issues, to work through the five steps to addressing your limits. Choose the case example you find most challenging and that most clearly pushes your limits as a therapist. In other words, try to select the one that would require the most explicit plan for you to address your limits to effectively meet the client's needs. Once you have done so, work through the five steps we described earlier.

Case 1

Tammi is 35 years old and identifies as an African American queer, cisgender woman. She is currently involved in a polyamorous relationship with an interracial (African American cisgender woman and Asian American cisgender man) married couple, Kim and Jacob Chiu. Kim identifies as queer as well, and Jacob identifies as heterosexual. Kim and Jacob are both 28 years old. Tammi recently moved in with the couple, and although the relationship was progressing well when Tammi had her own place, the three have been fighting a lot since Tammi moved into the Chiu's residence. In particular, Jacob is feeling less and less a part of the relationship. The three would like to work on their issues and present to you for relationship counseling.

Case 2

Bill is 58 years old and identifies as a White, heterosexual, cisgender man. He is single, with no children. He was recently diagnosed with Stage 4 lung cancer and has only 3 to 6 months to live. Bill shares that he never smoked and has tried to live a healthy lifestyle. He is seeking therapy at the recommendation of his physician, who noticed Bill has been showing symptoms of depression, as well as angry outbursts. During his intake session, Bill shares that he sees no point in engaging in therapy because he is just waiting to die.

Case 3

Macy is 17 years old and identifies a White, heterosexual, cisgender woman. She is 8 weeks pregnant and is seeking therapy to decide what to do with the baby. She is leaning toward having an abortion, but she worries she will never forgive herself if she does so because she believes abortion is a sin. She is not sure who the father of the child is. She has also not told her parents or family she is pregnant because she is worried about what they would think of her. She feels pressure to make a decision about the baby immediately because she thinks she will soon get to the point at which her family will realize she is pregnant.

Case 4

Simon is 30 years old and identifies as a biracial (White and Mexican American), heterosexual, cisgender man. He is homeless, and in your initial session you struggle to maintain focus because he has a strong odor. During the session, Simon admits he contracted HIV 6 months ago and that he regularly uses intravenous drugs and has unprotected sexual intercourse. He views his behavior as problematic but does not see himself changing his lifestyle. Instead, he wants to work on obtaining a job and affordable housing.

Addressing Limits With a Current Client

To this point, we have done a lot of practice with hypothetical scenarios, but now we would like you to apply the themes and skills of this chapter to your actual work with clients. We hope the structure we provided—or something like it that fits your personality and context—can help you develop a rhythm of practice that involves making the most of your experience and opportunities for learning, supervision, and collaboration. The major barriers are factors that would keep you from (a) letting people know where you are regarding limitations, and (b) being willing to reach out consistently and accept help and support.

In this final exercise, we would like you to apply the steps for acknowledging and addressing limits with a current client. Take some time and think about a client with whom you are currently working that you feel least confident about being able to achieve a successful outcome. Another idea is to select a client who has a cultural identity you know little or nothing about or a cultural identity you struggle with or toward which you experience negative countertransference. Once you have selected a case, work through the five steps we described earlier. After you have worked through the five steps, take some time and think and journal about what it was like to complete this activity. How did completing this activity influence or change your perspective of your client? Did you learn anything new about the client as a result of this exercise? Did you learn anything new about yourself?

Case Example: Karla, Julia, and Jeff

Let us return to the example of Karla, who was seeing Julia and Jeff in couples therapy. Recall that Jeff and Julia made a critical comment about Karla's age, which triggered her insecurities about her age and lack of experience, especially seeing couples. Take a minute to consider how Karla might use the steps discussed earlier to address her limitations.

Karla does seem to be aware of her limitations, which is a good place to start. She should also seek supervision to identify any other limitations she may not be aware of and also to help identify the strengths and resources she already possesses (e.g., she completed additional training in couples therapy). Karla may also investigate Jeff's diagnosis and the typical progression of his disease, as well as consider what role being an interracial couple has played in the couple's relationship. The following week, the couple returned for their second session, and with the support of her supervisor, Karla directly addressed some of her anxieties about her limits with the couple through dialogue.

Karla:	You know, last week felt a little anxiety provoking for me.
Jeff and Julia:	Us too.
Karla:	I thought that might be true. What might have made you nervous?
Julia:	Well, that you are so young, for one.
Jeff:	Yeah, we weren't sure how you would be able to help.
Karla:	Well, I want to thank you both for being so honest about that. I think therapy works a lot better when you both feel you can be honest with me, and you can count on the same from me. I hear that you are concerned about

my age. What exactly about my age makes you nervous?

Julia: We really need help. We really need to figure out if our marriage can work at all, and I am just not sure you will be able to do the job.

Karla: I can't give you guarantees about whether I will get everything right, but I do think I can help. For example, you both shared that communication and intimacy are areas you have been struggling with. I think I can help with that. Could we try? And, let's continue to talk about how both of you are feeling. I'll check in with you pretty regularly to see if it feels like things are moving forward, if that's OK. If they're not, we can discuss other options. How does that sound?

Jeff and Julia: OK.

Do you have any reactions to this follow-up dialogue between Karla, Jeff, and Julia? What do you think of Karla's strategy to bring up the limitation and discuss it with the couple? Through supervision and consideration of the strengths that Karla did bring to the therapy process, she was able to regulate her anxiety and engage the couple authentically. In addition, by accessing resources about Jeff's condition, additional information about couples therapy (including research on interracial couples), and seeking support, Karla is creating a strong foundation for moving forward in light of her limits.

Conclusion

Inevitably, we will run into situations or clients that test our limits as therapists. This can be an anxiety-provoking experience, especially when the limits have to do with clients' cultural identities or the intersection between their cultural identities and our own. Because of this, it is essential to have a plan to not only recognize our limits when they occur but also to address them and move forward in our work.

Continuing the Journey of Cultural Humility

9

All endings are also beginnings. We just don't know it at
the time.

—Mitch Albom, *The Five People
You Meet in Heaven*

We have reached the end of this book, but our hope is that
this is only the beginning of your development and growth
in cultural humility, learning about yourself, and effectively
working with cultural identities in therapy. We view the
development of cultural humility as a lifelong process, and
our desire is that you would continue to invest in this area
of your life and work.

Still, for this book, it is time to bring things together and
commit to lasting changes that will make us more culturally
humble people. What would it take for this book to make a
difference in the kind of therapist you are, not just for a few
days or weeks but for 5 or 10 years and beyond? One possibility is that you can take the things you have learned in
this pages and use them to make commitments that change
your sense of identity, including the kind of therapist you
aspire to be.

Donnie: I am a father of two children. The moment I
became a father for the first time, my life changed

http://dx.doi.org/10.1037/0000037-010
Cultural Humility: Engaging Diverse Identities in Therapy, by J. N. Hook, D. Davis,
J. Owen, and C. DeBlaere

forever because the father role came with clear cultural expectations regarding what it would mean for me to be a good father. In a similar way, we imagine that who you are as a therapist is an important part of your identity, and we hope that the themes we discussed in this book provide you with the chance to revisit, in a variety of ways, the kind of therapist you aspire to become, especially in terms of seeing clients from a variety of cultural identities and backgrounds and working with cultural identities in the therapy room.

The psychological literature on cultural humility and developing a multicultural orientation is relatively new (Mosher, Hook, Farrell, Watkins, & Davis, 2016), and we are aware that this book is a beginning. We hope that new theory will build on our initial ideas. Our knowledge of what kind of self-awareness is most important for strengthening relationships and promoting positive outcomes for clients will sharpen. Likewise, our knowledge of how to form, maintain, and repair relationships with clients when cultural ruptures occur will also deepen over time. However, as many others have noted (e.g., Fowers & Davidov, 2006), expertise in working with cultural identities in therapy is more than developing a set of skills, it is an identity and way of life. So to end this book, we as a team wanted to remind you of the key themes herein and provide you with a set of personal challenges that involve putting these themes into practice.

A New Way of Thinking About Working With Diversity

First, let's take stock of what we have learned so far. Chapter 1 focused on a new theoretical framework regarding what is needed for doing therapy with clients from a variety of cultural identities. This framework assumes clients and therapists create the process and narratives of therapy together, and having a strong multicultural orientation that values diversity can provide a way of engaging with clients that facilitates a vibrant, emotionally responsive relationship that allows clients to feel safe and grow. The three pillars of a multicultural orientation involve (a) cultivating a stance of *cultural humility* in which one remains open to the client's experience and adopts a receptive stance that allows for positive and responsive emotional engagement; (b) pursuing *cultural opportunities* through leaning into cultural interactions or conversations even when this feels vulnerable, difficult, or scary; and (c) developing a way of life that increases one's *cultural comfort* for working with a range of culturally diverse clients.

Challenge 1: Find a multicultural orientation buddy. Our first challenge to you is to find at least one other person invested in developing their multicultural orientation and commit to working on this process together. Working on one's multicultural orientation can be a difficult process, and at times it can be a struggle to stick with it. Having support will help to ensure that you can persist and even grow through the tough times.

> *Cirleen:* I am the practicum supervisor for first-year doctoral students. One thing I recommend and then remind my students often is that it is a good idea to take the time to develop strong relationships with the other students in their cohort and program during their first year. This is important for several reasons. First, no one in your life is going to understand what your graduate program is like better than those who are in the program with you. These people are the ones who can empathize with your stress and triumphs. Let one of those sources of stress and triumph be the development of your multicultural orientation. Also, once you graduate, you will take positions in different types of settings that may or may not support your efforts at promoting cultural understanding and humility. You will need your buddy. Trust me. You will need to have at least one person you trust who you can call to discuss a challenging situation or process an interaction.
>
> As an early career psychologist, my community of buddies has been critical to my growth as a therapist and person. Once I was out of graduate school, I lacked some of the inherent structures that can promote cultural growth. For instance, our research team in my doctoral program was composed of passionate social justice advocates. I was bombarded with ideas and new ways of thinking almost daily. Relatively early on in my first faculty position, I realized I was missing this community of people. I had maintained a connection with several of my colleagues from graduate school but felt the need to add to this group. Through participation in professional psychological organizations, I was able to connect with other individuals who had a deep commitment to diversity and social justice, and they helped me to develop my multicultural orientation in this phase of my professional development.

Self-Awareness: Examining the Log in Your Own Eye

We often judge others who are culturally different. Cultural humility is antithetical to judgment because it involves an open and curious stance toward cultural differences. Like the parable in which we are encouraged to examine the log in our own eye instead of pointing out the speck in another person's eye, the self-awareness component of cultural humility invites us to examine our own cultural limitations. Thus, in Chapters 2 and 3, we focused inward because self-awareness often precedes shifts in one's expression of cultural humility in therapy. In Chapter 2, we focused on what it looks like to gain greater self-awareness in a holistic way, including with regard to your knowledge, motivations, relational experiences, and meta- or epistemic cognitions. We invited you to consider your most important cultural identities and cultural beliefs and values, as well as the relationship or intersection between your cultural identities and experiences of power, privilege, and oppression.

In Chapter 3, we refined our discussion to focus on becoming more comfortable with exploring cultural differences, as well as identifying and reducing your cultural biases and exploring what to do with your power and privilege. In this way, self-awareness provides the starting place for working on reducing your biases and being more comfortable engaging with clients who are different from you. We invited you to engage in learning activities about cultural groups that you do not know much about, actively work on reducing your cultural biases, and develop a plan for how to use your experiences of power and privilege to fight for justice.

Challenge 2: Find places where your cultural worldview and perspective is challenged and stay there. When it comes to cultural beliefs and values, people often gravitate toward communities in which people share the same values and perspectives. This occurs even in professional organizations (e.g., the American Psychological Association) that appear to be culturally heterogeneous. Our worlds can quickly become smaller and smaller unless we make an explicit commitment to put ourselves in situations in which our cultural worldview and perspective are challenged.

Donnie: Sometimes being challenged means finding new communities and forming new relationships that are outside your comfort zone. Other times, being challenged means staying in communities, even though you may have personally changed. In my first few years in the profession, I was part of several professional psychological communities interested in the integration of spirituality and counseling (e.g., Christian Association of Psychological Studies). These groups were important to my development as a psychologist and helped me explore and develop my perspective of what it meant to be a Christian and a psychologist. It was helpful to hear other people talk about issues involved with integrating these identities in their lives.

These groups helped me gain a sense that part of my role is to take a seat at the table and become a good citizen within the broader profession. For me, this stands in contrast to a tendency within some of my communities to pull away, wanting "Christian music," "Christian schools," or "Christian psychology." As I started to feel more comfortable in my professional psychological groups, however, I noticed feeling less connected to conversations happening in other Christian communities. Sometimes I felt a tension in my Christian community and felt like people did not understand some of the ways I was growing and changing. An easy way to resolve these tensions might have been to leave, but I was committed to sitting with the discomfort and working to seek greater integration.

What I realized looking back is that "sitting at the table" is key to having one's worldview challenged. Real change and growth occur within the context of community and having relationships with real people. Each of us has had to strategically work to expand our relationships according to our areas of developing expertise. It is easy to join communities that resonate strongly with our values, but it is also important to seek relationships that will expand our ability to form strong relationships with people with different values and perspectives.

Challenge 3: Develop a plan to grow in cultural humility in areas of limitations. A key aspect of cultural humility involves having an accurate sense of one's strengths and limitations. Instead of looking for ego-boosting evidence and attempting to justify ourselves and our position, cultural humility involves sincerely wanting to see and understand ways we can do a better job meeting the needs of our clients. More than anything, cultural humility involves a willingness to continue to seek feedback. We never fully "make it" or "arrive" at a place where we do not need feedback from other people to help us see our potential limitations. Believing one has made it or arrived might work in a variety of other professional areas, but it simply does not work when the intention is to cultivate one's cultural humility. We must adopt a stance that is responsive to continual change and growth.

Josh: It has been important to me to continue to seek out feedback for how I engage with cultural humility in my personal and professional relationships, as well as in the context of teaching the graduate multicultural counseling course. This process isn't always easy. Even though I am committed to the process, I still struggle sometimes to maintain an open and nondefensive stance when receiving feedback about my struggles or limitations. For example, I was part of a discussion in which students expressed frustration about a lack of engagement and support about social justice issues. At first, I felt the pull to argue and defend myself. Don't they notice how I'm trying to implement issues related to social justice in my coursework? Don't they see me trying to integrate social justice issues in my research and writing?

When I felt these reactions coming on, I tried to press the pause button on my response and see whether there was anything I could learn from this feedback. Once I took a breath and thought about it, I realized my reactions were defensive, and I had to ask myself some tough questions. How much did I value social justice and advocacy, even when it was inconvenient or difficult for me? How involved had I been in supporting the students in their work on advocacy and social justice? How much was I infusing my coursework with activities and discussion related to advocacy and social justice? These were tough questions, and they didn't have easy answers. But if I want to continue to grow and develop in my cultural humility, I have to be open to this type of feedback. I have to sit with the feedback, even if it is uncomfortable and see what it might have to teach me. I have to view feedback as a gift and not back away from it or avoid it.

Self-awareness is only the first step. For self-awareness to lead to growth, it is crucial to engage in the process of responding to what you have learned. In this book, we suggested some general strategies, but you will need to take these strategies and contextualize them to your professional goals, cultural identities, and developmental needs. As you do this, our main encouragement is to stay realistic and to focus on follow-through. It's easy to overpromise. Develop professional rhythms in which you assess, set new goals, monitor progress, and assess again. Make strategic investments that will build on your strengths and help soften some of your limitations.

Donnie: For example, as I was starting my doctoral program, I realized I had considerable experience with spiritual clients. I completed a master's program specifically focused on the integration of spirituality into counseling and completed nearly 500 hours within a religiously affiliated counseling center that was different from my personal faith. I was also working with a doctoral mentor who focused on similar issues. So, in my clinical work, I explicitly decided to focus on other aspects of diversity. For example, I realized I needed and wanted a better understanding of gender in my clinical work. So, in my second year, I co-led a group on men's issues with a staff member with that expertise. This put me in a position to grow quickly. I had a strong supervisor who was aware of my goals. He gave me lots of readings. He got to know me personally and as a clinician and could contextualize what I was reading within our supervision. The next year, I reassessed and set new training goals. The key is strategically turning awareness into action. Awareness alone does little good. Neither does making a bunch of unrealistic plans. Learn to regularly assess areas for potential growth and put yourself in places where growth can occur.

Infusing Cultural Humility Throughout the Entire Process of Therapy

In Chapter 4, we started to focus on the implications cultural humility has for the various aspects of the psychotherapy process, including intake, diagnosis, case conceptualization, treatment planning, and use of interventions and techniques. Given that the multicultural orientation framework is intended to be pantheoretical—not loyal to or derived from any particular theory of psychotherapy—this chapter was necessarily a conversation starter and will require elaboration within various theoretical communities.

We do acknowledge that some theoretical traditions may have elements that are in greater alignment or misalignment with some of the core themes of the multicultural orientation model, especially as practiced within certain settings or professional communities. For example, if you primarily conduct therapy using a structured manualized therapy approach, this may not line up neatly with our suggestion to cocreate a treatment plan with clients, infusing cultural considerations along the way. Our main suggestion is to take what you can from what we have presented and think about ways in which you might creatively integrate aspects from the multicultural orientation model into your chosen theoretical approach. Also, some communities may not view issues related to culture and diversity to be of high importance. If you are brave, you might consider how you could use some of the key ideas in our framework to challenge the assumptions within the community of people who share your theoretical orientation.

Challenge 4: Seek explicit ways to integrate cultural humility into each part of your process of therapy. The psychology profession creates opportunities to think about how culture might affect business as usual. For example, a common question on internship interviews involves giving someone a case to conceptualize. After the interviewee discusses their conceptualization of the client for a while, the follow-up question might ask how knowing that the client is from another racial or ethnic background might affect one's conceptualization and treatment plan. This sort of perspective taking is important and can generate ideas worth exploring, but in Chapter 4, we explored more specific ways to incorporate culture into several aspects of the psychotherapy process. We discussed some specific ideas and activities, but actualizing this professional commitment will require ongoing creativity based on your current setting and developmental needs.

> *Jesse:* I try to infuse cultural humility throughout the course of my therapy work. For me, this process starts with the acknowledgment that I know I am going to make some mistakes—I am not perfect (or even close) in how I address culture in the therapy room. However, having grown up in a working-class family, I believe that what I lack in natural talent, I can make up in dedication, caring, and loyalty. In my work with clients, I am frequently humbled by what they bring to the therapy room—much of which is outside my personal experience. Cultural humility for me is a way of being with my clients, an attunement to cultural opportunities, and trust in the process of psychotherapy—even the ups and downs. I try to ground myself

before every session, through mindfulness, to be better connected with my clients (including their cultural identities) and let go of the other distractions in daily life. Moreover, I attempt to fully put myself in the shoes of my clients—to truly understand how they live, how they think, how they feel, and why they do what they do. This immersion is at the heart of cultural humility.

Challenge 5: See whether you can use cultural humility to initiate change within the community of people who share your theoretical orientation. As noted earlier, after reading through Chapter 4, an important next step will be to contextualize the multicultural orientation framework within your theoretical tradition and community of people who share your theoretical orientation. This process will require ongoing professional dialogue and development and refinement of one's theory and practice.

Josh: When I began to focus more of my professional and personal work in the area of cultural humility, one of my struggles was figuring out how to integrate this framework within the broader community of psychologists interested in the intersection of psychology and religion. My sense was that cultural humility was a difficult concept for some religious psychologists because it can be challenging to remain humble when a client challenges one of your deeply held religious or moral values. But I believed it was important, so I tried to start the discussion. I wrote an autobiographical paper sharing my experiences developing cultural humility in my work (Hook, 2014). I conducted research about what it looked like to be culturally humble about one's religious and spiritual perspective (Owen, Jordan, et al., 2014; Woodruff et al., 2014). I gave presentations about cultural humility at conferences in this community. And I used my blog to disseminate some of what I was learning related to the intersection of cultural humility and religion or spirituality.

I have received a variety of reactions to my attempts to integrate cultural humility in this professional community. Some people have thanked me for giving words to things they were struggling with themselves and encouraged me to do even more. Others have not necessarily agreed with me but have been interested in engaging in the discussion and dialogue. Still others have been critical or questioned whether I was moving away from my faith, which was hurtful and difficult to navigate. Although the reactions have been varied, the process has been good for me. It has been challenging to refine my thinking on cultural humility and even see some of the limitations of the model. We imagine you may encounter difficulties or struggles yourself when trying to integrate the multicultural orientation framework within your professional community. Our hope is that you would stick with it, even when it is difficult. Even when tough and challenging, the process of dialogue and engagement is likely to result in movement and advancement for how to positively engage cultural identities in a variety of theoretical approaches.

Cultural Humility During the Formation, Maintenance, and Repair of Therapy Relationships

Chapters 5 through 8 focused on what it looks like to express cultural humility throughout the process of a therapy relationship. We need cultural humility to form a strong working alliance with clients (Chapter 5), repair relationships after cultural offenses (Chapter 6), and navigate value conflicts when they arise (Chapter 7). Moreover, because one of the core components of cultural humility involves an awareness of our limitations, it is inevitable that we will experience situations during our therapy work in which we struggle and run into a limit. A big part of what it means to be a culturally humble therapist is to have the humility to admit limitations and to get help (Chapter 8).

We function best when we are integrated into a community. What should be quite clear by now is that cultural humility is not something you can develop through taking a single course or by reading a book. In fact, it does not make sense to think of cultural humility as something you possess as an individual alone. The world is just too complex. Imagine a person in today's society who tried to function only on the information they could access by personal experience or memory. This person would fail in almost any industry. Tools such as Google and PsycINFO make large quantities of information highly accessible. Making good decisions requires humility—knowing when you have limits and having a good sense of the tools available to help address those limits. These examples should make us aware of how dependent we are on others to best serve our clients' needs. We are functioning within a broader system with a charge to help improve the mental health of those who trust us with their psychological welfare. We have limitations, and to grow and become more culturally responsive, we have to invest in our various personal and professional communities.

Challenge 6: Continuously explore and assess your privileged and marginalized identities, as well as their potential impact on your ability to form a strong working alliance with clients. A critical requirement of this challenge is to recognize first that our identities are not stagnant. They are fluid and can be influenced by life events, context, and contacts with others. We are not suggesting that all your identities will change, but the idea that your constellation of identities today will be identical to your constellation of identities 5 years from now or maybe even 5 months from now is a fallacy. If you accept this point about your identities possibly moving or shifting over time, you will recognize the need to consistently explore your identities for areas of privilege and marginalization and the ways your current constellation of identities could affect your work with clients.

> *Cirleen:* As I shared in the Introduction, I am a first-generation college student. Despite the fact that my parents did not graduate from college, there was never a question that I would obtain a college degree. Eventually, I did obtain a bachelor's degree, then a master's, and finally a doctorate. Within my lifetime, the educational attainment within my family shifted greatly. Thus, although being a first-generation college student remains a part of my identity and allows me to relate to others with a similar experience, I now also have to integrate my identity as a highly educated person into my overall constellation of the identities that make up who I am. Interestingly, it took some time for this identity to become salient for me. It didn't feel easy to integrate "doctor" into my understanding of myself. However, by not doing so, I was creating a point of potential disconnect with my clients—both the highly educated and less educated ones. By not acknowledging this identity, I was not acknowledging my privilege, and I was missing points when this could have been a salient factor for my clients. I was also less integrated myself, which wasn't great for working with clients (or for life in general).
>
> Now, in addition to having a doctoral degree, I am a professor. I not only obtained a high level of education but I also now do education for a living. Again, because this isn't exactly something I imagined for myself, I tend to minimize the status that may be associated with my occupation (beyond the fact that I have a so-called occupation or career), and again, I have to process what this identity means to me and how it may affect my interactions with others. So, this is a process. As I develop and my identities shift and change, I will try to recognize those shifts and explore how they affect my relationship to power and privilege and the ways in which I develop my relationships with others, including my clients. It is crucial for us to continually examine our cultural identities, including the intersection between our identities and experiences of power, privilege, and oppression.

Challenge 7: Refuse to dismiss or deny the perspectives of clients. This commitment might appear simple on the surface, but it is difficult to accomplish. Inevitably, our set of identities (i.e., who we are) makes it easier for us to hear certain perspectives and harder for us to hear other perspectives. We each have mental ruts, narratives, and loyalties that can make it hard to fully understand the lives and experiences of our clients. In addition, we want to see ourselves as good and moral people. We want to believe our behavior helps clients and does not harm them. So we are motivated to defend our honor and perspective on life, including our interactions with clients. But sometimes we do hurt or offend clients. A key expression of cultural humility involves owning our tendency to view ourselves well, which can make us susceptible to justification and defensiveness in the context of conflict. To counteract this tendency across all our relationships, we must refuse to dismiss or deny the perspectives of others, even when we strongly disagree with their values or worldview.

> *Donnie:* I once had a client who was very defensive. She had recently gone through a bad breakup. I got the sense that she did not like men, and she expressed as much when we explored this issue. After a session or two, she seemed frustrated. I wasn't sure why. I remember starting to challenge her on the basis of a few ideas I had discussed in supervision. She stopped coming to therapy after her third session. I don't know for sure why she didn't come back to therapy, but if had it to do over again, I would try something different. I remember feeling defensive and ultimately blaming her for being a "resistant client." The blame may have been masked behind some complex conceptualization, but the conclusion was that the issue was with my client, not me. In hindsight, I needed to listen when I noticed signs of damage to our relationship. I'm not sure what she would have said if I had slowed down and asked.

Make a commitment to soften your defensive reactions and explore signs of cultural rupture with your clients. Let go of your need to be "right" and instead focus on being open and curious toward your client's experience. Having a therapist who is right does the client little good. What clients need is a therapist who will model effective ways of exploring and working through conflict and hurts.

Challenge 8: Consistently work to stretch your zone of toleration for connecting with clients who hold different cultural beliefs and values. Some cultural limitations will resolve with intentional effort. However, we all have some cultural issues or biases that are fundamental to who we are, and it may take consistent effort over a long period to experience significant growth and learning in these areas. In his work with couples, John Gottman said that some problems are perpetual—they reflect differences that can be managed respectfully but that will never completely disappear (Gottman & Silver, 1999). One aspect of cultural humility involves acknowledging parts of our identity that may require lifelong processes of growth and refinement.

> *Donnie:* Religion and spirituality is one of those areas for me. I am deeply committed and believe that I will always consider myself a person of faith. At the same time, the communities I am involved with (e.g., religious and professional) are deeply divided on other issues of diversity, including gender roles, sexuality, and race and ethnicity (or other political issues that have racial overtones).
>
> I remember one conversation that stands out in my mind as an example of how a person can work to increase their cultural zone of toleration over time. I attended a conference

in which Ralph Hood gave a talk that included a documentary he made on religious traditions that practice snake handling (Hood, 2009). What stood out to me was how respectful he was toward that religious tradition. For example, he systematically debunked some common misperceptions of that group, including information about the likelihood of being bitten (much smaller than one might expect). Deeply curious, after the talk, I asked Ralph whether he had ever tried snake handling himself. He quickly responded, "Oh, no! I do not share that belief, so I would not mock their beliefs in that way." Ralph's reaction shifted my perspective. I still had major reservations about that particular faith perspective, but I realized why he is one of the few psychologists who has ever been trusted to study this community. He deeply respected their way of life—not in a manner that was condescending but with genuine, full-bodied respect.

Sometimes our cultural perspectives and biases change more slowly, but we do believe it is possible to put yourself in relationship contexts that will lead to greater cultural humility and an increased zone of tolerance for developing relationships with others who hold cultural beliefs and values that are different from your own. Through these relationships, we can internalize more complex ways of understanding cultural differences.

Challenge 9: Own your cultural limitations when you recognize them. As described in Chapter 8, one expression of cultural humility is remaining committed to owning limitations that arise in clinical work. When we respond to our current level of awareness, we set the stage for growth and increased awareness. In contrast, adopting a defensive stance closes the door to growth. This is the danger of "competence" language. As soon as we think we have made it or arrived, we become less receptive to learning and growing.

Jesse: As a clinical supervisor, I remember recognizing a significant limitation for both the treating therapists (cotherapy model) and myself in the treatment of a couple who was engaging in BDSM (i.e., bondage/discipline, domination/ submission, sadism/masochism) behaviors, as well as intimate partner violence. The difficulty I had with this particular case was that the line between consensual sexual expression on the one hand and emotional manipulation and physical abuse on the other hand was quite blurred for this couple. It was difficult to figure out whether their sexual practices were a normal variant of sexual expression that should be respected or whether the behaviors were abusive and dangerous (especially to the female client, who was on the receiving end of the sometimes violent behavior). The treating therapists were still new to couples therapy, and I had never encountered this type of dynamic in a couple in my practice. I quickly sought consultation from a trusted colleague. After discussing the case, we determined that because of the complexity of the case, combined with the cotherapist's inexperience and my own lack of experience with these issues, it would be best to transfer the case to a more experienced therapist.

Final Thoughts

At the beginning of this book, we suggested a shift in perspective that involves adopting a multicultural orientation that values diversity. We are all deeply affected by identity-related wounds associated with privilege and marginalization. Our privilege can blind us to the pain of others and make us comfortable treating others as less, rather than equally, deserving of dignity and respect. Likewise, we have experiences of marginalization and hurt, but these experiences do not necessarily show us a way forward to work through our pain, help alleviate the pain of others, or effectively engage relationships or systems in advocating for greater levels of justice.

One of the best ways to change who you are as a person is to change your commitments. Commitments have the power to shape our future because they involve clarifying the kind of people we hope to become, making specific plans, and making ourselves accountable to follow through. With this in mind, we presented nine challenges. We have made these challenges to each other, and we invite you to share them with us. We cannot actualize these commitments alone. We need one another to work out these commitments in real life.

References

Ackerman, S. J., Hilsenroth, M. J., Baity, M. R., & Blagys, M. D. (2000). Interaction of therapeutic process and alliance during psychological assessment. *Journal of Personality Assessment, 75,* 82–109. http://dx.doi.org/10.1207/S15327752JPA7501_7

Allport, G. W. (1954). *The nature of prejudice.* Reading, MA: Addison-Wesley.

American Psychiatric Association. (2013). *Diagnostic and statistical manual of mental disorders* (5th ed.). Arlington, VA: Author.

American Psychological Association. (2003). APA guidelines on multicultural education, training, research, practice, and organizational change for psychologists. *American Psychologist, 58,* 377–402. http://dx.doi.org/10.1037/0003-066X.58.5.377

Ashmore, R. D., & Del Boca, F. K. (1981). Conceptual approaches to stereotypes and stereotyping. In D. L. Hamilton (Ed.), *Cognitive processes in stereotyping and intergroup behavior* (pp. 1–35). Hillsdale, NJ: Erlbaum.

Bacon, L. (2010). *Health at every size: The surprising truth about your weight.* Dallas, TX: BenBella Books.

Barber, J. P., Gallop, R., Crits-Christoph, P., Frank, A., Thase, M. E., Weiss, R. D., & Connolly Gibbons, M. B. (2006). The role of therapist adherence, therapist competence, and alliance in predicting outcome of individual drug counseling: Results from the National Institute Drug Abuse Collaborative Cocaine Treatment Study. *Psychotherapy Research, 16*, 229–240. http://dx.doi.org/ 10.1080/10503300500288951

Beck, J. T. (1995). *Cognitive therapy: Basics and beyond.* New York, NY: Guilford Press.

Becker, D., & Lamb, S. (1994). Sex bias in the diagnosis of borderline personality disorder and posttraumatic stress disorder. *Professional Psychology: Research and Practice, 25*, 55–61. http://dx.doi.org/10.1037/ 0735-7028.25.1.55

Benish, S. G., Quintana, S., & Wampold, B. E. (2011). Culturally adapted psychotherapy and the legitimacy of myth: A direct-comparison meta-analysis. *Journal of Counseling Psychology, 58*, 279–289. http:// dx.doi.org/10.1037/a0023626

Binder, J. L., & Strupp, H. H. (1997). Supervision of psychodynamic psychotherapies. In C. E. Watkins, Jr., (Ed.), *Handbook of psychotherapy supervision* (pp. 44–62). Hoboken, NJ: Wiley.

Bordin, E. S. (1979). The generalizability of the psychoanalytic concept of the working alliance. *Psychotherapy: Theory, Research & Practice, 16*, 252–260. http://dx.doi.org/10.1037/h0085885

Brown, K. W., & Ryan, R. M. (2003). The benefits of being present: Mindfulness and its role in psychological well-being. *Journal of Personality and Social Psychology, 84*, 822–848. http://dx.doi.org/10.1037/ 0022-3514.84.4.822

Brown, S. L., & Brown, R. M. (2006). Selective investment theory: Recasting the functional significance of close relationships. *Psychological Inquiry, 17*, 1–29. http://dx.doi.org/10.1207/s15327965pli1701_01

Budge, S. L. (2015). Psychotherapists as gatekeepers: An evidence-based case study highlighting the role and process of letter writing for transgender clients. *Psychotherapy, 52*, 287–297. http://dx.doi.org/10.1037/ pst0000034

Burkard, A. W., & Knox, S. (2004). Effect of therapist color-blindness on empathy and attributions in cross-cultural counseling. *Journal of Counseling Psychology, 51*, 387–397. http://dx.doi.org/10.1037/ 0022-0167.51.4.387

Cabral, R. R., & Smith, T. B. (2011). Racial/ethnic matching of clients and therapists in mental health services: A meta-analytic review of preferences, perceptions, and outcomes. *Journal of Counseling Psychology, 58*, 537–554. http://dx.doi.org/10.1037/a0025266

Caplan, P. J., & Cosgrove, L. (2004). *Bias in psychiatric diagnosis.* Lanham, MD: Rowman & Littlefield.

Carmody, J., & Baer, R. A. (2008). Relationships between mindfulness practice and levels of mindfulness, medical and psychological symptoms and well-being in a mindfulness-based stress reduction program. *Journal of Behavioral Medicine, 31*, 23–33. http://dx.doi.org/10.1007/s10865-007-9130-7

Chang, D. F., & Berk, A. (2009). Making cross-racial therapy work: A phenomenological study of clients' experiences of cross-racial therapy. *Journal of Counseling Psychology, 56*, 521–536. http://dx.doi.org/10.1037/a0016905

Chapman, G. D. (1992). *The five love languages: The secret to love that lasts.* Chicago, IL: Northfield.

Cole, E. R. (2009). Intersectionality and research in psychology. *American Psychologist, 64*, 170–180. http://dx.doi.org/10.1037/a0014564

Comas-Díaz, L. (2012). *Multicultural care: A clinician's guide to cultural competence.* Washington, DC: American Psychological Association. http://dx.doi.org/10.1037/13491-000

Constantine, M. G. (2007). Racial microaggressions against African American clients in cross-racial counseling relationships. *Journal of Counseling Psychology, 54*, 1–16. http://dx.doi.org/10.1037/0022-0167.54.1.1

Constantine, M. G., Hage, S. M., Kindaichi, M. M., & Bryant, R. M. (2007). Social justice and multicultural issues: Implications for the practice and training of counselors and counseling psychologists. *Journal of Counseling & Development, 85*, 24–29. http://dx.doi.org/10.1002/j.1556-6678.2007.tb00440.x

Constantine, M. G., & Ladany, N. (2000). Self-report multicultural counseling competence scales: Their relation to social desirability attitudes and multicultural case conceptualization ability. *Journal of Counseling Psychology, 47*, 155–164. http://dx.doi.org/10.1037/0022-0167.47.2.155

Cornett, C. (1993). *Affirmative dynamic psychotherapy with gay men.* Northvale, NJ: Aronson.

Cornish, J. A. E., Schreier, B. A., Nadkarni, L. I., Metzger, L. H., & Rodolfa, E. R. (2010). *Handbook of multicultural counseling competencies.* Hoboken, NJ: Wiley.

Crawford, E. P. (2011). *Stigma, racial microaggressions, and acculturation strategies as predictors of likelihood to seek counseling among Black college students* (Unpublished doctoral dissertation). Oklahoma State University, Stillwater.

Cross, W. E., Jr. (1995). The psychology of nigrescence: Revising the Cross model. In J. G. Ponterotto, J. M. Casas, L. A. Suzuki, & C. M. Alexander (Eds.), *Handbook of multicultural counseling* (pp. 93–122). Thousand Oaks, CA: Sage.

Dana, R. H. (2005). *Multicultural assessment: Principles, applications, and examples.* Mahwah, NJ: Erlbaum.

Davis, D. E., DeBlaere, C., Brubaker, K., Owen, J., Jordan, T. A., II, Hook, J. N., & Van Tongeren, D. R. (2016). Microaggressions and perceptions of cultural humility in counseling. *Journal of Counseling & Development, 94,* 483–493. http://dx.doi.org/10.1002/jcad.12107

Davis, D. E., Worthington, E. L., Jr., & Hook, J. N. (2010). Humility: Review of measurement strategies and conceptualization as a personality judgment. *The Journal of Positive Psychology, 5,* 243–252. http://dx.doi.org/10.1080/17439761003791672

Davis, D. E., Worthington, E. L., Jr., Hook, J. N., Emmons, R. A., Hill, P. C., Bollinger, R. A., & Van Tongeren, D. R. (2013). Humility and the development and repair of social bonds: Two longitudinal studies. *Self and Identity, 12,* 58–77. http://dx.doi.org/10.1080/15298868.2011.636509

de Shazer, S. (1988). *Clues: Investigating solutions in brief therapy.* New York, NY: Norton.

Devine, P. G. (1989). Stereotypes and prejudice: Their automatic and controlled components. *Journal of Personality and Social Psychology, 56,* 5–18. http://dx.doi.org/10.1037/0022-3514.56.1.5

Drinane, J. M., Owen, J., Adelson, J. L., & Rodolfa, E. (2016). Multicultural competencies: What are we measuring? *Psychotherapy Research, 26,* 342–351. http://dx.doi.org/10.1080/10503307.2014.983581

Eells, T. D. (2007). *Handbook of psychotherapy case formulation* (2nd ed.). New York, NY: Guilford Press.

Farrell, J. E., Hook, J. N., Ramos, M., Davis, D. E., Van Tongeren, D. R., & Ruiz, J. M. (2015). Humility and relationship outcomes in couples: The mediating role of commitment. *Couple and Family Psychology: Research and Practice, 4,* 14–26. http://dx.doi.org/10.1037/cfp0000033

Finkenauer, C., & Buyukcan-Tetik, A. (2015). To know you is to feel intimate with you: Felt knowledge is rooted in disclosure, solicitation, and intimacy. *Family Science, 6,* 109–118. http://dx.doi.org/10.1080/19424620.2015.1082012

Finn, S. E., & Tonsager, M. E. (1997). Information-gathering and therapeutic models of assessment: Complementary paradigms. *Psychological Assessment, 9,* 374–385. http://dx.doi.org/10.1037/1040-3590.9.4.374

Foster, R. P. (1998). The clinician's cultural countertransference: The psychodynamics of culturally competent practice. *Clinical Social Work Journal, 26,* 253–270. http://dx.doi.org/10.1023/A:1022867910329

Fowers, B. J., & Davidov, B. J. (2006). The virtue of multiculturalism: Personal transformation, character, and openness to the other. *American Psychologist, 61,* 581–594. http://dx.doi.org/10.1037/0003-066X.61.6.581

Frank, J. D., & Frank, J. B. (1991). *Persuasion and healing: A comparison study of psychotherapy.* Baltimore, MD: Johns Hopkins University Press.

Freud, S., & Strachey, J. (Ed. & Trans.). (1964). *The standard edition of the complete psychological works of Sigmund Freud.* Oxford, England: Macmillan.

Galla, B. M. (2016). Within-person changes in mindfulness and self-compassion predict enhanced emotional well-being in healthy, but stressed adolescents. *Journal of Adolescence, 49*, 204–217. http://dx.doi.org/10.1016/j.adolescence.2016.03.016

Gottman, J. M., & Silver, N. (1999). *The seven principles for making marriage work: A practical guide from the country's foremost relationship expert.* New York, NY: Three Rivers Press.

Graham, J., & Haidt, J. (2010). Beyond beliefs: Religions bind individuals into moral communities. *Personality and Social Psychology Review, 14,* 140–150. http://dx.doi.org/10.1177/1088868309353415

Graham, J., Haidt, J., & Nosek, B. A. (2009). Liberals and conservatives rely on different sets of moral foundations. *Journal of Personality and Social Psychology, 96,* 1029–1046. http://dx.doi.org/10.1037/a0015141

Graham, J., Nosek, B. A., Haidt, J., Iyer, R., Koleva, S., & Ditto, P. H. (2011). Mapping the moral domain. *Journal of Personality and Social Psychology, 101,* 366–385. http://dx.doi.org/10.1037/a0021847

Greenberg, L. S. (2004). Emotion-focused therapy. *Clinical Psychology & Psychotherapy, 11,* 3–16. http://dx.doi.org/10.1002/cpp.388

Haidt, J. (2012). *The righteous mind: Why good people are divided by politics and religion.* New York, NY: Vintage Books.

Haidt, J. (2013). Moral psychology for the twenty-first century. *Journal of Moral Education, 42,* 281–297. http://dx.doi.org/10.1080/03057240.2013.817327

Hayes, J. A., McAleavey, A. A., Castonguay, L. G., & Locke, B. D. (2016). Psychotherapists' outcomes with White and racial/ethnic minority clients: First, the good news. *Journal of Counseling Psychology, 63,* 261–268. http://dx.doi.org/10.1037/cou0000098

Hayes, J. A., Owen, J., & Nissen-Lie, H. A. (2017). The contributions of client culture to differential therapist effectiveness. In L. G. Castonguay & C. E. Hill (Eds.), *How and why are some therapists better than others? Understanding therapist effects* (pp. 159–174). Washington, DC: American Psychological Association.

Heider, F. (1958). *The psychology of interpersonal relations.* Hoboken, NJ: Wiley.

Helms, J. E. (1990). *Black and White racial identity: Theory, research, and practice.* New York, NY: Greenwood Press.

Hilsenroth, M. J., Ackerman, S. J., Clemence, A. J., Strassle, C. G., & Handler, L. (2002). Effects of structured clinician training on patient and therapist perspectives of alliance early in psychotherapy. *Psychotherapy: Theory, Research, Practice, Training, 39,* 309–323. http://dx.doi.org/10.1037/0033-3204.39.4.309

Hilsenroth, M. J., & Cromer, T. D. (2007). Clinician interventions related to alliance during the initial interview and psychological assessment. *Psychotherapy: Theory, Research, Practice, Training, 44,* 205–218. http://dx.doi.org/10.1037/0033-3204.44.2.205

Hilton, J. L., & Von Hippel, W. (1996). Stereotypes. *Annual Review of Psychology, 47,* 237–271. http://dx.doi.org/10.1146/annurev.psych.47.1.237

Hood, R. (2009, January). *Them that believe: The power and meaning of the Christian serpent-handling tradition*. Paper presented at the meeting of the Institute for Research on Psychology and Spirituality, La Mirada, CA.

Hook, J. N. (2014). Engaging clients with cultural humility. *Journal of Psychology and Christianity, 33*, 277–280.

Hook, J. N., Davis, D. E., Owen, J., Worthington, E. L., Jr., & Utsey, S. O. (2013). Cultural humility: Measuring openness to culturally diverse clients. *Journal of Counseling Psychology, 60*, 353–366. http://dx.doi.org/10.1037/a0032595

Hook, J. N., Farrell, J. E., Davis, D. E., DeBlaere, C., Van Tongeren, D. R., & Utsey, S. O. (2016). Cultural humility and racial microaggressions in counseling. *Journal of Counseling Psychology, 63*, 269–277. http://dx.doi.org/10.1037/cou0000114

Hook, J. N., Watkins, C. E., Jr., Davis, D. E., & Owen, J. (2015). Humility: The paradoxical foundation for psychotherapy expertise. *Psychotherapy Bulletin, 50*(2), 11–13.

Hook, J. N., Watkins, C. E., Jr., Davis, D. E., Owen, J., Van Tongeren, D. R., & Ramos, M. J. (2016). Cultural humility in psychotherapy supervision. *American Journal of Psychotherapy, 70*, 149–166.

Horvath, A. O., Del Re, A. C., Flückiger, C., & Symonds, D. (2011). Alliance in individual psychotherapy. *Psychotherapy, 48*, 9–16. http://dx.doi.org/10.1037/a0022186

Huey, S. J., Jr., Tilley, J. L., Jones, E. O., & Smith, C. A. (2014). The contribution of cultural competence to evidence-based care for ethnically diverse populations. *Annual Review of Clinical Psychology, 10*, 305–338. http://dx.doi.org/10.1146/annurev-clinpsy-032813-153729

Imel, Z. E., Baldwin, S., Atkins, D. C., Owen, J., Baardseth, T., & Wampold, B. E. (2011). Racial/ethnic disparities in therapist effectiveness: A conceptualization and initial study of cultural competence. *Journal of Counseling Psychology, 58*, 290–298. http://dx.doi.org/10.1037/a0023284

Insel, T. R. (2013). *Post by former NIMH director Thomas Insel: Transforming diagnosis*. Retrieved from: http://www.nimh.nih.gov/about/director/2013/transforming-diagnosis.shtml

Johnson, R. A. (1991). *Owning your own shadow: Understanding the dark side of the psyche*. New York, NY: HarperCollins.

Jones, C. P. (2000). Levels of racism: A theoretic framework and a gardener's tale. *American Journal of Public Health, 90*, 1212–1215. http://dx.doi.org/10.2105/AJPH.90.8.1212

King, P. M., & Kitchener, K. S. (1994). *Developing reflective judgment: Understanding and promoting intellectual growth and critical thinking in adolescents and adults*. San Francisco, CA: Jossey-Bass.

Kirchhoff, J., Strack, M., & Jager, U. (2009). Apologies: Depending on offence severity the composition of elements does matter. In F. Garoff (Chair), *Preventing violent conflict: Psychological dimensions*. Symposium conducted at the meeting of the European Congress of Psychology, Oslo, Norway.

Kocet, M. M., & Herlihy, B. J. (2014). Addressing value-based conflicts within the counseling relationship: A decision-making model. *Journal of Counseling & Development, 92*, 180–186. http://dx.doi.org/10.1002/j.1556-6676.2014.00146.x

Kruger, J., & Dunning, D. (1999). Unskilled and unaware of it: How difficulties in recognizing one's own incompetence lead to inflated self-assessments. *Journal of Personality and Social Psychology, 77*, 1121–1134. http://dx.doi.org/10.1037/0022-3514.77.6.1121

Lambert, M. J., & Shimokawa, K. (2011). Collecting client feedback. *Psychotherapy, 48*, 72–79. http://dx.doi.org/10.1037/a0022238

Locke, D. C., & Bailey, D. F. (2013). *Increasing multicultural understanding* (3rd ed.). Thousand Oaks, CA: Sage.

Luft, J. (1969). *Of human interaction*. Oxford, England: National Press.

Mahalik, J. R., Good, G. E., & Englar-Carlson, M. (2003). Masculinity scripts, presenting concerns, and help seeking: Implications for practice and training. *Professional Psychology, Research and Practice, 34*, 123–131. http://dx.doi.org/10.1037/0735-7028.34.2.123

Maxie, A. C., Arnold, D. H., & Stephenson, M. (2006). Do therapists address ethnic and racial differences in cross-cultural psychotherapy? *Psychotherapy: Theory, Research, Practice, Training, 43*, 85–98. http://dx.doi.org/10.1037/0033-3204.43.1.85

McIntosh, P. (1988). *White privilege and male privilege: A personal account of coming to see correspondences through work in women's studies*. Retrieved from http://www.collegeart.org/pdf/diversity/white-privilege-and-male-privilege.pdf

Mehr, K. E., Ladany, N., & Caskie, G. I. L. (2010). Trainee nondisclosure in supervision: What are they not telling you? *Counselling & Psychotherapy Research, 10*, 103–113. http://dx.doi.org/10.1080/14733141003712301

Metzger, L. L. H., Nadkarni, L. I., & Cornish, J. A. E. (2010). An overview of multicultural counseling competencies. In J. A. E. Cornish, B. A. Schreier, L. I. Nadkarni, L. H. Metzger, & E. R. Rodolfa (Eds.), *Handbook of multicultural counseling competencies* (pp. 1–21). Hoboken, NJ: Wiley.

Morton, E. (2012). *The incidence of racial microaggressions in the cross-racial counseling dyad* (Unpublished doctoral dissertation). Saint Louis University, Saint Louis, MO.

Mosher, D. K., Hook, J. N., Farrell, J. E., Watkins, C. E., Jr., & Davis, D. E. (2016). Cultural humility. In E. L. Worthington, Jr., D. E. Davis, & J. N. Hook (Eds.), *Handbook of humility* (pp. 91–104). New York, NY: Routledge.

Myers, D., & Twenge, J. M. (2012). *Social psychology* (11th ed.). New York, NY: McGraw-Hill.

Nevid, J. (2013). *Psychology: Concepts and applications* (4th ed.). Belmont, CA: Wadsworth.

Neville, H. A., Lilly, R. L., Duran, G., Lee, R. M., & Browne, L. (2000). Construction and initial validation of the Color-Blind Racial Attitudes Scale (CoBRAS). *Journal of Counseling Psychology, 47*, 59–70. http://dx.doi.org/10.1037/0022-0167.47.1.59

O'Neil, J. M. (2008). Summarizing 25 years of research on men's gender role conflict using the gender role conflict scale new research paradigms and clinical implications. *The Counseling Psychologist, 36*, 358–445. http://dx.doi.org/10.1177/0011000008317057

Owen, J. (2013). Early career perspectives on psychotherapy research and practice: Psychotherapist effects, multicultural orientation, and couple interventions. *Psychotherapy, 50*, 496–502. http://dx.doi.org/10.1037/a0034617

Owen, J., Drinane, J., Tao, K. W., Adelson, J. L., Hook, J. N., Davis, D., & Foo Kune, N. (2017). Racial/ethnic disparities in client unilateral termination: The role of therapists' cultural comfort. *Psychotherapy Research, 27*, 102–111. http://dx.doi.org/10.1080/10503307.2015.1078517

Owen, J., Drinane, J., Tao, K. W., Gupta, D., Zhang, Y., & Adelson, J. (2016). *An experimental test of microaggression detection in psychotherapy: Therapist multicultural orientation.* Manuscript submitted for publication.

Owen, J., & Hilsenroth, M. J. (2011). Interaction between alliance and technique in predicting patient outcome during psychodynamic psychotherapy. *Journal of Nervous and Mental Disease, 199*, 384–389. http://dx.doi.org/10.1097/NMD.0b013e31821cd28a

Owen, J., Imel, Z., Adelson, J., & Rodolfa, E. (2012). "No-show": Therapist racial/ethnic disparities in client unilateral termination. *Journal of Counseling Psychology, 59*, 314–320. http://dx.doi.org/10.1037/a0027091

Owen, J., Imel, Z., Tao, K. W., Wampold, B., Smith, A., & Rodolfa, E. (2011). Cultural ruptures in short-term therapy: Working alliance as a mediator between clients' perceptions of microaggressions and therapy outcomes. *Counselling & Psychotherapy Research, 11*, 204–212. http://dx.doi.org/10.1080/14733145.2010.491551

Owen, J., Jordan, T. A., II, Turner, D., Davis, D. E., Hook, J. N., & Leach, M. M. (2014). Therapists' multicultural orientation: Cultural humility, spiritual/religious identity, and therapy outcomes. *Journal of Psychology and Theology, 42*, 91–99.

Owen, J., Leach, M. M., Wampold, B., & Rodolfa, E. (2011). Client and therapist variability in clients' perceptions of their therapists' multicultural competencies. *Journal of Counseling Psychology, 58*, 1–9. http://dx.doi.org/10.1037/a0021496

Owen, J., & Lindley, L. D. (2010). Therapists' cognitive complexity: Review of theoretical models and development of an integrated approach for training. *Training and Education in Professional Psychology, 4*, 128–137. http://dx.doi.org/10.1037/a0017697

Owen, J., Tao, K., & Rodolfa, E. (2010). Microaggressions and women in short-term psychotherapy: Initial evidence. *The Counseling Psychologist, 38*, 923–946. http://dx.doi.org/10.1177/0011000010376093

Owen, J., Tao, K. W., Drinane, J. M., Hook, J., Davis, D. E., & Foo Kune, N. (2016). Client perceptions of therapists' multicultural orientation: Cultural (missed) opportunities and cultural humility. *Professional Psychology: Research and Practice, 47*, 30–37. http://dx.doi.org/10.1037/pro0000046

Owen, J., Tao, K. W., Imel, Z. E., Wampold, B. E., & Rodolfa, E. (2014). Addressing racial and ethnic microaggressions in therapy. *Professional Psychology: Research and Practice, 45*, 283–290. http://dx.doi.org/10.1037/a0037420

Owen, J., Thomas, L., & Rodolfa, E. (2013). Stigma for seeking therapy: Self-stigma, social stigma, and therapeutic processes. *The Counseling Psychologist, 41*, 857–880. http://dx.doi.org/10.1177/0011000012459365

Owen, J. J., Tao, K., Leach, M. M., & Rodolfa, E. (2011). Clients' perceptions of their psychotherapists' multicultural orientation. *Psychotherapy, 48*, 274–282. http://dx.doi.org/10.1037/a0022065

Pascual-Leone, A., Andreescu, C. A., & Greenberg, L. S. (2016). Emotion-focused therapy. In A. Carr & M. McNulty (Eds.), *The handbook of adult clinical psychology: An evidence-based practice approach* (2nd ed., pp. 137–160). New York, NY: Routledge.

Pedersen, P. (1987). Ten frequent assumptions of cultural bias in counseling. *Journal of Multicultural Counseling and Development, 15*, 16–24. http://dx.doi.org/10.1002/j.2161-1912.1987.tb00374.x

Pedersen, P. (1990). The multicultural perspective as a fourth force in counseling. *Journal of Mental Health Counseling, 12*, 93–95.

Peek, L. (2005). Becoming Muslim: The development of a religious identity. *Sociology of Religion, 66*, 215–242. http://dx.doi.org/10.2307/4153097

Perls, F., Hefferline, R. F., & Goodman, P. (1951). *Gestalt therapy: Excitement and growth in human personality*. New York, NY: Dell.

Pettigrew, T. F., & Tropp, L. R. (2006). A meta-analytic test of intergroup contact theory. *Journal of Personality and Social Psychology, 90*, 751–783. http://dx.doi.org/10.1037/0022-3514.90.5.751

Phinney, J. S., & Ong, A. D. (2007). Conceptualization and measurement of ethnic identity: Current status and future directions. *Journal of Counseling Psychology, 54*, 271–281. http://dx.doi.org/10.1037/0022-0167.54.3.271

Pyszczynski, T., Greenberg, J., Solomon, S., Arndt, J., & Schimel, J. (2004). Why do people need self-esteem? A theoretical and empirical review. *Psychological Bulletin, 130*, 435–468. http://dx.doi.org/10.1037/0033-2909.130.3.435

Racker, H. (1982). *Transference and countertransference*. London, England: Karnak Books.

Richardson, T. Q., & Molinaro, K. L. (1996). White counselor self-awareness: A prerequisite for developing multicultural competence. *Journal of Counseling & Development, 74,* 238–242. http://dx.doi.org/10.1002/j.1556-6676.1996.tb01859.x

Rosario, M., Schrimshaw, E. W., & Hunter, J. (2011). Different patterns of sexual identity development over time: Implications for the psychological adjustment of lesbian, gay, and bisexual youths. *Journal of Sex Research, 48,* 3–15. http://dx.doi.org/10.1080/00224490903331067

Roysircar, G. (2004). Cultural self-awareness assessment: Practice examples from psychology training. *Professional Psychology: Research and Practice, 35,* 658–666. http://dx.doi.org/10.1037/0735-7028.35.6.658

Rusbult, C. E. (1983). A longitudinal test of the investment model: The development (and deterioration) of satisfaction and commitment in heterosexual involvements. *Journal of Personality and Social Psychology, 45,* 101–117. http://dx.doi.org/10.1037/0022-3514.45.1.101

Safran, J. D., & Muran, J. C. (2006). Has the concept of the therapeutic alliance outlived its usefulness? *Psychotherapy: Theory, Research, Practice, Training, 43,* 286–291. http://dx.doi.org/10.1037/0033-3204.43.3.286

Salvatore, J., & Shelton, J. N. (2007). Cognitive costs of exposure to racial prejudice. *Psychological Science, 18,* 810–815. http://dx.doi.org/10.1111/j.1467-9280.2007.01984.x

Schwartz, S. H. (1992). Universals in the content and structure of values: Theory and empirical tests in 20 countries. In M. Zanna (Ed.), *Advances in experimental social psychology* (Vol. 25, pp. 1–65). New York, NY: Academic Press.

Seelman, K. L. (2014). Transgender individuals' access to college housing and bathrooms: Findings from the National Transgender Discrimination Survey. *Journal of Gay & Lesbian Social Services, 26,* 186–206. http://dx.doi.org/10.1080/10538720.2014.891091

Shelton, K., & Delgado-Romero, E. A. (2011). Sexual orientation microaggressions: The experience of lesbian, gay, bisexual, and queer clients in psychotherapy. *Journal of Counseling Psychology, 58,* 210–221. http://dx.doi.org/10.1037/a0022251

Skinner, B. F. (1953). *Science and human behavior.* Oxford, England: Macmillan.

Smyth, J. M., & Pennebaker, J. W. (2008). Exploring the boundary conditions of expressive writing: In search of the right recipe. *British Journal of Health Psychology, 13,* 1–7. http://dx.doi.org/10.1348/135910707X260117

Sue, D. W. (2001). Multidimensional facets of cultural competence. *The Counseling Psychologist, 29,* 790–821. http://dx.doi.org/10.1177/0011000001296002

Sue, D. W. (2010). *Microaggressions in everyday life: Race, gender, and sexual orientation.* Hoboken, NJ: Wiley.

Sue, D. W., Arredondo, P., & McDavis, R. J. (1992). Multicultural counseling competencies and standards: A call to the profession. *Journal of Counseling & Development, 70,* 477–486. http://dx.doi.org/10.1002/j.1556-6676.1992.tb01642.x

Sue, D. W., Bernier, J. E., Durran, A., Feinberg, L., Pedersen, P., Smith, E. J., & Vasquez-Nuttall, E. (1982). Position paper: Cross-cultural counseling competencies. *The Counseling Psychologist, 10,* 45–52. http://dx.doi.org/10.1177/0011000082102008

Sue, D. W., Capodilupo, C. M., Torino, G. C., Bucceri, J. M., Holder, A. M. B., Nadal, K. L., & Esquilin, M. (2007). Racial microaggressions in everyday life: Implications for clinical practice. *American Psychologist, 62,* 271–286. http://dx.doi.org/10.1037/0003-066X.62.4.271

Sue, D. W., Carter, R. T., Casas, J. M., Fouad, N. A., Ivey, A. E., Jensen, M., . . . Vazquez-Nutall, E. (1998). *Multicultural counseling competencies: Individual and organizational development* (Vol. 11). Thousand Oaks, CA: Sage.

Sue, D. W., & Sue, D. (2013). *Counseling the culturally diverse: Theory and practice* (6th ed.). Hoboken, NJ: Wiley.

Sue, S. (1976). Clients' demographic characteristics and therapeutic treatment: Differences that make a difference. *Journal of Consulting and Clinical Psychology, 44,* 864. http://dx.doi.org/10.1037/0022-006X.44.5.864

Sue, S. (1977). Community mental health services to minority groups. Some optimism, some pessimism. *American Psychologist, 32,* 616–624. http://dx.doi.org/10.1037/0003-066X.32.8.616

Sue, S., Fujino, D. C., Hu, L. T., Takeuchi, D. T., & Zane, N. W. S. (1991). Community mental health services for ethnic minority groups: A test of the cultural responsiveness hypothesis. *Journal of Consulting and Clinical Psychology, 59,* 533–540. http://dx.doi.org/10.1037/0022-006X.59.4.533

Sue, S., McKinney, H. L., & Allen, D. B. (1976). Predictors of the duration of therapy for clients in the community mental health system. *Community Mental Health Journal, 12,* 365–375. http://dx.doi.org/10.1007/BF01411075

Sue, S., & Zane, N. (1987). The role of culture and cultural techniques in psychotherapy. A critique and reformulation. *American Psychologist, 42,* 37–45. http://dx.doi.org/10.1037/0003-066X.42.1.37

Sullivan, H. S. (1954). *The psychiatric interview.* New York, NY: Norton.

Tao, K. W., Owen, J., Pace, B. T., & Imel, Z. E. (2015). A meta-analysis of multicultural competencies and psychotherapy process and outcome. *Journal of Counseling Psychology, 62,* 337–350. http://dx.doi.org/10.1037/cou0000086

Tao, K. W., Whiteley, A., Noel, N., & Ozawa-Kirk, J. (2016, November). Challenging essentialism in multicultural counseling: A grounded theory study of multicultural competence in white psychotherapy dyads. In J. Owen and Z. E. Imel (Chairs), *Multicultural processes in psychotherapy.* Panel discussion presented at the North American Society for Psychotherapy Research Conference, Berkeley, CA.

Tao, K. W., Whiteley, A., Noel, N., Ozawa-Kirk, J., & Owen, J. (2016, August). White therapy dyads and missed cultural opportunities. In J. Owen (Chair), *Social justice in counseling: Opportunities to consider intersectionality and invisible difference.* Symposium conducted at the annual convention of the American Psychological Association, Denver, CO.

Teyber, E., & McClure, F. H. (2011). *Interpersonal process in therapy: An integrative model* (6th ed.). Belmont, CA: Brooks/Cole.

Thompson, V. L. S., & Alexander, H. (2006). Therapists' race and African American clients' reactions to therapy. *Psychotherapy: Theory, Research, Practice, Training, 43,* 99–110. http://dx.doi.org/10.1037/0033-3204.43.1.99

Tracey, T. J. G., Wampold, B. E., Lichtenberg, J. W., & Goodyear, R. K. (2014). Expertise in psychotherapy: An elusive goal? *American Psychologist, 69,* 218–229. http://dx.doi.org/10.1037/a0035099

Utsey, S. O., Ponterotto, J. G., & Porter, J. S. (2008). Prejudice and racism, year 2008—still going strong: Research on reducing prejudice with recommended methodological advances. *Journal of Counseling & Development, 86,* 339–347. http://dx.doi.org/10.1002/j.1556-6678.2008.tb00518.x

Vera, E. M., & Speight, S. L. (2003). Multicultural competence, social justice, and counseling psychology: Expanding our roles. *The Counseling Psychologist, 31,* 253–272. http://dx.doi.org/10.1177/0011000003031003001

Vygotsky, L. S. (1978). *Mind in society: The development of higher psychological processes.* Cambridge, MA: Harvard University Press.

Wachtel, P. L. (1993). *Therapeutic communication: Principles and effective practice.* New York, NY: Guilford Press.

Waehler, C. A. (1996). *Bachelors: The psychology of men who haven't married.* Westport, CT: Praeger.

Wampold, B. E. (2001). Contextualizing psychotherapy as a healing practice: Culture, history, and methods. *Applied & Preventive Psychology, 10,* 69–86.

Wampold, B. E. (2007). Psychotherapy: The humanistic (and effective) treatment. *American Psychologist, 62,* 857–873. http://dx.doi.org/10.1037/0003-066X.62.8.857

Wampold, B. E., & Imel, Z. E. (2015). *The great psychotherapy debate: The evidence for what makes psychotherapy work* (2nd ed.). New York, NY: Routledge.

Webb, C. A., DeRubeis, R. J., & Barber, J. P. (2010). Therapist adherence/competence and treatment outcome: A meta-analytic review. *Journal of Consulting and Clinical Psychology, 78,* 200–211. http://dx.doi.org/10.1037/a0018912

Weinrach, S. G., & Thomas, K. R. (2002). A critical analysis of the multicultural counseling competencies: Implications for the practice of mental health counseling. *Journal of Mental Health Counseling, 24,* 20–35.

Whaley, A. L. (2001). Cultural mistrust and mental health services for African Americans: A review and meta-analysis. *The Counseling Psychologist, 29,* 513–531. http://dx.doi.org/10.1177/0011000001294003

Whaley, A. L., & Davis, K. E. (2007). Cultural competence and evidence-based practice in mental health services: A complementary perspective. *American Psychologist, 62,* 563–574. http://dx.doi.org/10.1037/0003-066X.62.6.563

Wood, D., Bruner, J. S., & Ross, G. (1976). The role of tutoring in problem solving. *The Journal of Child Psychology and Psychiatry, 17,* 89–100. http://dx.doi.org/10.1111/j.1469-7610.1976.tb00381.x

Woodruff, E., Van Tongeren, D. R., McElroy, S., Davis, D. E., & Hook, J. N. (2014). Humility and religion: Benefits, difficulties, and a model of religious tolerance. In C. Kim-Prieto (Ed.), *Positive psychology of religion and spirituality across cultures* (pp. 271–286). New York, NY: Springer.

Worthington, E. L., Jr. (1988). Understanding the values of religious clients: A model and its application to counseling. *Journal of Counseling Psychology, 35,* 166–174. http://dx.doi.org/10.1037/0022-0167.35.2.166

Index

About the Authors

Joshua N. Hook, PhD, received his doctorate in counseling psychology from Virginia Commonwealth University. Currently, he is an associate professor of psychology at the University of North Texas, where he teaches the graduate multicultural counseling course. He is a licensed clinical psychologist in the state of Texas. His professional interests include humility, religion/spirituality, and multicultural counseling. In his free time, he enjoys blogging (http://www.JoshuaNHook.com), cheering on the Chicago Bears, and trying not to get injured doing CrossFit.

Don Davis, PhD, received his doctorate in counseling psychology from Virginia Commonwealth University. Currently, he is an assistant professor of counseling psychology and counselor education at Georgia State University. His professional interests include humility, forgiveness, and religion/spirituality. He teaches courses on group counseling as well as on measurement. He also teaches an advanced seminar on humility, drawing on contemplative spiritual practices in counseling. In his free time, he likes biking, complaining about the Georgia Tech football team, and playing with his two kids, Catherine (age 7) and Adam (age 3).

Jesse Owen, PhD, received his doctorate in counseling psychology from the University of Denver (DU) in 2005. He is currently an associate professor and chair of the Counseling Psychology Department at DU. He worked at Gannon University and the University of Louisville prior to joining the faculty at DU. He is a licensed psychologist and has had a private practice at times over the past decade. His research focuses on psychotherapy processes and outcomes as well as romantic relationships. More specifically, his work in psychotherapy focuses on therapists' multicultural orientation and expertise. Personally, he enjoys outdoor activities and quality time with family and friends.

Cirleen DeBlaere, PhD, received her doctorate in counseling psychology from the University of Florida and is currently an assistant professor of counseling psychology at Georgia State University. Her professional interests include the identity and experiences of individuals with marginalized identities, particularly people with multiple marginalized identities (e.g., LGBTQ people of color, women of color), resilience, cultural humility, and multicultural counseling and supervision. She teaches graduate courses in multicultural issues, personality theory, and clinical supervision. In her free time, she enjoys hiking, watching classic episodes of the Golden Girls, and quality time with her beloved black lab, Maggie.